Growing Wings Self-Discovery Workbook:
18 Workshops to a Better Life
Volume Two

Exploring the Multi-Faceted Self

from the Blue Wing Workshops Self-Discovery Series

Susan D. Kalior
M.A. in Education in Counseling
Human Relations and Behavior
B.S. in Sociology

Blue Wing Publications, Workshops, and Lectures
Tualatin, Oregon

Growing Wings Self-Discovery Workbook-Volume Two:
18 Workshops to a Better Life
Exploring the Multi-Faceted Self
from the Blue Wing Workshops Self-Discovery Series
Copyright©2012 by Susan D Kalior
First Printing Feb 2012
ISBN 978-0-9795663-7-0
Editor: Paula Warren
Proofreader: Shoshana Hurwitz
Cover Designer: Laura C. Keyser

Blue Wing Publications, Workshops, and Lectures
P.O. Box 947, Tualatin, OR 97062
sdk@bluewingworkshops.com
www.bluewingworkshops.com
Readers' comments are welcome.

Other Books by Susan D. Kalior

Growing Wings Self-Discovery Workbook: 17 Workshops to a Better Life-Volume One
The Other Side of God: The Eleven Gem Odyssey of Being
The Other Side of Life: The Eleven Gem Odyssey of Death
Warriors in the Mist: A Medieval Dark Fantasy
The Dark Side of Light: A Medieval Time Travel Fantasy
Johnny, the Mark of Chaos
Jenséa, an Angel's Touch

Growing Wings Self Discovery Workshops

For information on workshops in Portland, Oregon
or on how to arrange a workshop in your location,
contact: sdk@bluewingworkshops.com

Manufactured in the United States of America

Dedication

This workbook is dedicated to the multitudes whom,
from all walks of life,
opened their lives to me
that I might better see into the soul of humankind.

Acknowledgements

To my wise father, who is my greatest sounding board in all I write, I thank you. To my sister Cindy and my brother Mark, who so lovingly support all my endeavors, thank you. To my children Sara and Stephen, who have so often served as motivators to help me fly higher, you mean so much. To Laura, (who designed my cover), Jennifer, and Matt, my nieces and nephew, whose love I feel seeping into me over the miles—you too. Thank you dear aunts, Linda, Mary, and Gail, for caring about my work and about me. Yes, my family is close! Thank you to Cyndi Myers (e), my dear friend, whose feedback on this workbook was invaluable. Thank you Paula Warren, my old cherished friend for coming back into my life and contributing your expertise in helping me bring this workbook into fruition. Cyndi, Paula, you are my family too. While self-actualization is ever my goal, my life sparkles with these precious people in it. Family is not always in a bloodline, nor does it end when our loved ones pass away. To my belated mother, I feel you still . . . inspiring me to be—an original.

I would like to make a special acknowledgment
to my proofreader, Shoshana Hurwitz,
who did an outstanding job. I highly recommend her.

Table of Contents

Introduction to Self-Discovery: Volume Two

Light the world with who you are,
then you will have done your part to change it.

We are more than our bodies. We are more than what we can consciously perceive. We are more. In light of that, this workbook is designed for the individual to step behind self-image and behold the many psychological facets and dimensions that make up his or her human being. The psychological profession has barely begun to scratch the surface in this endeavor. These workshops are for the true explorers of human nature, for those who seek to understand the underpinnings of who they are deep within, beyond social programming.

Only when we peer into ourselves and see what is going on in there can we begin to notice and appreciate the complex kaleidoscopic design that shapes our personality. In this, it becomes apparent that what we refer to as "I" is not by any means simplistic. *Everyone* is complicated and so unique that no outer world advice, way, philosophy, or religion can be *one hundred percent* right for anyone. And yet, the ambiguity of our own complexity often drives us outward to adopt *other* people's ideas, idioms, philosophies, or religions that at least, in part, resonate with who we *think* we are.

Although every perception, way, philosophy, or religion has a place and purpose, if we do not detect a pulse on our own uniqueness, then we tend to behave as a robot taking commands from the social conscience telling us how we must behave in order to physically, mentally, emotionally, and even spiritually survive. With a multitude of commands coming from here, there, and everywhere pointing the way to salvation, no wonder we get confused. Who are we . . . really? And what is right for us as an individual?

Though there are many dimensions to what we call "self," the most identifiable are the Outer Self, the Inner Self, and the Quintessential Self. The Outer Self is the persona we project to the world. It is the image we try to become in order to secure acceptance and appreciation from others, and hence ourselves. If we cannot attain the desired image, depression or anxiety set in. And if we do, we are stressed to maintain it. Most desired images, such as a do-gooder, sex symbol, or ultimate warrior, are prototypes propagated by influential people, various social circles, the commercial world, and indeed society itself. Tying self-worth to any image is like trying to harbor a cloud; the result is always fleeting. And trying to get psychological nourishment by becoming an image is like trying to feed our reflection in a mirror. We go hungry. The masks we wear, while acceptable, if not applauded by those around us, can leave us bereft in our secret, silent moments behind closed doors. Those who seem to have it all on the outside are sometimes the saddest on the inside because their *true* self is unexpressed.

Behind the constructed mask of the Outer Self is the Inner Self. It is the private part of us that devises ways to survive in the world, to absolve our underlying fear, and to find an acceptable avenue of self-expression. This effort gives rise to various aspects of our personality: the Sage, the Judge, the Warrior, the Nurturer, the Pleaser, the Leader, the Victim, the Martyr, the Scaredy Cat, the Fury, the Fabricator, the Rebel, the Skeptic, the Traitor, the Innovator, the Hero, and the Healer. These aspects, like people in a village, collide, collude and vie for attention, creating internal conflict (arguing with ourselves). The Warrior in us wants to fight, but the Scaredy Cat in us says no. The Rebel in us wants to rebel, but the Pleaser in us, disliking confrontation, overpowers it.

Sometimes our internal aspects work together toward victory or a heroic end. The Fury propelled by the Nurturer might explode onto a scene to fight injustice. The Leader paired with the Innovator might take point and execute a brilliant solution to a troubling situation.

Sometimes, certain parts of us, not ready to be fully developed, emerge only in specific circumstances. The Leader in us is ready to lead children, but not adults. The Rebel in us can say no to women, but not men. Then, there are other aspects of ourselves that go dormant, or have been dormant, waiting to be triggered by a life event or to rise at a specific pinnacle in our development. The Innovator in us, buried in duty for years raising children, might emerge boldly with some new passion when the children grow up and leave home.

Throughout our lives, these various selves within our self establish pecking orders. Depending on who we are, this pecking order might remain the same or change as we enter new life phases. Maybe after decades of taking abuse, the Inner Hero might rise and take a bold stand. Maybe after years of behaving recklessly due to underlying trauma, the Inner Healer heals the source of what has made us reckless, and we settle down.

While the faces of our personality can be roughly labeled Hero, Warrior, Victim, etc, they each have individual variations with their own special flair. Just as no two snowflakes are exactly alike, neither are two people, nor the aspects within them. And for as many aspects of ourselves that we think we know about, there are many more that we do not. However, for the purpose of this self-exploration, the focus is on the more archetypal aspects that are the most prevalent in our human being, the ones that dominate our lives, and the ones we need to bring out of the shadows to champion us.

This workbook is designed to help you get better acquainted with the many basic characters within you that together make up what we call "I." In this, you will be more enabled to shift out of unsavory moods to a more congenial state of mind. Prolonged moods such as chronic depression or anxiety are examples of getting stuck in an aspect of our self such as our Inner Victim, Fury, or Skeptic. Shifting moods requires shifting to another aspect of our self. We are like the crystal with many facets, and we can perceive life through any facet we choose.

Deeper, beyond the facets of our personality, at the core of our being, is our Quintessential Self. The Quintessential Self is the essence of who we are *beyond our conscious analysis* and outer world judgment. Unlike the many faces of our Inner Self that can be twisted, marred, or psyched into creating drama, the Quintessential Self is always pure, innocent, sincere, and wise. It senses its place in the universe beyond what we can consciously explain, and therefore has no doubts about its worth or validity.

Our Quintessential Self watches over its many aspects, like children who leave home and get swept into outer world currents, creating (as they should) a life story. Involved in the drama, our Inner Self often loses touch with the Quintessential Self. When this happens, we feel lost inside. The craving to touch nature is about a need to reconnect with this purest part of ourselves. Likewise, the need to be creative is our Quintessential Self, saying, "Remember me?" When we adhere to our Quintessential Self, we feel the most alive.

This does not, however, diminish the value of our other personality aspects, even though they are capable of taking us on seeming wild goose chases into the outer reaches of forgetting who we are. Even if an aspect keeps getting us into trouble, it cannot be thrown away or snuffed, nor should it be, even if it were possible. Every aspect can enrich our lives if we take the time to deal with it as we would an ailing loved one. For example, the Skeptic who has turned cynical and is drowning in pain, needs aid, not annihilation. In this, we can tune up our various aspects, like strings on an instrument, to be more harmonious.

Each workshop in this workbook is dedicated to tuning up one aspect by exploring it, understanding it, and embracing it, *despite* the role it has played in your life or the consequences it has generated. And like a stairway, each workshop completed will bring you closer to your core being, which is your Quintessential Self. It is in that core where we find calmness, relief from our woes, and behold our beauty—the greatest beauty imaginable. Here, in the beauty, our Inner aspects feel their oneness with each other, cease fighting for control, and can better work together to help us through this crazy life. Maybe it is a tall order to make peace on Earth, but maybe, just maybe, it is not so tall an order to make peace with ourselves.

Once the inner friction amongst our "selves" is calmed, like tossing waters that still, our total self in its unique configuration can be better seen and cherished, despite age, appearance, or social position. Our image then is no longer a reflection of the outer world, but of *our* true self (the divine individual that we are) emanating from our core being. Discovering our true self is the greatest journey we can ever take, and emanating it into the world is the greatest mission we can ever have.

It is this author's hope that this workbook will contribute to your ability to get in touch with, and remain centered in—your Quintessential Self. In this, your true being will shine in the outer world, despite what happens to you, or what is going on around you. And in that, each step you take upon your life journey will forge a one-of-a-kind path, lighting your footprints like stars in the sky. This is your legacy. You were here. This was you. You and no other. This was your splash of paint in the canvas of life, your specialness, your beauty, your contribution. You will be among those who make extraordinary imprints in the world by simply being—yourself.

To that end, the next leg of the journey to the center of you—begins now.

Workshop Guidelines

*This workbook will help you explore yourself at *this time* in your life. It is important to fill in the date at the beginning of each workshop. A year from now, or a year ago, answers might be different. Reviewing the workbook from time to time often resurrects insights and inspiration, and can prove to be a wonderful asset to keep as a revered journal.

*Write directly in the book. Use a pencil so that you may change answers as needed. Exploring the self is like journeying through layers. You might be writing an answer, when a deeper truth arises, and crossing previous answers out in pen can prove messy and hard to read later. Feel free to use colored pencils, especially in exercises that require drawings. Drawings are not about good art. They are tools to help you see yourself.

*It is suggested that you have a supplementary journal should you need more space than is available to record your explorations or if you need to extend an exercise. A spiral notebook works nicely. Simply note in the workbook, see journal, page 1, etc.

*Even if you feel at times that there are too many questions in an exercise, and you are tempted do just a few, push yourself to do them all. The exercise is designed to help you dig deeper, so it is important that you scrape up everything inside you and get it out so you can see it. And if there is not enough space for you to express it all, use your supplementary journal.

*Do not skip the **Healing and Balancing Exercises.** They are invaluable. Suggestions are made for hand placement, however, feel free to place your hands where they feel best: crown of head, forehead, base of throat, heart, base of breastbone, just below the navel, or the base of your spine.

*Do not skip the **Relaxation and Creative Visualization Experience** at the end of each workshop. This is perhaps the most important part of the workshop. Initial exploration through question and answer opens the door. The Creative Visualization experience is about walking through that door to discover personal truths that lie beyond conscious analysis. In the depths of our incorporeal being, the purest insights can be found, as well as a kind of universal wisdom. General guidelines are provided; however, feel free to diverge into your own experience whenever the flow takes you there. Trust that you will experience what you need in order to be a healthier, wiser, and more balanced person.

*The **Relaxation and Creative Visualization Experience** requires instrumental music. Music selection is important. Select instrumental music that makes you feel good: classical, New Age, or any music that is of gentle, sweeping, or dynamic beauty. This kind of music tends to initiate emotional catharsis, catalyze insight, and spark experiences that promote positive life change. If you have selected music that you have not yet heard, listen to it before using it with the Relaxation and Creative Visualization Exercise. It is essential that you find the music emotionally moving and not irritating. You can use the same music for each Relaxation and Creative Visualization Experience, or you can change it as you please.

*It is suggested that you complete no more than one workshop per day so that the full benefit is reaped. However, if something inside you calls to complete more than one workshop per day, trust yourself. Make the most of each workshop and each exercise, taking time to ponder the questions, even if it takes days. Sometimes letting a question stew for a while can help you dig deeper and pull out even more rewarding revelations.

*It is suggested that you do not skip workshops, or do them out of order. They are designed as a progression, leading to the finale at the end. However, if you sense that you are not ready to do a particular workshop, by all means, skip it.

*Before answering questions, search your mind and heart honestly. Set the intent to understand yourself better. The deeper you probe and the more honest your answers, the more you will discover about yourself. No one ever need see this workbook. It is yours and yours alone.

*While most chapters feature one aspect of the human psyche with many variations, three remain pure: the Sage, the Healer, and the Hero. Hence, these chapters will not share the exact same format as the others. This in no way diminishes the beauty and value of the other aspects of our psyche.

These workshops are not designed to replace other forms of therapy. If you feel you need therapy, it is suggested that you seek a therapist. If you are in therapy, it is suggested that you consult with your therapist regarding this workbook.

*These workshops are the culmination of this author's years in higher education, extra curricular training, extensive experience as a psychotherapist, sociological studies, decades of facilitating self-discovery workshops, and thirty years of in-depth meditation. However, the self-discovery process works best when you trust your own sense of things. Therefore, *always* respond in a manner healthy to yourself.

Materials Needed:
Pencils, colored pencils, spiral notebook, a machine that plays music, and music that is comforting and/or inspiring.

Glossary for Growing Wings Self-Discovery Workbook-Volume Two

The Terms

Authenticity: emanating our true self into the outer world.
Pseudo-Reality: a reality that seems real but is fabricated by our mind.
Self-Actualization: the flowering of who we truly are.
Significant Other: a mate, family member, good friend or any other who is significant to us.
Social Conscience: the collective view of a social group.
Social Programming: outer world influences that affect our perceptions.
Social Perception: how others view us, and how we view others.
Inner Self: the many aspects of us that make up our personality.
Inner Aspect: one face of our personality.
Outer Self: the image we project to others.
Quintessential Self: our core essence from which all our Inner Aspects spring.
True Self: our total self in its unique configuration, like a one of a kind snowflake.

Our Inner Aspects

The Sage: the part of us that is intrinsically wise.
The Judge: the part of us that draws subjective conclusions followed by a verdict.
The Warrior: the part of us that responds to challenge with "fight" and a will to succeed.
The Nurturer: the part of us that is compelled to nourish, love, and bring comfort.
The Pleaser: the part of us that pleases others to secure what we need from them.
The Victim: the part of us that feels *unfairly* hurt.
The Martyr: the part of us that sacrifices (at our own expense) to benefit others.
The Leader: the part of us that takes command, and/or trail blazes.
The Scaredy Cat: the part of us that is driven by fear.
The Fury: the part of us that is driven by rage.
The Traitor: the part of us that betrays ourselves or others.
The Rebel: the part of us that defies conformity and oppression.
The Skeptic: the part of us that questions what seems to be.
The Fabricator: the part of us that creates stories to entertain, manipulate, or justify actions.
The Innovator: the creative, inventive, and resourceful part of us.
The Hero: the noble part of us that behaves bravely even when we don't relish the idea.
The Healer: the part of us that knows what needs healing and proceeds to repair.

THE BOOK OF

_____

(YOUR NAME)

WORKSHOP ONE
THE SAGE "I am wise."

Everyone has an Inner Sage, sometimes explained as the tiny voice deep down inside us. Even if we trust other people's wisdom over our own, our Inner Sage is there, waiting for us to listen. In the wheel of our being, it is positioned smack dab in the center, like an apostle committed to our Quintessential Self that resides in pureness, beneath the hub at our core. From this central position, the Sage observes with equal measure, the many faces of our personality, that like spokes, join the rim of the outer world. If we are too influenced by the outer world and lose touch with our Quintessential Self, the shape of our wheel can get distorted and make us wobble. When we ask our Inner Sage for wisdom, it will urge us to sink into our Quintessence, rather than adhere to the social programming that can take us further from it.

Finding this calm state of mind requires us to be still, quiet, and listen to our deepest self, beyond the chatter in our heads. This is called meditation. In meditation, we fall away from outer world turbulence and sink into the center of our being. In that center, we grow calm, regenerate, and see what we could not see before. We gain *insight*, which gives us clarity about our life, and often about life itself. When we do this, wisdom pours into our consciousness effortlessly, and we receive epiphanies great and small.

This centered place, which we can train ourselves to live in most of the time, also gives us an overview to connect the dots of our life events and get a broader picture of our overall life story. We can see the good that came from our hardship, have compassion for our struggles, and glimpse the psychological games we are currently playing. Sometimes the games work for us, and sometimes they just cause us more work. In seeing this greater picture, we can make adjustments that better serve our well-being.

Although it might seem daunting to explore the Inner Sage at the beginning of this workbook (given that we in the Western World are trained to reach out for advice and guidance), it is the most powerful aspect we have in helping us better our current reality. No one can ever know what is better for us as an individual than that still small voice that lives within us all. You have an Inner Sage, a wise one, a powerful one. Do not doubt it for a minute. By embracing it first, you can practice using it throughout the workbook.

We cannot truly know the wisdom of our Inner Sage until we give it a whirl in the driver's seat of our lives. It will handle situations differently than any other aspect within us. Furthermore, it will not give the same guidance to you as it might to another, for we all have different natures and needs, however, all Sages, fundamentally share the same Universal Wisdom.

Universal Wisdom #1: *We can regain or maintain an inner calm no matter what happens to us or what is going on around us.* Most distress is caused by a perception that an outer world occurrence is causing us to lose some control over our lives. Although it is natural to feel derailed when we get in a car accident, contract a disease, lose a job or a loved one, or are singled out or trounced upon, it is our *perception* of the occurrence, and not the occurrence itself, that is causing the distress. We can only be shaken by the outer world if we allow those events to shake our inner world. We can always maintain control of our lives if we keep control of ourselves. Sitting in the eye of the storm, out of the fray, can be quite empowering.

Universal Wisdom #2: *Those who are the most offensive are those who are the most afraid.* The Sage, seeing beyond the facade of others, will behold the fear in those who are trying to offend it. While the abusers are posturing like parrots, poofing out to appear larger, tougher, and more dangerous than they really are, the Sage will see through this camouflage and behold the abusers gaping psychological wounds. Given that the abusers (who need to feel powerful) will only feel relief if the attacked respond with anger, sadness, or fear, the Sage will remain neutral. In this, the abusers will walk away and find less well-adjusted targets to torment.

Universal Wisdom #3: *We can never change another; we can only change ourselves.* Our Inner Sage is a natural psychologist and can help us end stressful psychological games we play with others in an attempt to coerce them into behaving as we wish. For instance, a husband chronically treats his wife with disrespect. She yells at him. He glares, goes to the bar, comes home drunk, then makes tender love to her. Over and over this happens. She keeps the game going because she has learned that in order to get affection, she must play it. However, if she were to allow her Inner Sage to rise at the beginning of the "game," she might say calmly to the husband, "I feel disrespected when I'm around you, so I am going to go spend my time in a way that makes me feel better." She has released her end of the tug-of-war rope and just walked away. She no longer looks to him for respect; she has given it to herself.

The husband is left holding his side of the rope with no one to play the game. He will probably keep trying to entice her back into the game, but if she resists, his behavior *will* change. If he has the capacity to grow, he will treat her better, and their relationship will jump to the next level. If he isn't ready to grow, he will do more drastic things to recover the power he thinks he lost. Eventually, he will destroy the relationship, but the wife, who just keeps shining her self-respect brighter and brighter in that scenario, will neither need him, nor want him anymore anyway. She can then attract, with her self-respect, one who can return it.

Universal Wisdom #4: *Refrain from helping others if it keeps them weak.* For example, the Sage rising in a woman who has a strong Inner Warrior and always fights her sister's battles for her, might guide her to hold back and give the dependent sister a chance to develop her own Inner Warrior. In this case, inspiring her sister to make her own stands would be more helpful than making those stands for her.

Universal Wisdom #5: *Sometimes humans need drama to air out psychological wounds.* For example, an oppressed man with bottled emotions, when scratched by the family cat, might emotionally explode and roar about all that has bothered him for decades. Like an abscess that has been pierced, repressed emotions that had turned toxic are finally drained. Even though shocked by his behavior, the man will not only more clearly see what was clouded within him, but also understand what can happen when he stuffs his feelings. He then learns to start constructively speaking up to get his needs met, instead of trying to make them die. The Sage knows this explosion is a healing event and will rebel against anyone who would shame the man for his outburst.

Universal Wisdom #6: *We are each responsible for our own happiness.* The Sage knows that even if others do make us happy, to rely on them or to expect them to do so, leads to eventual conflict in those relationships. Always accountable for its own state of being, the Sage knows when to touch and when to detach from others because it is not afraid to love, nor does it need the love of others to feel loved. It knows it can stand on its own if it must.

Universal Wisdom #7: *Authenticity nourishes the process of Self-Actualization.* The Sage is a true champion of authenticity. It puts on no act, hides behind no facade, needs no affirmation, has no need to control, and cannot be hurt because its true self is no mystery.

Getting into the habit of running your thoughts and feelings by your Inner Sage can help bring balance to your life, *if* balance is what you seek. Sometimes we enjoy our turbulent drama, and there is nothing wrong with playing it out. Humans are curious and often seek experiences to see what it would be like, even if we know we are setting ourselves up for some pain. However, should the drama become overwhelming, our Inner Sage will still be there to help us release the drama and move on.

This workshop is designed to help you locate and further familiarize yourself with the wisest part of your being. If you feel unfamiliar with this part of yourself, this workshop might be akin to exercising new muscles, and feeling uncomfortable, you might be tempted to skip it. Do not. Developing your Inner Sage is *vital* to enriching your life. You will be surprised how much "lighter and brighter" your days shall be even in the face of challenge.

Or, your Inner Sage might already be your best ally, and feeling it is already developed, you might be tempted to skip this workshop. Embrace it anyway. This is an opportunity to make your Inner Sage an even stronger force in your life. We are never done growing wiser.

The Sage is an advocate for your own becoming; it is the torch that holds the shining flame of your Quintessential Self.

The Sage in a Nutshell
* Is guided by wisdom, not intellect.
* Does not blindly follow, but neither does it need to lead.
* Never claims to "know it all," for there is always more to know.
* Does not succumb to social pressure that compromises well-being.
* Champions authenticity, even if it rocks the boat.
* Is secure within itself.
* Does not judge others, and therefore does not try to change them. The Sage knows that
  the only person it can change is itself, and in that, it has an effect on those around it.
* Acts on what *feels* healing and balanced, rather than what sounds or looks right.
* Never acts rashly, or gets carried away with any emotion, unless it senses that the act
  will be healing and productive.
* Wears no mask, and therefore never *pretends* to be a Sage.
* Remains vigilantly open to all things.

Exploring Your Inner Sage.

Exercise One

This exercise is designed to bring forth your Inner Sage. Place an X by *all the answers* in each question that fit what your Inner Sage might say or do. Remember, the purpose is not to get the right answers (because they are fairly obvious), but to spotlight your Inner Sage and observe the role it plays or does not play in your life, and to be aware of what emotion you are feeling (good, resistant, irritated) when you X the sage-like answers. Say silently as you answer each question, "I give my Inner Sage permission to shine through me."

1. You are walking down the street and a stranger insults you. What might your Inner Sage say or do?

____Return the insult.   ____Not feeling insulted, don't respond.

____Smile gently with a knowing eye.

____Glare.

____Stay calm and enjoy the day.

____Boo-hoo.

____Give yourself a silent compliment.

____Respond with, "I hope you feel better."

2. You get rejected by someone who you thought cared about you. What might your Inner Sage do?

____Get drunk.

____Don't take it personally.

____Go jogging.

____Fume.

____Cry.

____Meditate.

____Plan revenge.

____Make the best of it.

3. Someone berates your best friend. What might your Inner Sage do?

____Glare.

____Chew that person out.

____Feel embarrassed for being associated with that friend.

____Realize that criticism is in the perception of the beholder.

____Respond by saying, "You are entitled to your perception."

____Feel paralyzed and can't take any action at all.

____Respond by saying, "My perception of my friend is nothing short of amazement."

____Don't respond, refusing to give credence to someone skewed opinion.

When you X'd the sage-like answers, what emotion did you generally feel? _____

If you felt positive, you likely use your Inner Sage often or are eager to do so.

If you felt neutral, you are likely exploring this aspect and are not sure how you feel about it.

If you felt resistant, you likely have other aspects that override it, such as your Inner Fury.

Exercise Two

Answer the following questions honestly. If your answers aren't sage-like, it doesn't matter. There are no wrong answers, just different ways that yield different results. The only thing that matters is, do your responses serve you *better or worse* than another might?

1. When insulted (in general), my *typical* response is_____

_____

The general result is _____

In tapping your Inner Sage, what might you do to improve that result?_____

_____

2. When rejected (in general), my *typical* response is _____

_____

The general result is _____

In tapping your Inner Sage, what might you do to improve that result?_____

_____

3. When someone I care about is insulted behind his/her back, my _typical_ response is _____

_____

The general result is _____

In tapping your Inner Sage, what might you do to improve that result? _____

_____

Exercise Three

Recall two times your Inner Sage emerged and you surprised yourself with how well you handled a situation and the consequent result. Example #1: I usually _yell when my husband comes home exceptionally late without calling,_ but this one time I _went out and meditated under the stars. When he came home, I was so calm and quiet that he couldn't understand why I wasn't mad._ The result was _he became increasingly flustered showing his insecurity and I felt very empowered without saying an unkind word to him._ Example #2: I usually _just stay quiet and am secretly hurt when people mouth off at me,_ but this one time _when my brother yelled at me, I felt strong inside myself and shook my head saying confidently, "Hmm, interesting opinion," and then walked away. He kept trying to get my attention by yelling more. I held my stance, saying calmly, "Interesting opinion," and he finally left me alone._ The result was _he doesn't yell at me anymore._

1. I usually_____

when_____

but this one time_____

_____

The result was_____

_____

2. I usually_____

when_____

but this one time_____

_____

The result was_____

_____

Exercise Four

Take a moment and imagine your Inner Sage. Now move into your Inner Sage. Be the Sage. As the Sage, see your human form in the distance. Walk up to your human form and share your insights. Fill in the blanks below. You can have more than one answer. For now, ignore the letters P T N at the end of each statement.

I am your Inner Sage. I have been watching you for a long while.

I notice that when you are walking along a populated street, you mostly appear_____

_____ P T N
(Examples: kind to people making conversation, mean to people or ignoring everyone, etc.)

I notice in public on an ordinary day, that you mostly appear_____

_____ P T N
(Examples: sad and walking with your head down, joyful and put together with a clean look, etc.)

When you talk to people in general, you mostly_____

_____ P T N
(Examples: are aloof and try to get away as quick as you can, go on and on about only yourself, etc.)

When you are alone and have free time, I notice you mostly_____

_____ P T N
(Examples: watch TV and play video or computer games, get out of the house as quick as possible, etc.)

When you are sad, you tend to_____ P T N
(Examples: mope about and get depressed, go find someone to talk to, etc.)

When you are mad, you tend to_____ P T N
(Examples: bark at everyone, stuff it, confront the issue, meditate, etc.)

When you are afraid, you tend to_____ P T N
(Examples: turn to a psychic, pretend like you are not, calm down and act rationally, fly off the handle, etc.)

When you are happy, you tend to_____ P T N
(Examples: celebrate with drugs or alcohol, go somewhere fun, feel guilty, sabotage it, etc.)

If someone pours good attention on you, you mostly_____ P T N
(Examples: get really shy, beam and accept it, put yourself down, etc.)

If someone criticizes you, you tend to_____ P T N
(Examples: bark at them, criticize back, listen, consider it, beat yourself up, take it with a grain of salt, etc.)

When someone is attracted to you, but the attraction isn't mutual, you tend to_____

_____ P T N
(Examples: run and hide so they will never know, try to go to bed with them anyway, etc.)

When you are attracted to someone, you tend to_____ P T N
(Examples: pretend you aren't, flirt, keep your composure, shut down etc.)

When you are lonely, you tend to_____ P T N
(Examples: mope, call someone, go somewhere, grab onto anyone who will let you, join a group, etc.)

When you are anxious, you mostly_____ P T N
(Examples: bite your nails, take drugs or alcohol, bark at people, become a recluse, eat, meditate, etc.)

When you are excited, you mostly_____ P T N
(Examples: jump up and down, hide it, share your excitement with others, get drunk, etc.)

When you are in emotional pain, you mostly_____ P T N
(Examples: turn to drugs and alcohol, cry alone, call everyone you know hoping they can ease your pain, etc.)

When you are confronted, you mostly_____ P T N
(Examples: get defensive, listen to consider it, ignore the confronter, beat yourself up, etc.)

When a loved one dies, even if it is a pet, you tend to_____ P T N
(Examples: go into deep depression, distract yourself, turn to drugs or alcohol, talk about it, meditate, etc.)

When you succeed at something, you tend to_____ P T N
(Examples: be nice to everyone around you, start the next project, do something to punish yourself, etc.)

When you are down on yourself, you_____ P T N
(Examples: drink alcohol, put others down, do something creative, exercise, meditate, etc.)

If you notice something nice about someone, you mostly_____ P T N
(Examples: compliment them, keep it to yourself, brag about yourself, etc.)

When you are in a crowd, you mostly_____ P T N
(Examples: feel claustrophobic and try to escape, get dizzy, love it, etc.)

Now, go back to each statement and circle the P (for Positive) by statements that reflect reactions that satisfy you. Circle T by statements that reflect reactions you'd like to tweak. Circle N for Neutral by the statements that don't affect you much one way or another. When you are finished, count the number of each and fill in the blanks below.

Positive ____   Tweak____   Neutral____

Do not be concerned about any topic you feel needs tweaking. It just means you are willing to honestly look at yourself and are committed to improving your life.

Exercise Five

The following is an exercise in learning how to shift your focus to your Inner Sage. State an upsetting situation, then explain how you can bring out your Inner Sage to make the situation better. Example #1: *My internet connection is on the fritz and it will take two days to be corrected,* I can bring out the Sage by *telling myself that I can turn this seeming setback into something productive, such as using my waiting time to clean the house, do my art, jog, and go out with my friend.* Example #2: *My livelihood is threatened.* I can bring out the Sage by *telling myself to calm down, embrace my self-worth no matter what happens, and know that one way or another I will make the best of the situation.*

When you answer the questions, keep in mind the following:

* The Sage makes the best out of every situation.
* The Sage advocates inner calmness and confidence to resist playing psychological games.
* The Sage will steer you to behave in ways that feel healing to you.
* The Sage knows hardship leads to growth.
* The Sage does not try to change people; it gives itself what it needs.
* Outcomes do not define your worth. Say, "I am worthy no matter what happens."
* People's opinions do not define your worth. Say, "I am worthy despite people's opinions."
* It can still be a good day even if obstacles arise. Say, "This is a good day because I can strengthen my patience and tenacity."
* When you can't do something about a situation, say, "It will all work out for the best beyond what I can see or understand."
* Acting like a sage is not the same as tapping your Inner Sage. Your Inner Sage knows if it is better for *you* to make a stand or rise above the situation.
* There are no wrong answers; your Inner Sage guides you to act in ways that are healthiest *for you.*

1. My best friend insults me. I can bring out the Sage by_____

_____

2. My boss tells me my work is sub-par. I can bring out the Sage by_____

_____

3. I get caught cheating on a test. I can bring out the Sage by_____

_____

4. I catch my mate sleeping with someone else. I can bring out the Sage by_____

_____

5. My child, or a child I know, screams that she hates me. I can bring out the Sage by_____

_____

6. Someone cuts in front of me in a line. I can bring out the Sage by_____

_____

7. I've been mugged, and I'm shaken up. I can bring out the Sage by_____

_____

8. My friend falls asleep when I'm talking to him. I can bring out the Sage by_____

_____

9. Someone badmouths me behind my back. I can bring out the Sage by_____

_____

10. My Significant Other really hurts my feelings. I can bring out the Sage by_____

_____

Exercise Six:

State what currently upsets you the most.

_____

Now say to yourself, "I am calming down to let the waters still." See yourself in the center of a circle, calm and still. Focus on this instead of the commotion around the periphery of the circle. Stay focused; stay centered. Stirring inside your heart is the beauty of your Quintessential Self. This beauty in your heart begins to shine. The shine turns brighter, growing beyond your heart, radiating all around your body. Now the shine stretches beyond your body, outward, engulfing the periphery of the circle you are sitting in.

You realize that your problems goad you into growing and flowering. So, instead of letting your upset control you, you focus on staying centered, growing, and flowering. In centeredness, it is easy to act in ways that feel healthy to your well-being and to make choices that reflect your self-respect. Your upsetting situation doesn't feel so bad any more because it is catalyzing you to grow into a new and better level of existence, and that is the true prize.

At any stressful moment, close your eyes, take a few slow, deep breaths, and see yourself in the center of a circle, perfectly calm, and open to your Quintessential Self. Let its beauty flow into you, fill you, and glow around you.

Circle the answer that feels truest. My Inner Sage is:

rarely active   moderately active   highly active

Healing and Balancing Exercise for Your Inner Sage

Place one hand over your forehead.
Place the other hand on the crown of your head.
Concentrate deeply. Repeat silently or aloud for at least two minutes:
"I carry the wisdom of all great sages."

Relaxation and Creative Visualization Exercise
Lie in a comfortable position. Play instrumental music that makes you feel good: classical, New Age, or music that is of gentle, sweeping, or dynamic beauty. When the music is playing, close your eyes. Inhale through your nose deeply, and exhale through your mouth slowly; do this eight times. Visualize that you are inhaling the power of the universe, which purifies and attunes you physically, emotionally, mentally, and metaphysically. When you exhale, all the tensions and worries leave your body and go back into the universe where they dissolve and blend into the pure life force.

Tighten and loosen your muscles slowly in this order:

Feet. Tighten. Loosen. Take a slow, deep breath, and exhale.
Calves. Tighten. Loosen. Take a slow, deep breath, and exhale.
Thighs. Tighten. Loosen. Take a slow, deep breath, and exhale.
Hips and buttocks. Tighten. Loosen. Take a slow, deep breath, and exhale.
Back. Tighten. Loosen. Take a slow, deep breath, and exhale.
Arms. Tighten. Loosen. Take a slow, deep breath, and exhale.
Hands. Tighten. Loosen. Take a slow, deep breath, and exhale.
Neck and shoulders. Tighten. Loosen. Take a slow, deep breath, and exhale.
Face. Tighten. Loosen. Take a slow, deep breath, and exhale.

Then completely relax and take eight more slow, deep breaths. Inhale the universal life energy through your nose and exhale tension through your mouth.

Set the intent: *Whoever I am, whatever I am, whatever I need, whatever is right for me—so be it. I open to insight. I open to receive.*

Now that you are completely relaxed, focus on the point between your eyebrows. See yourself moving inward, deeper and deeper into your vast being. Deeper and deeper you go, moving toward the center of who you are, your inner core, your Quintessential Self. Do this for a while . . . .

You are now very close to your inner core, your Quintessential Self. You see a brilliant ball of light, as big as a house. As you come toward the light, you notice your Inner Sage standing next to the great ball of light. Staring into the light, you are awed by its beauty, unabashed and unaffected by the outer world. And the most amazing thing is . . . that this light is you, your true self. Experience this for a while . . . .

Now focus on your Inner Sage. As the ambassador of your Quintessential Self, it is always with you when you journey in the outside world. It is there to remind you who you *really* are when you get confused. Move closer to your Inner Sage. Behold the wisdom beaming from its eyes. Move closer, closer, so close that you have now merged with your Inner Sage. You are one with your Inner Sage. Experience this for a while . . . .

You and your Sage, merged as one, walk into the brilliant light of your Quintessential Self. A wave of strength hits you like a warm water current. The warmth of this energy fills you. You feel charged, purified, and empowered. The energy in you shines around you. Now it shines stronger and brighter in all directions, spanning all space and time. And now it transcends space and time. Experience this for a while . . . .

This is who you truly are, and you know you can count on your Inner Sage to always bring you back to the center of your being into your Quintessential Self when you need to feel your worth and your power. Bask in this experience until the music ends . . . .

When you open your eyes, you will feel the strong presence of your Inner Sage, knowing you can use it always to keep you calm in the eye of any storm. Knowing this, you will feel confident and at peace.

Record your experience.

_____

_____

_____

_____

_____

_____

_____

_____

Draw a picture or symbol that summarizes this experience. Example: _A ball of light._

Create a key phrase that summarizes this experience. Example: _I am pure._

_____

When needed, say the phrase silently and visualize the picture or symbol. This will reactivate the experience and generate a peaceful, empowered, clear state of mind.

Δ
Gem of Wisdom
It's all right to have the drama, but when the drama is having you,
your Inner Sage can pull you back into the quiet eye of the storm.

Live the Mystery

Date_____

WORKSHOP TWO
THE JUDGE "My perception is the right one."

"I know what I know, and I am right." The Judge is the part of us that claims to know the answer. Although this "knowing" is subjective, the Judge will fixate on cementing chosen perceptions as a way to make sense of a world in which it feels overwhelmed. What was complicated becomes simplified. Verdicts are made. New evidence is rejected. The Judge will try to convince those around it to adopt its perceptions in an attempt to fortify a pseudo reality, that for, whatever reason, it needs to sustain. The Judge's followers are generally those who prefer to adopt the reality of another, rather than explore their own.

While this is human and completely natural, it does have consequences. The cementing of *any* judgment *insures* our life experiences will reflect it. A verdict of "Everyone is good" will result in many adventures into the lion's den getting bit by lions. A verdict of "They are all out to get me" will result in a life of paranoia and distress. A verdict of "Life is unfair" will result in seeing everything colored with injustice, and living with a bitter heart. A verdict of "I do not measure up, will result in a lot of head hanging depression in a sad gray world—forever.

Given this, the Judge is perhaps one of the most powerful characters within us, constantly making verdicts that influence our mood, and hence our reality. We judge ourselves. *Did I do good, bad, wrong, right? Am I worthy? Do I fall short?* We judge our circumstance. *It's all over for me* or *I think I will make it.* We judge others. *This person is an idiot; that person is amazing.* We judge issues. *This is right; that is wrong.* We judge things. *This is the best; that is the worst.* And we judge ideologies. *I believe in this; I don't believe in that.*

Even though our Inner Judge can bind us to limited realities, it also deserves our thanks. We can thank it for helping us make decisions to get us moving. *After weighing all the options, I will take the job!* And we can thank it for keeping us out of harms way. *That person looks suspicious; I will keep my distance.* Sometimes the Judge will review new case material and rescind its verdict. *"I see things differently now. I change my judgment.* And sometimes it makes a verdict that will give us a rest from spinning our wheels. *This isn't going to work; I give up!* Then after a while of shutting down (and calming down), we try again.

We also tend to judge ourselves by how others judge us. When judged negatively, we feel the sting *if* our Inner Judge concurs. *They are right; I'm not good enough.* If our Inner Judge does not concur, we remain relatively unaffected. *They don't know what they are talking about; I'm more than good enough.* Admittedly, however, remaining unaffected isn't easy because what people think of us seems to matter. The more insecure we are within, the more approval we need without.

On the other side of the coin, we also tend to judge others the way we judge ourselves. *It was immoral of you to have an affair; I would never do such a thing.* Or, *I had an affair once too, I know the reasons for doing it are always more complicated than it seems.*

Our Judge's judgments are usually, at least in part, a reflection of the social paradigm of our culture at the given time. For example, in today's Western World, we are programmed to believe that if we aren't happy, something is wrong. To be happy, we must appear thin, young, strong, sexy, and attractive. We must be clean, educated, and financially solvent. We must be perfect friends, lovers, and parents, adored by many, and rejected by none. That is a lot to achieve. And if we don't, we tend to feel bad about ourselves, and hence unhappy. The more our Inner Judge concurs with the social standard, the more it colludes with our Inner Traitor to beat us over the head with our seeming imperfections. *You are fat! You are old! You are poor, sloppy, weak. You are a bad lover, bad parent, bad person. You aren't sexy enough, smart enough, rich enough. . . .* No wonder we are chronically anxious.

Our Inner Judge usually falls into one, more than one, or a combination of the following types: the Smoke and Mirrors Judge, the Blaming Judge, the Self-Condemning Judge, the Bossy Judge, the Snap to Judge-Judge, the Emotional Judge, the Rational Judge, or the Wise Judge. While some of these types may not apply to you, they will likely apply to others you know. Armed with this understanding, you will be better able to either improve your relations, or at the very least, steer clear of the fallout.

The Smoke-and-Mirrors Judge. We know this Judge has risen when we express in generalities what has personally upset us. In this, we disguise the source of pain from which our judgment springs. "Men are pigs" is really about how we have been personally hurt by men. "Women are leaches," is really about how women have taken advantage of us. "College professors are jerks" is really about how college professors have mistreated us in the past. "Your thinking is stupid," is really about us secretly feeling stupid. This technique keeps others from poking at psychological wounds we don't want to acknowledge and, least of all, expose.

The Blaming Judge. We know this Judge has risen when we blame others for our own mistakes. Every mishap is the fault of another. This blame stems from deep-seated feelings of inadequacy spawned from a tormented past. The only way we can feel better is to decide we are perfect and incapable of error. For us to be perfect, this means every one else falls short. We project onto others the grief we deny in ourselves. In short, we make others suffer to avoid feeling our own pain.

The Self-Condemning Judge. This Judge is also fond of blame, but the blame is inverted. Second-guessing everything we do, the Self-Condemning Judge uses hindsight as a gavel to deliver verdicts that begin with, "I should have . . . ." The Self-Condemning Judge always makes us feel we could have done better. It is fueled by a need to be perfect. When we agree with our Judge about all our imperfections, we find it difficult to take compliments, and easy to accept blame. This Judge will order our Inner Traitor to punish us for anything we've ever done that didn't turn out right. It won't care that we did our best. It won't take into consideration that our past behavior was contingent on many variables: our environment, what was going on around us, how the people in our lives were treating us, what we were thinking and feeling, what had happened to us in the past that made us behave as we did, what underlying fears and angers drove us to certain actions, what hopes we had then, and the pain we suffered. With all these variables, if we went back in time *without* our hindsight, we would have no choice but to respond the same way. Hindsight gives us perspective, but the Self-Condemning Judge does not care. This Judge can be harsh, and its condemnation can chip away at our self-esteem and thwart our confidence to forge ahead.

The Bossy Judge. The Bossy Judge believes it knows what is right for others. It crams its verdicts down the throats of whom it has judged. *Listen to what I say; I know what is best for you. If you don't listen to what I say, you are doing the wrong thing.* While the Bossy

Judge usually has good intentions, it has a hard time conceiving that other people can actually figure out what is best for them all on their own.

The Snap-to-Judge Judge. This Judge has a lightning mind and makes judgments before having all the facts, or any facts. *You're late; you don't respect me!* (The person is late because he was in a car accident.) *That woman is on drugs.* (The woman looks spacey because her mom just died.) This type of Judge can change verdicts on a dime, and often has a reputation of blowing hot and cold because it fails to ever think things through before rendering its verdicts. We know this Judge is on center stage when we keep changing our minds, or regret our rash conclusions that caused more trouble than they were worth.

The Emotional Judge. This Judge is controlled by its emotions. Emotionally fraught from neglect, a man might glare at his mate, thinking, I *sentence you with my wrath for neglecting me!* If the mate responds by sharing a few kind words with a warm hug, the Emotional Judge may change its verdict: *I will let you off the hook because I need your love.* It pretty much bypasses any reason behind the neglect (the husband might be having an affair).

The Emotional Judge is also known to hold marathon grudges: *My friend betrayed me, and I haven't talked to her in ten years* or sustain life-long verdicts to deflect certain life experiences: *I will never trust love again; I haven't dated for seven years.* Making all its verdicts based on emotion, the Emotional Judge often finds itself in some very challenging situations: *I know the job only pays minimum wage, but it will be fun!* (Later on, it becomes difficult to pay the bills.) *I know he just got out of prison for swindling women, but I don't care, I love him!* (Six months later, he has run off with all her savings.)

We know this Judge is at the helm when the decisions we have made, based solely on emotion, more often than not, come back to bite us.

The Rational Judge. This Judge logically weighs out the consequences for an impending decision. *If I do this, that might happen; if I do not do that, then this might happen.* It thinks everything out and makes decisions based on facts over feelings. When this Judge is on center stage we might ignore what we want and make judgments based on what logically seems best. Living logically and ignoring emotions can sometimes lead to a deep inner sadness because our emotional needs are not met. If we are not meeting our own emotional needs, there is a good chance we aren't meeting anyone else's either.

The Wise Judge. This Judge makes judgments in the name of growth and moving on. Its favorite attorney is the Sage. With the Sage's broad perception, it takes into account the bigger picture, examining various angles, close up and far back, seeing the details as well as the grand overview.

This Judge accepts the case the Sage makes on behalf of ourselves and others. It goes something like this: "Have compassion, Judge. Our pitfalls teach us about what does and does not work. Without mistakes, we remain stagnant and afraid to try new things. If we were to choose the perfect mate, and have the perfect job, and the idyllic fantasy children, in a beautiful paid-for home, and never knew debt, or suffering, or disappointment, we would be disconnected from the bounty that life has to offer. Suffering is how we measure joy. Challenge is how we measure triumph. We can never know who we truly are until we push ourselves to fix things that have seemingly gone wrong in our lives. Discomfort catalyzes growth. We would not eat if we did not get hungry. We would not build shelter if we did not get cold. We would not fight to stay out of harm's way if we did not feel pain. We would not have all our adventures in love if we did not need touch and appreciation. The past is a learning experience, and the future an experience that will help us learn, and every experience transforms us into more than we were. Look at the big picture, Judge. I ask for a verdict of Innocent!"

The Wise Judge in its infinite wisdom replies, "It is true. I would not have self-hatred fester for a mere bout of insecurity, fear, or loneliness. We learn through trial and error. We crawl before we walk, and we walk before we run. Our follies are just scenes in the play, and every hardship, if we look deeply enough, lends something beautiful. Everything everywhere comes full circle: the seasons, the stars in the sky, our blood circulating in our body. The sharks kill the baby whale. The baby whale provides food for a thousand ocean creatures for weeks. The vengeful person, bitter from a string of rejections finally has a breakdown, and in that breaking is reborn. And in that rebirth, the sun feels brighter than ever before, even before the string of rejections began. Never could this experience happen if we did not take a journey of barking and biting and being barked at and bitten. In this, I support the human effort to survive. Yes, my verdict is Innocent!"

This Wise Judge's verdict of Innocent does not mean that people get away with misbehavior because this Judge knows that life has natural consequences that cannot be defied. What goes up must come down. What we put out, we get back. Eventually the givers will take and takers will fall. Natural law transcends all judgment.

Balancing the Inner Judge

Given our whole life experience is a reflection of what we believe, if we are suffering too much, it might be well to examine the beliefs our Inner Judge endorses. Whole wars are fought driven by conflicting religious and ideological beliefs. Who is right, really? Can anyone say definitively and unequivocally? Or is it just what we choose to believe?

The way we raise our children, the mates we choose, and our life attitude are all symptomatic of our underlying beliefs. If our beliefs enrich our lives, it doesn't really matter how subjective they are. However, if our beliefs are taking us down a road to ruin, it's time for pruning the weeds that are causing the problem. Although our problems seem as if they are "out there," they aren't. What we *see* going on out there is just a manifestation of what is going inside of us. While the various characters within us will vie for a role in our lives, the parts they want to play cannot be executed without the Judge's okay. *Yes, it's okay for me to act this way. No, I must behave differently.*

Just as a hermit crab outgrows its shell, we too eventually begin to feel squashed in the confines of stubbornly held verdicts. When we refuse to open our minds to broaden and deepen our perceptions, we are refusing to grow. Since we can't stop our growth, we get uncomfortable and sooner or later we break down and are forced to rebuild our way of thinking.

This workshop is designed to help you get better acquainted with the workings of your Inner Judge, examine its verdicts, and determine if they are *currently* serving you, even if they once served you quite well. You will see how your responses to life events are less about *what is* and more about what your Inner Judge *decrees the events mean.* And if your Inner Judge's perceptions are keeping you in an unsavory life situation, this workshop will help your Inner Judge evolve by opening its mind to see a bigger picture, whereupon old verdicts can be thrown out and wiser judgments rendered.

The Judge in a Nutshell
* Believes it is right.
* Makes decisions based on its subjective *perceptions.*
* Has a hidden agenda to compliment or condemn itself or others.
* Does not always know best.

* The Smoke-and-Mirrors and Blaming Judges project their suffering onto others.
* The Self-Condemning Judge feels that you are less adequate than other people.

Judge Types

Smoke-and-Mirrors Judge: "I judge in generalities."
Blaming Judge: "It's your fault, not mine."
Self-Condemning Judge: "It's my fault, not yours."
Bossy Judge: "Listen to me; I know what is right for you."
Snap-to-Judge Judge: "I jump to conclusions."
Emotional Judge: "My verdicts are based on emotion."
Rational Judge: "My verdicts are based on reason."
The Wise Judge: "We are all doing our best."

Exploring Your Inner Judge.

Exercise One

This exercise will help you clarify the different Judge types. In this, you might better be able to identify your own type(s). Next to each statement below, state which Judge type is rendering the verdict to the incident: "My romantic partner said I was overweight."

My romantic partner said I was overweight.

1. _____ I hate my partner for saying that.

2. _____ My partner must be having an affair.

3. _____ It's my partner's fault for feeding me all those rich foods.

4. _____ I am ugly and unappealing.

5. _____ My weight is fine; it's my partner who's overweight.

6. _____ I *have* gained some weight, so I'll cut down on sugar.

7. _____ I love myself no matter what.

8. _____ Our whole country is weight-obsessed.

Answers: 1. Emotional 2. Snap-to-Judge 3. Blaming 4. Self-Condemning 5. Bossy 6. Rational 7. Wise 8. Smoke-and-Mirrors

Exercise Two

Part One

This exercise will spotlight your Inner Judge's verdicts. State your Inner Judge's *current* verdicts on the following topics:

1. My father is/was_____

2. My mother is/was_____

3. Men are_____

4. Women are_____

5. Children are_____

6. Religion is_____

7. People are_____

8. Democrats are_____

9. Republicans are_____

10. Pornography is_____

11. Television is_____

12. Technology is_____

13. Alcohol is_____

14, Prescription drugs are_____

15. Recreational drugs are_____

16. Higher education is_____

17. Casual sex is_____

18. Romance is_____

19. Divorce is_____

20. Homosexuality is_____

21. Aging is_____

22. Foreigners are_____

23. Our world is_____

24. Our planet is_____

25. My body is_____

26. My mind is_____

27. My heart is_____

28. Success is_____

29. Failure is_____

30. I am_____

31. In order to feel okay about myself, I must_____

_____

Put this all together and you have *your* reality in a nutshell. If you are not content, your current task is to broaden your perceptions so that your Inner Judge can make new verdicts.

Part Two

Review the previous exercise. Take note of the judgments you have rendered that cause you distress. Rewrite them below; then after each statement, say to yourself . . . but maybe there is more to the picture. Example: If your judgment on people is, "People are selfish," write that and then say, "but maybe there is more to the picture."

1._____but maybe there is more to the picture.

2._____but maybe there is more to the picture.

3._____but maybe there is more to the picture.

4._____but maybe there is more to the picture.

5._____but maybe there is more to the picture.

6._____but maybe there is more to the picture.

If there are more, continue this exercise in your supplementary journal.

Exercise Three

Part One

Our judgments often rise because we have been hurt in some manner. In this next exercise, state times when you were hurt, the judgment you rendered upon yourself, the judgment you rendered upon your antagonist, and the type of Judge who drew these conclusions (can be a combination), and if your conclusions helped you or made things worse. Example: My feelings were hurt when *someone I loved and needed abandoned me.* The judgment I rendered on myself was *I am not good enough.* The judgment I rendered on my antagonist was *I wouldn't have been abandoned if I was somebody else.* The type of Judge that drew these conclusions was the *Self-Condemning Judge.* These verdicts hurt me because *ever since that incident, I have felt too inadequate to even date.*

1. My feelings were hurt once when_____

_____

The judgment I passed on myself was_____

The judgment I passed on who upset me was_____

At the time my Inner Judge was the_____

These verdicts   helped me / hurt me   because_____
            (circle the appropriate answer)

_____

2. My feelings were hurt once when_____

_____

The judgment I passed on myself was_____

The judgment I passed on who hurt me was_____

At the time my Inner Judge was the_____

These verdicts   helped me / hurt me   because_____
            (circle the appropriate answer)

_____

_____

3. My feelings were hurt once when_____

_____

The judgment I passed on myself was_____

The judgment I passed on who hurt me was_____

At the time my Inner Judge was the_____

These verdicts   helped me / hurt me   because_____
            (circle the appropriate answer)

_____

_____

Whatever judgments you made in the past were the judgments that, for whatever reason, you *needed* to make—then. You could not have done things differently. However, by honestly examining that past, you can change how you judge in the future. There are no mistakes. We are all fledglings trying to find our way through the maze of life. In this, we cannot avoid trial and error. Regret is only constructive for a short time in order to realize that what we said or did is not something we want to repeat. It is important that you love and forgive yourself, right now, this instant. And if you can open your mind to the bigger picture in all the incidents above where people hurt you, perhaps you can forgive them too.

If someone behaved coldly toward us, there are reasons. It's just that those reasons are mostly hidden beneath the surface, like the bulk of an iceberg. Without understanding the whole truth, judgments of others come easy, and sometimes these judgments hurt us. Now restate the three incidents above where you were hurt and say to yourself, *but maybe there is more to the picture.* Example: *My feelings were hurt once when I shared my heart and got rejected*, but maybe there is more to the picture.

1._____

but maybe there is more to the picture.

2._____

but maybe there is more to the picture.

3._____

but maybe there is more to the picture.

Part Two

If these three incidents were to occur today, what judgments would the Wise Judge pass on yourself and on the antagonist(s)? Be honest, think big, think personal transformation. If you already have seen the incident through the Wise Judge's eyes, stretch yourself and kick it up a notch. Example: *If I were to fall in love and get abandoned again today*, my Wise Judge's verdict on myself would be, *Your worth can never be defined by others.* The Wise Judge's ruling on my antagonist(s) would be, *Everyone is doing their best, even if it seems selfish.*

Before you begin, close your eyes for a moment, and say to yourself with meaning, "I love and forgive myself."

1. If_____occurred *today,* the Wise
   (incident #1.)

Judge's verdict on myself would be_____

The Wise Judge's verdict on my antagonist(s) would be_____

_____

2. If_____ occurred *today,* the Wise
   (incident #2.)

27

Judge's verdict on myself would be _____

The Wise Judge's verdict on my antagonist(s) would be_____

_____

3. If _____occurred *today,* the Wise
                                 (incident #3.)

Judge's verdict on myself would be_____

The Wise Judge's verdict on my antagonist(s) would be_____

_____

From now on, when you catch yourself making a judgment, practice running it by the Wise Judge. Your stress will greatly ease. Most of our stress is derived from judgments such as "It's all over for me." "I don't measure up." "They don't like me." "The world sucks." Once a broader view is had on whatever you are passing judgment, the picture changes. "Maybe it isn't all over for me." "Maybe I do measure up." "It doesn't matter if they don't like me." "The world might suck, but it is beautiful too."

Exercise Four

This workshop would not be complete without examining how our Inner Judge perceives our body. These judgments can seriously affect our mental, emotional, and physical health. Answer the following questions:

1. The things I like about my body are:_____

_____

_____

Are your answers mostly about physical attributes or function?_____

Our body is a great gift no matter how it appears or performs. It has a consciousness of its own, and it is imperative that we treat it like our best friend. It is not bad for being hungry or craving unhealthy foods. It is not bad if parts of it are ailing. It does not deserve to be punished for not matching the current socially acceptable prototype, which is nearly impossible to achieve. If you catch your Inner Judge judging your body unfavorably, change it to something kind. In this, you are appreciating the home it gives you to explore the physical world and have adventures. And you are detaching from the social consensus of how our bodies should appear, which currently, in general, *does not* promote overall well-being.

2. Imagine that you are all alone on a desert island for a whole week. The island is stocked with natural foods and a cozy dwelling for shelter, should you want it. No one can see you. You are free to play naked on the beach. Your skin revels in the warm sun and balmy breezes blow against your body. Cool water swirls around your bare feet. You eat sun-ripened fruits

and colorful vegetables that nourish your body. You chew these delicious foods that slide down your throat, filling your stomach, sending nutrients throughout your body making you feel strong. Look at your hands. How precious they are to work for you as they do. Look at your legs and feet and appreciate their function. Your heart, your brain, every aspect of your body serves you. And if you are impaired, there are yet many other parts of your body doing the best they can to help you out in life. Do we not owe our body a debt of gratitude? See yourself now, sitting under stars on a warm night, naked and feeling the majesty of all the beauty around you. Talk to your body kindly and appreciatively and record these kind words below.

Dear Body,

_____

_____

_____

_____

_____

_____

_____

When you feel your Inner Judge bringing down harsh verdicts on your body, say to yourself: "No, Judge. My body is my best friend, and I stand by it, no matter what it looks like. My body is okay. My body is beautiful to me, by *my* standard."

Exercise Five

Circle the answer that describes you best. How harshly do you judge yourself?

not harsh at all   a little harsh   kind of harsh   really harsh

Circle the answer that describes you best. How harshly do you judge others?

not harsh at all   a little harsh   kind of harsh   really harsh

Our judgments help us survive. But if we know we can reject the judgments that hurt us or others, we can live more joyfully. *The joy in living is not dependent on what happens to us, but what we do with what happens to us.*

Things to Keep in Mind:

*Broaden your perceptions: "If I could see the bigger picture from an objective overview, what might I see?"

*Preface your judgments with the word "maybe." *Maybe* men are . . . *Maybe* women are . . . *Maybe* the world is . . . *Maybe* I am . . .
*Accept that everyone is doing their best and will eventually learn by trial and error.

Healing and Balancing Exercise for Your Inner Judge

Place one hand on the crown of your head.
Place the other hand beneath your breastbone.
Concentrate deeply. Repeat silently or aloud for at least two minutes:
"Everyone is doing their best."

Relaxation and Creative Visualization Exercise

Lie in a comfortable position. Play instrumental music that makes you feel good: classical, New Age, or music that is of gentle, sweeping, or dynamic beauty. When the music is playing, close your eyes. Inhale through your nose deeply, and exhale through your mouth slowly; do this eight times. Visualize that you are inhaling the power of the universe, which purifies and attunes you physically, emotionally, mentally, and metaphysically. When you exhale, all the tensions and worries leave your body and go back into the universe where they dissolve and blend into the pure life force.

Tighten and loosen your muscles slowly in this order:

Feet. Tighten. Loosen. Take a slow, deep breath, and exhale.
Calves. Tighten. Loosen. Take a slow, deep breath, and exhale.
Thighs. Tighten. Loosen. Take a slow, deep breath, and exhale.
Hips and buttocks. Tighten. Loosen. Take a slow, deep breath, and exhale.
Stomach. Tighten. Loosen. Take a slow, deep breath, and exhale.
Back. Tighten. Loosen. Take a slow, deep breath, and exhale.
Arms. Tighten. Loosen. Take a slow, deep breath, and exhale.
Hands. Tighten. Loosen. Take a slow, deep breath, and exhale.
Neck and shoulders. Tighten. Loosen. Take a slow, deep breath, and exhale.
Face. Tighten. Loosen. Take a slow, deep breath, and exhale.

Then completely relax and take eight more slow, deep breaths. Inhale the universal life energy through your nose and exhale tension through your mouth.

Set the intent: *Whoever I am, whatever I am, whatever I need, whatever is right for me—so be it. I open to insight. I open to receive.*

Now that you are completely relaxed, give yourself over to the music that is playing. Focus on the center between your eyebrows and move inward, deeper and deeper . . . . and deeper. Do this for a while . . . .
    As you journey into your vast inner being, you move toward your Inner Judge. In the distance, you see your Inner Judge. As you approach it, notice the setting. Is it indoors or out, in darkness or light? Notice your Judge's appearance. Is it wearing heavy black robes, a flowing glittery gown, or is it just an obscure image? Notice its demeanor. Is it austere, kindly, or poker-faced? Observe for a while . . . .
    Now approach your Inner Judge and stand before it. Peer deeply into your Inner Judge's eyes to see what influences its rulings. Is it rage? Compassion? Pain? Detachment? Wisdom?

Perhaps it is a combination of these things, or maybe different things at different times. Look deeper into its eyes. Reach into your Inner Judge to see what drives it. Do this for a while . . .

You can feel your Inner Sage rising in you, filling your body. You are one with your Inner Sage. In your hand there appears a golden key. This is the key of wisdom. Offer your Inner Judge the golden key. Does it open its hand? Does it ignore you?

If the Judge accepts the key, watch what happens. If the Judge does not accept the key, watch what happens. If it won't take the key, set the key near it and step back.

Now bring an upsetting incident to mind when your Inner Judge judged you harshly and made you feel guilty. Take a moment to do this . . . .

As you focus on this incident you find yourself in that situation again, as if it just happened. You can see your Inner Judge clearly there before you, slamming down the gavel with a verdict of "guilty." But this time, you stare firmly into your Inner Judge's condemning eyes and summon the power of your Quintessential Self. You can feel the light of your Quintessential filling you with power. Empowered by your Quintessential Self you move into your Inner Judge like a spirit. You lift the Judge into the air, rising higher and higher above the upsetting situation.

From here, your Inner Judge can feel the wind and clear air. In the distance it can see the pulsing waves of the shore and the mountains tall. Nearer, it can see buildings and cars driving along on roads and people bustling about living many life stories as they struggle to survive and thrive. You can tell that your Inner Judge is beginning to feel the pulse of life, the collective heartbeat, and the natural rhythm in the cycles of all that exists.

Now, have your Inner Judge look down upon the upsetting situation. As it looks down, you can tell that it is seeing a bigger picture. Tell your Inner Judge that the incident was meant to happen just as it did because it pushed you toward personal evolvement. It's just that the evolvement happened so slowly, it was hard to notice. You feel your Inner Judge gasp a bit, as if inhaling wisdom and insight.

The whole scene changes and you are now beneath the ground as a seedling that has sprouted and is pushing its way through the soil to find the sun. You blindly struggle to forge a path, as you cannot see where you are going. All you know is that you are in pain, and you hope that if you can break ground, you will find some joy in your existence. Feel your struggle, your desperation, your deepest hope, your longing, and your need. Do this for a while. . .

Now you break ground, upsetting the surface. Your Inner Judge is before you—glaring because you have toppled some beings that were in your way when you broke through to the surface. But you didn't mean to topple anything or anyone; it just happened. You cry out to your Inner Judge, "Can't you see I have done the best I could! All I am trying to do is be all right! Am I so horrible for that? I need compassion and love, not condemnation." Now say the last part a few times: "I need compassion and love, not condemnation." . . . .

With all your heart, send this plea into your Inner Judge. Make your Inner Judge feel your suffering, your hope, your need. Fill your Inner Judge with your honest intentions, even though they have caused upset. Do this for a while . . . .

You feel your Inner Judge softening and compassion stirring. You notice that in the Judge's hand is the golden key you had offered it. The key dissolves into the Judge's hand. Your Inner Judge begins to glow, a warm golden glow that feels good to your eyes and balmy on your body, like the sun on a cold day. You feel your shoulder being touched. It is your Inner Judge. Your Inner Judge tells you, "I can see now how hard you have tried. I see you have done your best, given that "at the time" you could not see or understand the impact of your actions on those around you. I've changed my verdict. You are . . . innocent." The words echo in your brain. "I am innocent. I am innocent. I am innocent." Give yourself over to the words, to the meaning, "I am innocent." Do this for a while . . . .

You now feel relief from your Inner Judge's condemnation. You realize that we humans are never as horrible as we deem ourselves to be, for anything we have ever done or not done. You forgive yourself, and in that forgiveness, your whole reality changes, and you emerge into a new plateau of being. Bask in this experience until the music ends . . . .

When you open your eyes, you will feel cleansed of guilt and self-condemnation. You will feel lighter, brighter, and free of dark judgment. You will not even accept it from others. You will feel porous with joy . . . for you . . . are . . . innocent.

Record your experience.

_____

_____

_____

_____

_____

_____

_____

_____

Draw a picture or symbol that summarizes your experience. Example: *A heart.*

Create a key phrase that summarizes this experience. Example: *I am innocent.*

_____

When needed, say the phrase silently and visualize the picture or symbol. This will reactivate the experience and generate a peaceful, empowered, clear state of mind.

Δ
Gem of Wisdom
We are all innocent.

Live the Mystery

Date_____

WORKSHOP THREE
THE WARRIOR "I fight."

The Warrior is our stamina, the part of us that marches on through rain, wind, and fire, pushing past the opposition to achieve a desired goal. The opposition can be a group of people, one person, or even ourselves. The opposition can be an ideology: "I will fight against tyranny," a way of being: "I refuse to be poor!" or fear itself: "I will conquer my fear of . . . ."

Sometimes we fight with our mind, debating, persuading, or outwitting the opposition. Sometimes we fight with our hearts, melting the opposition with kindness. Sometimes we fight with our fists, repelling the enemy with physical force. And sometimes we fight with our spirit, forging ahead against all odds. The strength of our Inner Warrior will determine our skill in warding off and/or conquering our antagonists, how long we can last in a battle, our conviction to succeed, and our ability to create and maintain boundaries.

Just as we can't know a book by its cover, neither can we gauge our Inner Warrior's strength by how it appears to others. The Passive-Aggressive Warrior can look innocuous, yet have all kinds of not-so-noticeable ways to "win the game." A Spiritual Warrior can be quiet and deep, showing its strength like a gently flowing stream that slowly whittles down the rock that blocks its way to the sea. Even a flower can be mighty by simply withstanding the wind.

This is not to underestimate the power of the more overt Warrior who, when threatened, kicks on the gas and charges forward, hollering, "Everybody out of my way, I'm coming through."

Even when we have strong Inner Warriors, they still must contend with other aspects within us. For example, our Inner Warrior might jump onto center stage and engage in jaw-dropping battle when our Inner Martyr bursts on the scene, claiming center stage with hand over heart, proclaiming dramatically, " 'Tis better to suffer!" Or we might respond first as a Victim, needing to wallow a bit on center stage in a slump, whining and complaining before our more dominant Warrior leaps onto the scene with sword in hand, proclaiming to the Victim, "Enough of that; we have work to do!" And every now and then, we might go through periods in our lives when our Inner Warrior lays down arms and is prepared to die. This manifests as full-blown depression. Sometimes we need to be depressed for whatever reason and ignore our Inner Warrior, ever urging us to take action.

It can also be that our Inner Warrior is mighty in one area of our life but not another, such as protecting our children fiercely, but getting trounced upon at work. Or we might be proficient at physically guarding our boundary and warding off the enemy, but unable to confront our personal problems head-on. Our Warrior style might also change in various circumstances, such as using the Triumphant Warrior when competing, but the Gallant Warrior when defending a loved one. Or our Warrior style might change in different phases of our lives, such as Passive-Aggressive in our youth, but Spiritual in old age.

Our Inner Warrior will generally fall into one, more than one more, or a combination of the following types: the Triumphant Warrior, the Combative Warrior, the Passive-Aggressive Warrior, the Duty-Bound Warrior, the Gallant Warrior, the Spiritual Warrior, the Fledgling Warrior, or the Dormant Warrior. Even if you only recognize a few of these types in you, you will likely recognize all of them to some degree in other people you know. This can give you a leg up on understanding their Warrior nature in relation to your own. In this, you have a better chance to either improve those relations or at the very least—survive them.

The Triumphant Warrior. This Warrior's motivation is to *win*. Lusting to compete, it thrills in the triumph more than the actual prize. It can be clever, innovative, and persistent in its pursuit. It might strive toward winning without intent to cause harm, as in a competing for a job or award, luring its resistant lover into marriage, or playing a business deal like a chess game. Or it might be insensitive, clobbering anyone who gets in its way, such as dirty play in sports, hostile takeovers in business, or exploiting employees to make money. When the Triumphant Warrior rises in us, we enjoy challenges, work hard to do better than others, and find great joy in our success. This Warrior can help us get ahead in life. What we are willing to do to achieve that end will determine residual consequences, such as becoming a positive role model for others or winding up in jail for foul play.

The Combative Warrior. This Warrior's motivation is to *fight*. Colluding with the Fury, and sometimes the Traitor, it has a rash temper and is prone to knock people down a peg for a variety of reasons. It loves to argue, debate, confront, belittle, goad, bully, and may even incite physical brawls, or perpetuate an uprising. The reason for the fight is less important than the fight itself. Winning, though desired, is secondary to the goal of feeling mighty in battle. Confrontations are its way of bragging about how strong it is. They can go berserk at times, using the Fabricator to scare others away by acting crazy, enjoying the fear they can evoke.

The more balanced Combative Warriors only surface when threat comes knocking on their door, and rather enjoy the confrontation required to stabilize the situation (whether with words or fists).

The less balanced Combative Warriors often go around picking fights to keep their boxing gloves in motion because if they stop, the waters might still, and they fear what the reflection will show. Their survival depends on keeping the surface waters stormy so they never have to look too deep within themselves. They might use the Fury as a weapon to senselessly destroy anything or anyone. This is common in riots. When unbalanced, it is also capable of vicious retaliatory acts.

We know our Combative Warrior is not in balance when we take our distress out on others. We see this in the "wife-beater syndrome," the hen-pecked husband, sometimes in war, or even in those who just never have anything nice to say. This behavior is indicative of abuse or neglect in our early life, posttraumatic stress, and staggering insecurity. Unless the underlying wounds are healed, this bloodthirsty behavior will continue as a way for us to let off steam. In time, we will either self-destruct or wear ourselves out and succumb to the Healer (inner and outer) for help, and the Sage to guide us into more fruitful behavior.

The Passive-Aggressive Warrior. This Warrior's motivation is to get its needs met without confrontation. To that end, it psychologically manipulates its opponent. When our nature is such that going toe-to-toe with our antagonists such as a bossy mate, abusive boss, or hot-headed friend, will just get us stepped on, it is easier to find a softer, more clever way to survive and thrive. For instance, a husband wants to watch a boxing match on television, but his bossy wife is watching a game show. Instead of telling her he wants to watch boxing, he walks up behind her, rubs her shoulders, kisses her head, and says, "Honey, I ran a hot bubble bath for you and lit some candles so you could read that book you love so much." This manipulation can also be used to secure a favor, such as *If I give you great sex, you will buy me that new car.* Whenever we please others as a lure to "catch them" and trick them into doing our bidding, the Passive-Aggressive Warrior is in its finest form, operating on the old adage that you get more flies with honey than vinegar.

Sometimes the Passive-Aggressive Warrior fights by allowing its pain to surface, hoping its aggravator will submit out of pity. This isn't always a manipulation. In fact, it usually isn't. Those with gentler natures often skip mad and go straight to sad. There is power in honest emotion, and the Passive-Aggressive Warrior knows how to use it.

The Passive-Aggressive Warrior is also skilled at defusing potentially violent situations. For example, two inebriated men are arguing and on the threshold of a fistfight. A person, using the Passive-Aggressive Warrior, might intervene by telling them both warmly, "You are both so smart and you each have valid points, and gee, it's about to rain, let's get inside." Or if, for example, a woman in traffic accidentally cuts off a male driver. The woman, using her Passive-Aggressive Warrior, might counter the man's glaring face by mouthing *Sorry,* and blow him a kiss. The man's glare might soften and he may even laugh a little, flattered by the invisible kiss.

Less pleasant Passive-Aggressive Warriors string people along to get their way without having to fight for it. In order to avoid arguments, they will tell their opponents what they want to hear, then secretly do what they please. "Sure, I'll clean out the garage" is code for *I don't want to, leave me alone.* Or it might placate its opponent to buy time, and in the eleventh hour, renege with a rational excuse. "I know I said you could get a horse when you turned sixteen (never intended to get the horse), but we just don't have the money."

Sometimes the Passive-Aggressive Warrior sneaks up from behind and takes down its opponent without ever being identified, such as giving an anonymous tip to the police. In this, it prohibits any possible retaliation, knowing it does not fare well in a face-to-face fight.

The Duty-Bound Warrior. This Warrior watches over those it supports and protects out of a sense of duty. It is its nature to and gladly does anything necessary to meet the needs of those whom it has taken under its wing. It doesn't mind fighting or sacrificing to do whatever it takes to be the "rock" that others rely upon. For instance, it will make sure its family is fed and clothed (no matter what), and it will strive to meet all the obligations of a responsible person. These types of Warriors often have a problem enjoying the simple things such as beautiful colors, the songs of nature, or the texture of something soft. Ever the sentry at the gate, it is difficult for them to just run in the wind and enjoy life. They carry a heavy sword, holding it no matter how much their arm aches, fearing if they put it down, even for a moment, they will fail in their duty.

The Gallant Warrior. Although this Warrior can be combative, thrill in the win, and have a strong sense of duty, it is driven by *honor, adventure,* and even *love.* It emerges bravely in tenuous circumstances, sometimes against all odds, to defend itself or others for the greater good. It has no qualms about fighting for right, or at least what it thinks is right. It sometimes goes off on tangents only to discover later it jumped the gun, and the fight was either unnecessary or misdirected.

This Warrior is exemplified when we stand up for ourselves, fight for our loved ones, push through challenging situations to yield constructive results, fight off marauders to protect the innocent, stand up for the underdog, or speak out against injustice. The Gallant Warrior, paired with the Sage and Nurturer can move mountains with inspirational speech to surpass obstacles. The Rebel joining the team creates a social activist who creates potent change. Though the Gallant Warrior works closely with the Hero, the Hero differs in that it might save the day, but doesn't relish the mission. For example, the parent who jumps into a freezing lake to save his child, the abused spouse who forces herself to get strong, or the cancer Victim who rises tall to inspire others. The Gallant Warrior, however, will enjoy the challenge and revel in the victory.

The Spiritual Warrior. A spin off of the Gallant Warrior is the Spiritual Warrior. Collaborating with the Hero, Nurturer, Sage, and Healer, the Spiritual Warrior fights with honor, for honor, and with amazing stamina. Unlike the Gallant Warrior who is not opposed to using violence, its means are peaceful. It can bond with others to generate strength in numbers to withstand an oppressor, as did Gandhi when he non violently took India back from the British. It can also diffuse antagonists by reaching past their guard and touching their inner being. This sometimes happens in kidnapping cases, where the kidnapped personalizes herself to the kidnapper who then, out of compassion, releases her. It also happens when others are about to pounce on us and we circumvent it by acting kindly toward them. If the Spiritual Warrior is successful, the opponent(s) will feel bonded with those whom they want to crush, and they lose their urge to fight. Although this isn't a popular method, it can be quite powerful.

The Spiritual Warrior can also stand silent and alone, strong in itself, needing no outside approval or outer world battle. It has tremendous fortitude in any goal it undertakes. Sometimes, just enduring hardship in a fight toward self-actualization is the mark of perhaps the greatest Warrior of all. We know this Warrior is active in us when we push forward, even through seeming stone, to touch the sky, and when we dispel or prevent confrontation with our hearts.

The Fledgling Warrior. The Fledgling Warrior wants to fight, imagines fighting, but just can't seem to emerge, or at least not very much, or for very long. It often stews silently from lack of expression. This occurs when we want to speak up, stand up, defend, or fight, but it is as if something holds us back, maybe lack of confidence, fear of getting hurt, or the lack of wanting to hurt another. And if we do manage to make a stand, we often get blown away by our opponents, making us prefer the less frightening approach of the Passive-Aggressive Warrior. However, a major life event can catalyze the Fledgling Warrior, and without even trying, it bursts out of us like a firework, fighting in brilliant form. After that, it will rise more easily when needed.

The Dormant Warrior. The Dormant Warrior isn't necessarily against fighting and in fact admires Warriors in general. It just doesn't want to do the fighting and hopes it never must. This Warrior is stirred in us when we stick our head in the sand, waiting for others to pick up the sword and fight on our behalf. We might even enjoy the show, as long as we can just watch. This Dormant Warrior, like the Fledgling Warrior, when catalyzed by a major life event, can surprise us by suddenly emerging when least expected.

Balancing the Inner Warrior

The balanced Warrior is flexible, sometimes stepping out of the fray, sometimes stepping into it, sometimes fighting from behind the scenes, and sometimes leading the charge. As no two people or situations are exactly alike, only we can honestly look our Inner Warrior in the eye and determine if its behavior is helping or hindering our lives.

If your Inner Warrior is very strong, you might get so into taking on challenges that you can't see the forest for the trees because winning is all that matters, and when you look behind you, you see the wake of bodies you trampled to accomplish your goals. Or sometimes, even if you conquered your corner of the world with a measure of honor, you might, when reflecting on your feats, feel you could have had won by a bigger landslide. Or you might feel you can never get enough victories under your belt, and in hindsight, determine there were missed opportunities. Always looking at what hasn't been achieved, you many not realize how much you *have* achieved.

If your Inner Warrior is too overbearing, explosive, or ambitious without being tempered by your Inner Nurturer, you might frighten away those whom you actually want in your life, have trouble with emotional intimacy, and perhaps be unable to sustain healthy relationships. Eventually, this extreme aggression creates a backlash, and you might end up alone and lonely, feeling unloved, generally distrusted, and maybe even do jail time.

If your Inner Warrior is too thwarted, you will give up easily in more areas of your life than not, have difficulty making stands, and be subject to incessant abuse and suffering.

Even if your Inner Warrior's behavior lies somewhere in the middle, this workshop is designed to help you examine its workings, the consequences it currently generates, and make necessary modifications to empower your personal growth and bypass future pitfalls.

The Warrior in a Nutshell
* Is our stamina to endure and overcome challenges.
* Is our drive to succeed and thrive.
* Guards and/or tears down boundaries.
* Protects and/or strikes.

Warrior Types
The Triumphant Warrior: "I want to win."
Combative Warrior: "I want to fight."
Passive-Aggressive Warrior: "I fight indirectly."
Duty-Bound Warrior: "I am responsible."
Gallant Warrior: "I fight the good fight with enthusiasm and a taste for adventure."
Spiritual Warrior: "My weapon is compassion, wisdom, and endurance."
Fledgling Warrior: "I want to fight, but it's too hard."
Dormant Warrior: "I want others to fight for me."

Exploring Your Inner Warrior

Exercise One

This first exercise is to practice identifying the Warrior types so that you may better identify your own. Before each sentence, state the Warrior type that is speaking.

1. _____ "I enjoy arguing."

2. _____ "I defend the underdog."

3. _____ "I work hard to pay my bills."

4. _____ "I like to be number one in all I do."

5. _____ "I am frustrated because I can't stand up for myself."

6. _____ "I get others to solve my problems."

7. _____ "I just keep trying and I never give up."

8. _____ "I cleverly dodge direct confrontation to get my way."

Answers: 1. Combative 2. Gallant 3. Duty-Bound 4. Triumphant 5. Dormant
6. Fledgling 7. Spiritual 8. Passive-Aggressive

Exercise Two

This exercise will help you pinpoint your *predominant* Inner Warrior type. If it seems to be more than one, then your Warrior nature is likely a combination of types. Place an X by the answers that *currently* apply.

_____1. I often fight with compassionate words or actions. (Spiritual)

_____2. I often fight with insulting words. (Combative)

_____3. I pick fights when I am distressed. (Combative)

_____4. I want to speak up to defend myself, but it's just so hard. (Fledgling)

_____5. I have to quietly manipulate to get what I want or need. (Passive-Aggressive)

_____6. I usually stand up for my principles, even if it makes me unpopular. (Gallant)

_____7. I enjoy proving that I am the best. (Triumphant)

_____8. I might be able to take a stand, but I just can't seem to hold it. (Fledgling)

_____9. I push myself to do better for the sake of my loved ones. (Duty-Bound)

_____10. I will fight however I must to win my battles. (Triumphant)

_____11. If my honor has been compromised, I almost always make a bold stand. (Gallant)

_____12. When verbally assaulted, my self-respect shields me. (Spiritual)

_____13. When verbally assaulted, I might show my pain so the offenders will take pity and lay down their swords. (Passive-Aggressive)

_____14. I act compliant when I am bossed around, but then I go do what I want to do. (Passive-Aggressive)

_____15. I will do what I must to pay my bills. (Duty-Bound)

_____16. I like to argue. (Combative)

____17. I get mad when I see injustice, but I can't seem to do anything about it. (Fledgling)

____18. I usually stuff my negative thoughts and feelings. (Dormant)

____19. People often step in and help me because I have trouble helping myself. (Dormant)

____20. I don't care what I have to do when it comes to defending the innocent. (Gallant)

____21. If someone thinks she/he can do better than me, I will outshine them. (Triumphant)

____22. It is easy for me to diffuse arguments between people. (Spiritual)

____23. When people are afraid, I am their rock. (Duty-Bound)

____24. In the face of conflict, I often pretend all is well. (Dormant)

List the number of X's you have for each Warrior Type

Triumphant_____   Combative_____   Passive-Agressive_____   Gallant_____

Duty Bound_____   Spiritual_____   Fledgling_____   Dormant_____

By these numbers, list the Warrior type(s) that best depict your Inner Warrior.

_____

Exercise Three

This exercise will help you examine your reactions to emotional threat. State how you would most likely respond when in the situations listed below. You can have multiple answers. (Example responses: verbally defend myself, retreat at first but then face my antagonist head on, drink alcohol, ignore the problem, laugh in my antagonist's face, say something wise, shut down, etc.) Although we don't always respond the same way to every circumstance, or to every person, we generally will respond a *certain way* more often than not.

1. When someone important to me chews me out, I am most likely to_____

_____

2. When a stranger offends me, I am most likely to_____

_____

4. When someone insults someone I care about, I am most likely to_____

_____

5. When an innocent stranger is verbally harassed, I am most likely to_____

6. When someone tries to sabotage my efforts, I am most likely to_____

_____

7. When someone tries to sabotage someone I care about, I am most likely to_____

_____

8. When the competition is stiff for something I want, I am most likely to_____

_____

9. When I have a difficult climb ahead of me, I am most likely to_____

_____

10. In witnessing an act of prejudice upon a stranger, I am most likely to_____

_____

Given your answers, how do you feel *right now*? (Examples: mostly proud, generally satis-
fied, ashamed, worried, guilty, etc.)

_____

There are no right or wrong ways you need to be. Only you will know if your behavior is
working for you or causing problems. For instance, it might be better for you as an individual
to stay behind the scenes and not be brave or gallant by social standards. If you don't feel
equipped to handle certain consequences, it would be ill-advised for you to stick your neck
out. Or you might have a life philosophy that does not require you to jump into the fray of
things. On the other side of the coin, you might be a Gallant Warrior type, so gallant that
while you are out defending the world, your own family is neglected or your health suffers.
Or you might be a Combative Warrior type, pouncing upon your antagonists with ruthless
vigor, but if you are a prosecuting attorney that might not be a bad thing.

Considering these points, how do you feel about your Inner Warrior's responses now? (Examples: pretty good about myself, like I still need to strengthen my Inner Warrior, like I still
need to tone down my Inner Warrior in certain areas of my life, etc.)

_____

Exercise Four

To further examine how your Inner Warrior might hinder your personal growth, state times
when your Inner Warrior worked against you, the result, and how you could better handle
similar situations in the future. Example #1: My Inner Warrior worked against me once when
a work-related rival goaded me and I punched him. The result was I went to jail. In the fu-

ture, when my Inner Warrior has this impulse, *I will take my anger and channel it into becoming an even greater success than before.* Example #2: My Inner Warrior worked against me once when *there was a competition I really wanted to win,* so I cheated. The result was *I got caught, disqualified, and humiliated.* In the future when my Inner Warrior has this impulse *I will give my all to winning the competition honestly.*

If you are having trouble answering these questions because your Inner Warrior is less overt, think of passive-aggressive acts. Example: My Inner Warrior worked against me once when *I wanted to go to Europe with my spouse but he didn't want to go.* My Warrior emerged and I made him feel guilty about an affair he once had so he would agree to the Europe trip. The result was, he *got drunk, went driving, and got in a car accident.* In the future, when my Inner Warrior has this impulse, *I won't "play dirty" to get my way.*

1. My Inner Warrior worked against me once when_____

_____

The result was_____

In the future, when my Inner Warrior has this impulse, I_____

_____

2. My Inner Warrior worked against me once when_____

_____

The result was_____

In the future, when my Inner Warrior has this impulse, I_____

_____

3. My Inner Warrior worked against me once when_____

_____

The result was_____

In the future, when my Inner Warrior has this impulse, I_____

_____

4 . My Inner Warrior worked against me once when_____

_____

The result was_____

In the future, when my Inner Warrior has this impulse, I_____

_____

5 . My Inner Warrior worked against me once when_____

_____

The result was_____

In the future, when my Inner Warrior has this impulse, I_____

_____

If we can learn from our past behaviors, then those behaviors are merely stepping stones to our personal growth and self-actualization. Take a moment now to embrace yourself, no matter how you think your Inner Warrior may have failed you. You were doing the best you could *then* for the stage of growth you were in. Release any bad feelings about yourself that you have attached to these events. Close your eyes for a minute and do this now.

Exercise Five

This exercise will help you examine times when you regret *not* using your Inner Warrior, what held you back, how that incident makes you feel today, and what you can do in the future that might be better. Example #1: *Once when my child was unfairly accused by an authority figure, I didn't stand up for him.* I held my Inner Warrior back because *it was hard for me to stand up to authority figures.* The result was *his self-esteem plummeted.* Whenever I think of this I feel *guilty.* In the future, I will *take the plunge and defend my loved ones the best I can.* Example #2: I did not use my Inner Warrior once *when my girlfriend decided to date someone else who I knew was going to hurt her.* I held my Inner Warrior back because *after he hurt her, I wanted her to run back to me.* The result was *she got raped, and she never was the same after that.* Whenever I think of this, I feel *angry with myself.* In the future, *I will always defend those I care about even if it means I might not get what I want.*

1. I did not use my Inner Warrior once when_____

_____

I held my Inner Warrior back because_____

_____

The result was_____

_____

Whenever I think of this, I feel_____

In the future, I will_____

2. I did not use my Inner Warrior once when_____

_____

I held my Inner Warrior back because_____

_____

The result was_____

_____

Whenever I think of this, I feel_____

In the future, I will_____

3. I did not use my Inner Warrior once when_____

_____

I held my Inner Warrior back because_____

_____

The result was_____

_____

Whenever I think of this, I feel_____

In the future, I will_____

Be aware that maybe your inaction may have actually been for the best, a lesser of two evils so to speak. Do not be hard on yourself. If you "acted" then, something worse may have happened. Or, if you couldn't act and you believe if you had, things would have turned out better, keep in mind that at that time you could *not* behave any other way. We can't expect ourselves to run before we learn to walk. We can't expect to know all the answers before we are old enough and wise enough to know the important questions such as, "Who am I? What is love? How important is honor?" Accept that these things happened because your Inner Warrior was not developed enough and/or was overpowered by another aspect within you, such as the Scaredy Cat. Release any bad feelings about yourself that you have attached to these events. Close your eyes for a minute and do this now.

Exercise Six

List times when your Inner Warrior worked *for* you, the result, and how thinking of this makes you feel. Example: My Inner Warrior worked for me once when *I held my ground when someone was trying to take advantage of me.* The result was *I did not get swindled.* When I think of this I feel *proud that I did not give in.*

1. My Inner Warrior worked for me once when_____

_____

The result was_____

When I think, of this I feel_____

2. 1. My Inner Warrior worked for me once when_____

_____

The result was_____

When I think, of this I feel_____

3. My Inner Warrior worked for me once when_____

_____

The result was_____

When I think, of this I feel_____

Your Inner Warrior may have been more positively active in your life than you realize. Take a moment now to appreciate your Inner Warrior even if it needs to be tuned up or toned down. Close your eyes for a minute and do this now.

Exercise Seven

Now, for a moment become your Inner Warrior. Let it speak. Don't think too much, just let your answers flow like a stream.

I am _____'s Inner Warrior. My philosophy about fighting is_____
        (your name)

_____

When I feel the urge to fight, it is most frequently about_____

_____

On the occasions I give up, it is usually because_____

_____

My best warrior skill(s) are_____

I wish I could be more skilled at_____

It is hard for me to fight when_____

It is easy for me to fight when_____

I fight in full force when_____

I retreat when_____

I am proud of my warrior skills when_____

I am ashamed when_____

To be the best Warrior I can be (for who I am), my goal is to_____

You cannot change your Warrior nature, nor should you want to, because it is what it is for a reason. It is part of who you are and has great value. You can, however, as you advance in this workbook, infuse it with your Inner Sage (wisdom), your Inner Nurturer (compassion), your Inner Healer (regeneration), your Inner Leader (control), your Inner Rebel (individuality), your Inner Innovator (inspiration), and your Inner Hero (ability to save yourself). As your inner characters attune with each other, you become more attuned with yourself. Like ingredients that compliment each other in a gourmet dish, when your inner characters blend well together, you become your potential in all its glory.

Healing and Balancing Exercise for your Inner Warrior

Place one hand below your navel.
Place the other hand over your heart.
Concentrate deeply. Repeat silently, or aloud, for at least two minutes:
"I have the power to flourish."

Relaxation and Creative Visualization Exercise

Lie in a comfortable position. Play instrumental music that makes you feel good: classical, New Age, or music that is of gentle, sweeping, or dynamic beauty. When the music is playing, close your eyes. Inhale through your nose deeply, and exhale through your mouth slowly; do this eight times. Visualize that you are inhaling the power of the universe, which purifies and attunes you physically, emotionally, mentally, and metaphysically. When you exhale, all the tensions and worries leave your body and go back into the universe where they dissolve and blend into the pure life force.

Tighten and loosen your muscles slowly in this order:

Feet. Tighten. Loosen. Take a slow, deep breath, and exhale.
Calves. Tighten. Loosen. Take a slow, deep breath, and exhale.
Thighs. Tighten. Loosen. Take a slow, deep breath, and exhale.
Hips and buttocks. Tighten. Loosen. Take a slow, deep breath, and exhale.

Stomach. Tighten. Loosen. Take a slow, deep breath, and exhale.
Back. Tighten. Loosen. Take a slow, deep breath, and exhale.
Arms. Tighten. Loosen. Take a slow, deep breath, and exhale.
Hands. Tighten. Loosen. Take a slow, deep breath, and exhale.
Neck and shoulders. Tighten. Loosen. Take a slow, deep breath, and exhale.
Face. Tighten. Loosen. Take a slow, deep breath, and exhale.

Then completely relax and take eight more slow, deep breaths. Inhale the universal life energy through your nose and exhale tension through your mouth.

Set the intent: *Whoever I am, whatever I am, whatever I need, whatever is right for me—so be it. I open to insight. I open to receive.*

Now that you are completely relaxed, give yourself over to the music. Focus on the point between your eyebrows and journey inward, deeper and deeper into your vast being. Do this for a while . . . .
    Ahead, you see your Inner Warrior. As you approach, notice the setting, your Inner Warrior's appearance, and its demeanor. Do this for a while . . . .
    Now you are standing before your Inner Warrior, looking at it as it looks at you. Look deep into your Warrior's eyes . . . into its reality. Do this for a while . . . .
    Now you see in your Inner Warrior's eyes brief scenes of times when it helped you survive and thrive. Watch these scenes for a while. Do not try to remember; just watch what comes naturally, like watching a movie, even if you don't recall what you see . . . .
    You see some scenes now when your Inner Warrior overreacted. Do this for a while . . . .
    Now you see some scenes when your Warrior under reacted. Do this for a while . . . .
    While your Inner Judge may have once judged your Inner Warrior harshly for these times, you can now see that your Inner Warrior absolutely did the best it could at that moment, and at that time. When it overreacted, it was fueled by other aspects, such as the Fury. When it under reacted, it was held back by other aspects, such as the Scaredy Cat or Nurturer. And in these times when it over or under reacted, and didn't seem to serve you well, you realize it really did do all right, given all the variables.
    Behold your Inner Warrior now as if it were another human being separate from you. Take a moment to truly appreciate its effort to protect you, even if its actions backfired. You feel your Inner Nurturer stirring inside you and compassion rises. Looking into your Warrior's eyes, place your hand over your Inner Warrior's heart. Send your deep gratitude into it. And now your compassion . . . . And now your love . . . .
    This energy makes your Inner Warrior radiate a warm power. Love mixed in with its might makes it stronger. It is becoming empowered by your pure acceptance of its being. You can sense that it is evolving. Continue this for a while . . . .
    Now your Inner Sage stirs within you and flows wisdom through your hand into your Inner Warrior's heart as if giving it a shot of vitamins and minerals. You see your Inner Warrior evolving even more, shining now with a sense of honor that begins to define a life direction. You realize your Inner Leader and Inner Healer are also flowing their gifts into your Warrior. One by one, all your selves are flowing their energy, through your hand, into the Warrior's heart, paying tribute and lending their support. Experience this for a while . . . .
    With such a strong focus on your Inner Warrior, you now find yourself inside your Inner Warrior, and you can feel the charge of love and support you are receiving. This is your day, your moment of feeling appreciated for all your hard work. With all this support you feel that

you will now be able to handle outer world events with greater wisdom and compassion than ever before. You will shine so bright, you cannot be dimmed.

Bask in this experience until the music ends . . . .

When you open your eyes, you will feel the strong and wise presence of your Inner Warrior, ready and always there to be your very own knight or knightess in shining armor.

Record your experience.

_____

_____

_____

_____

_____

_____

_____

_____

Draw a picture or symbol that summarizes your experience. Example: *A noble sword.*

Create a key phrase that summarizes this experience. Example: *I am stronger than I know.*

_____

When needed, say the phrase silently and visualize the picture or symbol. This will reactivate the experience and generate a peaceful, empowered, clear state of mind.

Δ

Gem of Wisdom
Sometimes the armor we wear shields us from ourselves.

Live the Mystery

WORKSHOP FOUR
THE NURTURER "I love."

The Nurturer yearns to nourish and bring comfort. It lives to cultivate and watch things grow. In empathy, it forgives. In caring, it understands. Whether playing a minor, moderate, or major role, the Nurturer lives in us all. It is strong in parents, often in friends, and usually in lovers. It is there in the seeming cold-hearted, tied up and held hostage to keep their defenses strong. It is there in the seeming selfish, just inverted, sending the nourishment to themselves. Even hedonists who inhale pleasure are trying to nourish themselves, indulging in addictions that temporarily give them a fix. And in psychopaths too, it is there, locked away in the dudgeon of their being, punished for existing.

The Nurturer, when used in balance, can have a restorative affect on all it touches. Children flourish, friends grow closer, and strangers feel warmth in their hearts.

The act of nurturing is a truer expression of what we call love than the word love itself depicts. The word love has become so generic, it has multiple meanings, the most common of which is "need." *I love you* means *I need you*. However, need is not the same as love. When someone needs us, we might feel important, or maybe even smothered, but that is not the same as someone caring for us irrespective of our relationship with him or her. Further, when we need them, we need something *from* them, usually affirmation of our worth as a person, or maybe we just need someone to take care of us because we doubt our ability to take care of ourselves.

In romance, sexual attraction (sometimes chemistry) can turn into infatuation or what we call "being in love." Being in love is like a spell with a fairy tale quality derived from seeing others as we *want or need* to see them, and seldom as they are. When we see them as they are, often the spell breaks. And if they see us as we are, we fear abandonment. This is why the image game is so strong in romantic relationships.

Deep down, most realize that being "in love" is not same as love. While need and infatuation are nature's way of insuring propagation of the species, it has nothing to do with the authentic, pure connection between two people. However, there are couples who are in love and also love each other with respect and admiration. If the members of each couple are incompatible, or not self-examined, this is almost impossible to achieve. Unresolved issues of either, become obstacles for both. Further, if two people cannot see eye to eye, the romance dance becomes a series of missteps.

True love is about caring for others for *their* own sake, not ours. And if others truly love us, it is for our sake, not theirs. Many parents carry this kind of love for their children, and humanitarians often carry this kind of love for the world. This more unconditional love, however, falls into the realm of the Quintessential Self. Unaffected by the outside world, the Quintessential Self emanates from its original source. The Quintessential Self is who we are before we become, and it fuels us as we grow into what we are to be. The Nurturer, however, if offended, is not immune to taking its marbles and going home. It has a one-track mind to nurture, and if thwarted, it can fumble. It can also overdo, but be brought into balance by our Inner Warrior who can detach, and our Inner Sage who knows when to quit.

Sometimes the Nurturer is confused with the Pleaser, but they are not the same. Although the Nurturer often pleases others and enjoys pleasing, it differs from the Pleaser in that its motive is not to attain acceptance, love, and security; it just wants to bring comfort and joy to others.

Going through the motions of nurturing is not the Nurturer either. This "acting" like a Nurturer is often the Pleaser giving to get, or the Warrior doing its duty.

Our Inner Nurturer generally is one, more than one, or a combination of the following types: the Therapeutic Nurturer, the Cherry-on-the-Sundae Nurturer, the Sacrificial Nurturer, the Addicted Nurturer, or the Hedonist. While all these types may not apply to you, they will likely apply to others you know. In this, you might appreciate them more, or at least better understand their motives. You might even be able to hold up a mirror to those whose Inner Nurturer goes overboard with a proverbial message: "You need to do more for yourself."

The Therapeutic Nurturer. This Nurturer's goal is to help things flourish, be it a plant, animal, or human being. It instinctively softens the barriers of what it wants to nourish, and most often gains reception. It does not need praise or thanks. Its joy is simply in watching hardship turn into a growing experience. Therapeutic Nurturers collaborate with their Inner Healer and often are healers in the outer world, even if not professionally. However, the Inner Healer in its purity has a primary aim to cure ailments on any level, even if that involves some discomfort; the Therapeutic Nurturer's sole drive is to nourish what seems to be struggling.

The Therapeutic Nurturer is on stage when we tend our aphid-infested garden, prune our struggling trees, lovingly tender a child's cut finger, instill confidence in one who is flailing, comfort our distressed friends, visit our relative in the nursing home, or any number of things that involve giving a dose of compassionate caring to any who seem to need it.

Unable to watch anything suffer, it is sometimes guilty of robbing others of valuable life lessons. For instance, in an effort to erase the disappointment of a child who lost his birthday money of ten dollars because it fell out of his pocket while playing outside, the overly-nurturing mother, just to see him happy again, might give him a new ten-dollar bill saying, "Be more careful next time." She has unwittingly short-circuited her child's opportunity to be more careful with his money in the future. If the ten dollars were not replaced, the child actually *would be* less careless in the future and put his money in a safe place before going outside to play. Or if seeing him so sad is more than she can bear, she could strike a middle ground by allowing him to earn a new ten dollars by doing household jobs.

When our Therapeutic Nurturer is out of balance, we will over-coddle others and be so consumed with tending the "unhappy" that we've no time to enjoy the sun on our own face.

The Cherry-on-the-Sundae Nurturer. This Nurturer's goal is to generate smiles, make the cat purr, the dog's tail wag, and the birds sing louder. Loving to spread joy, the Cherry-on-the-Sundae Nurturer has a wide band of those whose days it tries to brighten. This Nurturer is active in us when we buy our animals gourmet pet food, throw a surprise party, send cards or presents to all whom we love, make habitats for the birds or squirrels in our yards, or compliment people because we so want to see them smile. The Cherry-on-the Sundae Nurturer doesn't need praise; it just wants its kindness to be received. Its reward is to see whomever or whatever it nurturers—joyful.

The Sacrificial Nurturer. This Nurturer unnecessarily over does. Driven solely to nurture others, it forgets to nurture itself. Our Sacrificial Nurturer is on stage when we expel more nurturing energy than we receive. This is apparent when we become emotionally malnourished and ask ourselves, "Who will nurture me?" It is also apparent when those whom we overly nurture begin taking us for granted, or maybe, feeling overwhelmed, retreat from our rain of constant kindness. In this, we might begin to feel like we are on the outside looking in, as if nobody cares for us as much as we care for them. We are left with a sudden need to receive from someone the pure nurturing we so often give away because we have failed to give it to ourselves. Depleted and alone, the Sacrificial Nurturer sits with the Martyr and the Victim, feeling sad.

When our Sacrificial Nurturer takes over, we need to stop nurturing others for a while and take time to nourish ourselves; perhaps take a bubble bath, paint, go to a movie, sing a song, hike in nature, buy ourselves a present, pursue a personal goal, or maybe just take a day to vegetate and do nothing.

The Addicted Nurturer. This Nurturer will use nurturing as a way to cope with feeling bad. Nurturing feels good, so instead of dealing with underlying issues, it throws its energy outward into good deeds that give it a high. Eventually, it will be swallowed by all the issues it is trying to escape and have a break down. When this happens to us, we are forced to deal with our own inner demons and have an amazing opportunity to grow.

The Hedonist. The Nurturer who uses physical pleasure in excess to comfort itself is the Hedonist. This is not to be confused with simply enjoying the taste of food or pleasuring in a sexual experience. It is when we take this need for pleasure to an extreme to drown out our psychological pain.

We are all a bit hedonistic from time to time indulging in a preponderance of sweets because we are depressed, or racking up the credit card because we feel better when we are shopping. This is normal human behavior and no cause for shame. Feeling shame only worsens our upset and fuels more hedonistic behavior. Trying to comfort ourselves is the most natural thing in the world and self-love is warranted even when shanghaied by our Inner Hedonist here and there, now and then.

However, extreme and chronic hedonistic behavior is often indicative of underlying psychological wounds from some sort of deprivation earlier in life. Hedonism is a drastic attempt to pour nourishment into that deep, dark emptiness by overeating, overspending, indulging in drugs, alcohol, pornography, or a variety of other things. Chronic indulgence counteracts the suffering that never goes away.

Sometimes it is not deprivation that creates full-time Hedonists, but having too much without ever taking consequences. Those who are accustomed to being showered with whatever they want and are spared from ever taking consequences for inappropriate behavior will be prone to stuff themselves with what ever brings them pleasure.

Eventually chronic Hedonists, whether filling an empty emotional hole, or sucking in too many pleasures just because they can, will pop like a balloon and be swamped with natural consequences: loneliness from being abandoned, failing health from eating fatty foods, a disease from sleeping with one too many bed partners, bankrupt from supporting their "fixes," or imprisoned for breaking the law. The only way chronic Hedonists will feel better is to consider the needs and joys of others and face the source of their pain.

Balancing the Inner Nurturer

When we nurture too much, we need to step back and give others a chance to nurture us. If stuff is always coming at them, there is never an exhale, and they are more likely to retreat from us than give back. Remember, giving back makes them feel good too. Sometimes it is kinder to not be so kind.

Balancing an Inner Nurturer who nurtures too much can be achieved by improving our relationship with our Inner Sage and Inner Warrior. Our Inner Sage signals us when to back off from spreading so much joy, and our Inner Warrior helps us detach and develop some boundaries.

On the other hand, when we nurture too little, our relationships can get rocky because our loved ones never feel loved. Withholding affection is a control tactic designed to keep our loved ones in our lives always wanting from us what they can't get, but ironically, they will inevitably slip away, lonely for emotional intimacy.

When our Inner Nurturer is balanced, we will have no problem expressing honest, positive feelings toward others because we can also nurture ourselves in ways that promote our well-being. Self-nurturing is about giving ourselves quiet time for deep thought, personal time for creative self-expression, time to tend our bodies with healthy food and exercise, and permission to actualize our dreams. But most of all, when we nurture ourselves, we pay attention to our own human struggle and give ourselves respect, compassion, and appreciation. When we nurture ourselves first and keep our own cup full, it will spill over to nurture others. Making ourselves a priority is NOT selfish.

Our Inner Nurturer, at its best, can bring much needed smiles to many, turn the surly into purring kittens, and punch a hole of relief to those enshrined in pain. It can lift us from the darkness, and help us grow into all we can be.

This workshop is designed to help you become more familiar with your Inner Nurturer. Is it blocked, free, out of control, or all of these at different times? What are its motives? What happens in your life when the Nurturer is in the driver's seat? In what ways might your Inner Nurturer be repressed? And if repressed, how does this affect your life? These answers and more can be found in the following exercises.

The Nurturer in a Nutshell
* Is an expression of love.
* Is compelled to foster comfort and joy.
* Can indulge others too much and itself too little.
* Can indulge others too little and itself too much.
* Works well with the Healer to promote well being.
* Lives to make compassionate connections.

Nurturer Types
* Therapeutic Nurturer: "I nourish the ailing."
* Cherry-on-the-Sundae Nurturer: "I spread joy."
* Sacrificial Nurturer: "I deplete myself to make others smile."
* Addictive Nurturer: "I constantly nurture because it makes me feel 'high.' "
* Hedonist: "I can't get enough comfort."

Exploring Your Inner Nurturer

Exercise One

This exercise will bring clarity to behaviors associated with various Nurturer types. State which kind of Nurturer is speaking: Therapeutic, Cherry-on-the-Sundae, Sacrificial, Addictive, or Hedonist.

1. _____ "Are you enjoying the two hundred gifts I sent you?"

2. _____ "I built my kids a tree house and they love it!"

3. _____ "My child had a bad day at school, but I assured him he was lovable and that he meant the world to me, and now he feels better."

4._____ "I ate three pies today."

5. _____ "I helped my kids with their homework last night in stead of studying for my own test, which I failed."

6. _____ "I gave my sister a great surprise party."

7._____ "I was upset, so I maxed out my credit card shopping for clothes."

8. _____ "I felt sorry for my friend who lost her job, so I happily invited her to live in my spare bedroom for a while.

9. _____ "Okay, I took care of everyone who needed my help, but now I have a splitting head ache."

10. _____ "I feel a bit down, I need to find someone to cheer up."

Answers: 1. Addictive 2. Cherry-on-the-Sundae 3. Therapeutic 4. Hedonist 5. Sacrificial 6.Cherry-on-the-Sundae 7. Hedonist 8. Therapeutic 9. Sacrificial 10. Addictive

Exercise Two

This exercise will help you explore how you nurture. State what brings out your Inner Nurturer and the act of nurturing that follows. If you find that your Inner Nurturer has difficulty expressing, list that too. Example #1: *When my mate smiles at me warmly,* it brings out the Nurturer, *but I can't say or do anything.* Or if you can express, share that. Example #2: When *my children go to bed,* it brings out the Nurturer and *I tuck them in and read them a story.* Example #3: When *I feel loving toward my mate,* it brings out the Nurturer and I *give her a back rub.* Example #4: When *I am hurting,* it brings out the Nurturer, and I *do something kind for myself.* Example #5: When *I see an injured bird,* it brings out the Nurturer, and I *try to help it.*

1. When_____

it brings out the Nurturer and I_____

_____

2. When_____

it brings out the Nurturer and I_____

_____

3. When_____

it brings out the Nurturer and I_____

_____

4. When_____

it brings out the Nurturer and I_____

_____

5. When_____

it brings out the Nurturer and I_____

_____

6. When_____

it brings out the Nurturer and I_____

_____

7. When_____

it brings out the Nurturer and I_____

_____

8. When_____

it brings out the Nurturer and I_____

_____

9. When_____

it brings out the Nurturer and I_____

_____

10. When_____

it brings out the Nurturer and I_____

_____

Given these answers, list the way(s) your Inner Nurturer generally expresses itself. (Examples: physical affection, warm words, acts of kindness, helping others with tasks, the look in my eyes, etc.)

My Nurturer generally expresses itself in the follow way(s):_____

_____

If your Inner Nurturer expresses itself in a variety of ways, it is strong in you.

If your Inner Nurturer's expression is limited to one or more ways, it is likely tempered by another aspect of yourself. For instance, those who wear a lot of emotional armor (the Warrior) are more likely to nurture by acting kindly rather than emotionally gush.

If your Inner Nurturer has difficulty expressing at all, it is likely repressed by another aspect of yourself such as the Scaredy Cat. For instance, those coming from abusive families often learn to button up their feelings and lock the door, for fear of being hurt again.

No matter where you fall on the scale of nurturing, you aren't doing anything wrong. You can't help how you are; you can, however, modify your behavior to change how you will be *if* you feel it will improve your life.

Exercise Three

This next exercise is to determine if your Inner Nurturer is helping or hurting your well-being. State how your various Significant Others (important people in your life) generally respond when you nurture them, how it makes you feel, and why. Example #1: When I nurture my *mate, she gets affectionate with me.* This makes me feel *even warmer toward her* because *she is reciprocating.* Example #2: When I nurture my *mate, he is non-responsive.* This makes me feel *unloved* because *my love seems to mean nothing to him.* Example #3: When I nurture my *children, they seem to take me for granted.* This makes me feel *unappreciated* because *I give a lot of myself when I nurture, and they don't seem to care.* Example #4: When I nurture my *friend, she lights up with joy.* This makes me feel *happy* because *she is so receptive.* Example #5: When I nurture my *mom, she complains about other things.* This makes me feel *frustrated* because *there seems to be nothing I can do to make her feel better.*

1. When I nurture my_____(response)_____

_____

This makes me feel_____because_____

_____

2. When I nurture my_____ (response)_____

_____

This makes me feel_____because_____

_____

3. When I nurture my_____(response)_____

_____

This makes me feel _____because_____

_____

4. When I nurture my_____(response)_____

_____

This makes me feel_____because_____

_____

5. When I nurture my_____(response)_____

_____

This makes me feel_____because_____

_____

Given these answers, state how you *most often* felt when you nurtured others. Circle the correct answer(s).

unappreciated   slightly appreciated   moderately appreciated   very appreciated

Depending on whom you were nurturing, your Significant Others responses may have varied, making you feel anything from unappreciated and disappointed to very appreciated and happy.

List the Significant Others whose responses left you disappointed.

_____

List the Significant Others whose responses made you happy.

_____

If *most* of your Significant Others are not responding well to your nurturing, it is likely due to one or more of the following reasons: Reason #1: Your Significant Others are spoiled and take your nurturing acts for granted. Reason #2: Your Significant Others are overwhelmed with your constant shower of kindnesses. Reason #3: Your Significant Others don't know you are actually nurturing them. For instance, if you are not warm with words or touch but in feeling affectionate toward your family, announce in a rather monotone voice that you have planned a family camping trip. Their response might be glum because they think you are just being bossy. Had you said, "I really miss us all having family time together; what do you think about us taking a trip somewhere?" the response may have been quite different.

Some people feel that bringing home a pay check or suggesting solutions to their loved one's problems is an expression of nurturing, not realizing how cold they seem with no warmth in their voice, or affection in their touch.

If only *certain* Significant Others don't respond well to your nurturing, it is likely due to one of two reasons. Reason #1: Their own Inner Nurturer is blocked and they are unable to receive your nurturing. Reason #2: They are responding positively, but you are not recognizing it because it is *different* than how *you* respond to nurturing. For instance, you tell your visiting brother you love him, and he doesn't seem to respond, however, before he leaves your house, he checks the oil in your car, and the air pressure in your tires.

This exercise is designed to help recognize how our Significant Others nurture. At best, it will help you recognize the signs that they care, even if it's not obvious. And at least it might help you understand that they may not be able to help being so stunted and you might have to give yourself more caring to compensate.

State the different ways your Significant Others nurture. Example #1: My *mate* nurtures by *doing things for me*. Example #2: My *daughter* nurtures by *using caring words*.

My _____ nurtures by_____

My _____ nurtures by_____

My _____ nurtures by_____

My _____ nurtures by_____

My _____ nurtures by_____

If in opening your mind to the various ways that others give and receive nurturing, you still feel like you are spinning your wheels in your nurturing efforts, STOP. Take the cues others give you. If you nurture too much, take a look at why you feel a need to throw your energy into a black hole. We often project our own needs onto others. Sometimes it is we who long to be nurtured, so we nurture others the way we wish others would nurture us. If we would reverse this flow and spend more energy nurturing and pampering ourselves, we would feel much better.

If you nurture too little, see what happens if you stretch your repertoire just a bit. You will see that the world will not crumble and your relationships will improve. While it might open a lid on what created your emotional armor (psychological wounds), it will also incite a giant leap in your personal growth.

We don't incite change in others by trying to change *them*, we do it by *changing ourselves*.

Circle the correct answer(s). When I nurture others *in general*, I *most often* feel:

energized   drained a little   drained a lot

If your answer is a mix of the above, that means sometimes you are nurturing in a healthy manner and sometimes you are giving too much. If you are nurturing in a healthy manner, you will usually feel energized, or maybe only a little drained. For instance, you get home late from work and are tired, but you still read your child a bedtime story. If you are enjoy reading the story, though tired, that is still a healthy nurture. However, if you really don't have the energy to read the story and you do it anyway, leaving you thoroughly drained, you are being the Martyr. It is okay to let others know from time to time that you just need to take care of yourself. In this, you give them a chance to nurture you.

What happens to those around you when you nurture too much, or if you have ever been nurtured too much, how did it make you feel?

_____

_____

What is the result?_____

_____

What can you do to feel better?_____

Exercise Six

This next exercise is designed to examine the affects of those who are deprived of nurturing. Answer the following questions:

1. In exercise three, on a scale of 1(easy) to 10 (impossible), how hard was it to think of times you nurtured others? _____

2. What happens to those around you when you do not nurture them enough *or* what has happened to you when you were not nurtured enough by a certain person or people?

_____

_____

_____

_____

3. If you withhold nurturing, what is in it for you, or what do you think was or is in it for whomever withheld nurturing from you?

_____

_____

_____

4. Explain how your relationships have faired with those whom you have withheld nurturing *or* with those who have withheld nurturing from you?

_____

_____

_____

5. Is this all right with you? _____ Why or why not? _____

_____

_____

6. Have you been in a relationship where nurturing was withheld from you?_____

7. How did it make you feel?_____

8. In what way has this lack of nurturing affected you or your ability to nurture? _____

_____

9. Think of one person whose withheld nurturing affected you the most, even if it occurred long ago. State below what you would like to tell that person.

_____, you have/had difficulty nurturing me. _____
(person's name)

_____

_____

_____

_____

Sometimes this lack of nurturing affects our own ability to nurture and sometimes it drives us to be overly nurturing, giving to others what we have so desperately needed ourselves. This is not to say that if you have an overly nurturing nature you were once deprived, but—it might. However, if you enjoy bringing comfort and joy to your loved ones, the plants, the birds, and the stranger passing by, be yourself and enjoy spreading joy!

If this exercise brought up any anger, breathe slowly and deeply for a moment. Each time you exhale, release your anger. See your anger moving into a large ball of white light before you and dissolving. This ball of white light is the pure energy of love. Love is love no matter where it comes from. You can tap the energy of love and receive it whenever you need. If you need love now, see the ball of light moving into you soaking you in caring, compassion, and pure unconditional love. Feel this for a few minutes before proceeding.

Self-Love. People's perceptions of us vary. But how we perceive ourselves is the key to how we experience our reality. Self-love, even with all our weakness and faults, is more powerful than the love we get from others because others most often love us *conditionally*. If they don't like us, they may not love us, so we tend to pull the wool over their eyes by only showing certain sides, or faces. Eventually when our insecurity emerges, tension rises in the relationship and the struggle to keep someone loving us causes great anxiety.

But if the love comes from within, deep and true, strong and pure, no matter how many people change their minds on us or the degree in which they love us, we remain stable in ourselves because NO ONE can take the love we have for ourselves away but us. LOVE IS LOVE, NO MATTER WHERE IT COMES FROM.

Exercise Seven

Let your Inner Nurturer speak. Move into it, no matter how weak or strong it might feel in you. Let this self express what it feels about you, about others, and about life.

I am _____'s Inner Nurturer. _____
　　　　(your name)

_____

_____

_____

_____

_____

_____

Circle the answer that best fits your Nurturer. The Nurturer in me is:

intense　　　　strong　　　　moderate　　　　weak　　　　almost nonexistent

Healing and Balancing Exercise for Your Inner Nurturer

Place one hand beneath your breastbone.
Place the other hand over your heart.
Concentrate deeply. Repeat silently or aloud for at least two minutes:
"I love myself no matter what."

Relaxation and Creative Visualization Exercise

Lie in a comfortable position. Play instrumental music that makes you feel good: classical, New Age, or music that is of gentle, sweeping, or dynamic beauty. When the music is playing, close your eyes. Inhale through your nose deeply, and exhale through your mouth slowly; do this eight times. Visualize that you are inhaling the power of the universe, which purifies and attunes you physically, emotionally, mentally, and metaphysically. When you exhale, all the tensions and worries leave your body and go back into the universe where they dissolve and blend into the pure life force.

Tighten and loosen your muscles slowly in this order:

Feet. Tighten. Loosen. Take a slow, deep breath, and exhale.
Calves. Tighten. Loosen. Take a slow, deep breath, and exhale.
Thighs. Tighten. Loosen. Take a slow, deep breath, and exhale.
Hips and buttocks. Tighten. Loosen. Take a slow, deep breath, and exhale.
Stomach. Tighten. Loosen. Take a slow, deep breath, and exhale.
Back. Tighten. Loosen. Take a slow, deep breath, and exhale.
Arms. Tighten. Loosen. Take a slow, deep breath, and exhale.
Hands. Tighten. Loosen. Take a slow, deep breath, and exhale.
Neck and shoulders. Tighten. Loosen. Take a slow, deep breath, and exhale.
Face. Tighten. Loosen. Take a slow, deep breath, and exhale.

Then, completely relax and take eight more slow, deep breaths. Inhale the universal life energy through your nose and exhale tension through your mouth.

Set the intent: *Whoever I am, whatever I am, whatever I need, whatever is right for me—so be it. I open to insight. I open to receive.*

Now that you are completely relaxed, give yourself over to the music. Focus on the point between your eyebrows and journey inward, deeper and deeper into your vast being. You are heading toward your Inner Nurturer. Do this for a while. . . .

Now you enter your Inner Nurturer's world. Move slowly into it and behold the setting, the colors, the atmosphere. Do this for a while . . . .

Ahead of you, you see your Inner Nurturer. Behold its appearance and what it is doing. Watch it for a while . . . .

As you watch your Inner Nurturer, scenes appear in your mind of when it rose in you. You behold the times it has played a part in your life. Watch for a while . . . .

What effect has your Inner Nurturer had on you? . . . .

What affect has it had on others? . . . .

Does your Inner Nurturer need something from you? . . . .

If so, what can you do to help it? . . . .

Move closer to it until you are before it. Look into its eyes and feel more deeply what it needs. Do this for a while . . . .

If it needs your endorsement, give it. If it needs you to give it permission to rest, give it. Perhaps it needs your appreciation or your understanding. Whatever it needs, give this to your Inner Nurturer now and watch how it changes as you do this . . . .

Now that you have given it what it needs, it looks much more balanced and beautiful. It gazes into your eyes with its great compassion. Its compassion soaks into you, reaching the saddest, most lonely parts of your being. Experience this for a while . . . .

The more you soak in this love, you realize that you do have the ability to love yourself. You can nurture yourself and you can allow yourself to be nurtured. And when you allow yourself to be nurtured, you naturally nurture those around you. By allowing your Inner Nurturer to love you always, you will never feel drained from nurturing others, or feel a need to over-nurture others just to feel joy. You feel joy, right now by letting your Inner Nurturer nurture you. There is a power in it. It's like you are shining inward, and the more you shine inward, the more you also shine outward. Bask in this experience until the music ends . . . .

When you open your eyes, you will feel sated with love. You will realize that love is an energy and you don't need someone else to give it to you in order to have it. You can feel loved anytime you choose.

Record your experience.

_____

_____

_____

_____

_____

_____

_____

_____

Draw a picture or symbol that summarizes your experience. Example: _A pink ball of light._

Create a key phrase that summarizes this experience. Example: _I love myself._

_____

When needed, say the phrase silently and visualize the picture or symbol. This will reactivate the experience and generate a peaceful, empowered, clear state of mind.

Δ

Gem of Wisdom
To purely nurture others and receive nurturing in kind
you must first nurture yourself.

Live the Mystery

5

WORKSHOP FIVE
THE PLEASER "If I please you, you will like me."

We attempt to secure love and safety in various ways. One common method is to please those with whom we seek positive affirmation. Seeking acceptance is not bad; it is human and by no means something that should be altogether shunned. It plays its part to help us get through life. Being alone can be frightening in a world where humans depend on each other to survive and thrive. Securing those connections often involves pleasing each other. If the pleasing is a two way street and not done at the expense of individuality, it can be quite exciting!

However, if in a relationship, one person is doing most of the pleasing, and to an excess, it can throw the whole relationship into a dysfunctional state. While both participants in these cases, might be perceiving the act of pleasing as an expression of love—it is not. While pleasing others can be an expression of love from the Nurturer, the Pleaser pleases in order to be liked. *If I please you, you will like me. If you like me, I am safe.* Our Inner Pleaser and our Inner Nurturer are very much *not* the same.

The Pleaser is evident in the child who strives to get straight A's to secure his parents' approval, or the teen taking drugs because all her friends are doing it. It is evident in the woman who keeps a perfect home, cooks delicious meals, works on her looks, and dotes on her man, even if he treats her badly. It can be seen in the man who lives beyond his means to shower his lover with expensive gifts to keep her from leaving him, or the woman who will adopt her mates way of thinking, calling it her own, in order to secure his allegiance. Although wanting to be liked is natural, if we try too hard, we can lose ourselves in those with whom we are trying to please. In this, we throw away who we are, to become what *we think* others want us to be.

Hiding our true selves to highlight another is an unconscious maneuver to avoid personal development because we feel unworthy of development and or we fear that if we do develop our individuality it will be sub par.

We know have been shanghaied by our Inner Pleaser when we go out of our way to get in the graces of those whom we have decided to depend upon, whether emotionally, physically, or even economically. While this is normal, healthy, and even lucrative in *moderation*, such as pleasing the boss to get a raise, or giving our pet that extra comfort so it won't run away, pleasing others excessively and constantly is not only stressful, but self-demeaning.

The need to continually please signifies heavy doubt about our intrinsic value as a human being. *I must please whom I want to love me, or I won't be loved.* In other words, we must enslave ourselves to secure the relationships we want to sustain. We *need* their approval, and we need it all the time. We might, for example, say yes to every request our child poses in hopes he will love us more, or cater to our mate all day in order to be held in his/her arms at night.

When pleasing others becomes our life mission, we put all our other needs on the backburner, such as getting rest, tending to our health, expressing honest thoughts and feelings, and having genuine fun. In suppressing our individuality, we lose our sparkle, and often the interest of whom we have been pleasing. Recipients of excessive pleasing eventually treat the pleaser with callous disregard. This does not necessarily mean that the recipients are horrible people. No matter who the excessive Pleaser tried to please, eventually he/she would evoke the worst in whoever's acceptance they seek. It is very difficult to admire those who prostitute themselves for us all to get a pat on the head.

Even industrial-strength Pleasers, in becoming the target of another Pleaser, will come to disdain the one who orbits around them in a constant state of doting. It is human nature to disrespect those who hide in the shadows, heads bowed in shame, and to be intrigued with those who brightly show their true colors.

When we feel people's desperation to manipulate us into giving them time and energy, it can feel like we are a wild horse that they want to pen in their corral. In this, it is natural to have an urge to "buck."

We may have been on both sides of the corral at some point in our lives. Sometimes just being infatuated with another person or having another infatuated with us can incite this behavior.

In short, when we please excessively, we set ourselves up to be disrespected because we are training others to *expect* us to please them. There are no thank you's, and hence we often feel unappreciated. Plus, we will never know if we can be loved for just being ourselves.

While these extremes are prevalent in many, our Inner Pleaser more commonly rises now and then and only in certain circumstances. We might be rather bossy at work but at home wait hand and foot on our mate hoping he or she will continue to love us. Or we might only want to please the boss at work, but be a control freak on the home front.

The more confident we are about our intrinsic value as a human being, the less our Pleaser will make an appearance. Instead of trying to please others in a quest *for love* (the Pleaser), we might please others as an expression *of love* (the Nurturer).

Sometimes what seems like the Pleaser is not. The woman who pleases her abusive mate so he won't hit her is actually using her Inner Warrior to hold it together so she can survive. The politician who tries to please her constituents is actually the Leader using that ploy to get elected. The Pleaser is distinctive in the fact that it thinks its only value rests in how well it can please others. It does not believe it can be loved any other way.

Our Inner Pleaser generally falls into one, more than one, or a combination of the following types: the Do-Gooder, the Peacemaker, the Manipulative Pleaser, the Competitive Pleaser, or the Social Pleaser. Given we all have our own nature, not all of the types will apply to you. You may however recognize them in others you know.

The Do-Gooder. This type of Pleaser strives to gain the attention of whomever it is trying to please by being the nicest, neatest, smartest, most thoughtful person that ever walked the face of the earth. It works hard to be "perfect" for someone or sometimes everyone. *If I am perfect I will please you. If I please you, you will love me. If you love me, I am safe.*

The Peacemaker. This Pleaser will do almost anything to avoid confrontation. It smacks a cap on any thoughts or feelings that might rock the boat in any relationship it relies upon. It's like the dog that rolls on its back, belly up, admitting defeat before it can be struck. This type of Pleaser just wants to get along with whomever it is pleasing, and will often absorb the brunt of the conflict just to get rid of it. If two people, one being Peacemaker, head for the front passenger seat of the car, the Peacemaker would say, "Let's not argue about who gets the front seat in the car. You can have it." *If I let you have your way, there will be no conflict, and you will want me in your life.*

The Manipulative Pleaser. This Pleaser is skilled at getting love and approval by manipulating its targets. For example, the act of wooing. Wooing, when done by the Nurturer, can be a genuine act of expressing affection through romantic gestures, but when done by the Pleaser, it is an act that *is an act* to "win" the person's commitment. Often the object of the wooing won't know the difference until the game is over, that is until he or she has given his or her heart to the wooer. It is an age-old story, that once love is secured, the wooer begins to neglect its prize, that is, until the prize gets antsy, where upon the wooer revs up its Inner Pleaser once more. This behavior is also common in children who please their parents only to get something they want; and once they do, their pleasing behavior disappears.

The Competitive Pleaser. This Pleaser competes with others to be the *most* pleasing. The Competitive Pleaser is evident in divorced parents who vie for their children's loyalty in a game of who can dazzle the kids most with outings, gifts, and an abundance of personal attention. Or sometimes it is the children who are competing for their parents' attention in a contest of who can gratify their parents the most. It is evident in the woman who strives to please the male eye by being the most attractive female in the room, or the student striving to please the teacher to become the "teacher's pet." Whenever the act of pleasing becomes a contest with another or others, the Competitive Pleaser is on stage.

The Social Pleaser. In collusion with the Traitor, this Pleaser will sacrifice not only its well-being, but sometimes the well-being of its Significant Others to secure social approval. It might insist its family members collude with it to display a pleasing front, fearing if its family fails to please, so will it. A mother might insist her child smile and be polite in public, all the time, even if the child is sad, mad, or even plagued with a tummy ache. If the Social Pleaser's family is invited for a chicken dinner and the chicken is undercooked, the Social Pleaser would rather its family eat the raw chicken and get sick than appear impolite. Although the Social Pleaser looks rather selfish under its veneer of being good, it only rises in us when we crave social acceptance so badly that we are willing to suffer almost any atrocity to get it. Peer pressure is a prime example. Again, approval equals security. *If you like me, I am safe.*

Balancing the Inner Pleaser

If you feel enmeshed in a constant battle to win approval, chronically repress your true thoughts and feelings, and are weary of working so hard to please another or others, you likely have a strong Inner Pleaser. When you are ready to nourish your individuality all this will subside, and you will begin to experience the wonder of your personal power to survive, thrive, and shine.

Or it might be that your Inner Pleaser makes only rare appearances and it is you who is the beneficiary of those who excessively dote. It might feel great for a while, but after a time, become an almost smothering experience and generate a feeling of resentment. The Pleaser might appear innocent and you might deem yourself somewhat of a heel for resenting someone who is lovely all the time, but you aren't.

However take note of the difference between rejecting a Pleaser who wants something from you and a Nurturer who needs nothing from you but a smile on your face. If you are resistant to being loved because it makes you feel vulnerable, you have some Warrior issues that won't let you take down your guard.

If so, know that people who please others excessively are suffering, even if they deny it. Never knowing from moment to moment, or day to day if the security they depend upon from another might disappear, they are always on edge. Afraid to show their true colors, they almost don't seem like a real person.

Sometimes relationships "look" fine between people, because one is making all the sacrifices to please the other who sits back and sucks it in. The one "overly" pleasing will slowly die inside, and the one being pleased will begin to take the Pleaser for granted. This inequity eventually topples them as a couple. After the toppling however, given they don't find new partners to repeat the pattern, they each have a chance for tremendous personal growth.

Whether you are the Pleaser, or the object of another's pleasing, when the Pleaser steps back and spends more time pleasing her/himself, the tables will begin to turn and others will step forward and have an urge to please the reformed Pleaser! Respect is restored, and all is well.

This workshop is designed to help you bring your Inner Pleaser into harmony with other aspects of yourself, and hence your outer world.

The Pleaser in a Nutshell
* Pleases to get approval, security, adoration, or a reward of some kind.
* Will please the most those from whom it needs something.
* Seeks to be viewed as "good."
* Does not like to rock the boat.
* Fears letting its true self emerge.
* In moderation, can be a healthy force in our lives.

Pleaser Types
* The Do-Gooder: "If I am perfect, you will like me."
* The Peacemaker: "If I don't make waves, you will like me."
* The Manipulative Pleaser: "I will please you in exchange for a favor."
* The Competitive Pleaser: "I will be the most pleasing and therefore be liked the best."
* The Social Pleaser: "I please whom I must to gain social acceptance."

Exploring Your Inner Pleaser

Exercise One

This exercise is designed to help you become more aware of how much energy you spend on pleasing others and determine if it is in your own best interest or not. State the top five people whom, in order of importance, you try to please, why, what pleasing acts you do, the toll it takes, and what you wish could be.

If there are many you try to please, this doesn't necessarily mean you have a strong Inner Pleaser. As human beings, we all want to be pleasing to someone, even if it is a prospective employer to get a job, or a parent whose aid we rely upon. There would be something wrong with us if we never sought to please anyone ever. Examples of people whom we might try to please are: family members, friend (s), acquaintances, peers, pets, spouse, lover, the public, the famous, the prestigious, powerful people, employers, the world, no one. Dig deep. Your Pleaser might be wearing a disguise and you will never get to know it if you collude with it and go into denial. If there are less than five you try to please, that's all right, if there are more than five continue this in your supplementary journal.

Example #1: I want to please *my spouse because I am afraid he will cheat on me*. To please him I *keep the house clean and myself looking attractive, make good meals for him, pump up his ego, tend to his every need if possible, give him good sex whenever he desires.* The toll it takes on me is that *I can never relax and I am tired a lot. I have to pretend all the time that I am fine when I am not.* I wish *that he would just love me for me and I wouldn't have to work so hard.*

Example #2: I want to please *my children because I want them to like me and hence love me. To please them I give them everything they want, and when I punish them I often lighten up later and let them off the hook.* The toll it takes *is that they only are nice to me when they get what they want and are disrespectful to me the rest of the time.* I wish *that they would just treat me better.*

Example #3: I want to please everyone because *then they will like me and I can like myself. To please them I try to help everyone, make everyone's day nicer, do lots of volunteer work, and go to church every Sunday.* The toll it takes is *that I feel drained a lot. I am so busy working hard that I never have time just to be with myself and enjoy life.* I wish that *I could just love myself without outside approval.*

1. I want to please_____because_____

_____

In an attempt to make this happen I_____

_____

The toll it takes is_____

_____

I wish_____

_____

2. I want to please_____because_____

_____

In an attempt to make this happen I_____

_____

The toll it takes is_____

_____

I wish _____

_____

3. I want to please_____because_____

_____

In an attempt to make this happen I_____

_____

The toll it takes is_____

_____

I wish_____

_____

4. I want to please_____because_____

_____

In an attempt to make this happen I_____

_____

The toll it takes is_____

_____

I wish_____

_____

5. I want to please_____because_____

_____

In an attempt to make this happen I_____

_____

The toll it takes is_____

_____

I wish_____

_____

Exercise Two

State the most extreme thing that you ever did, but didn't want to do, to please someone, why, the result, what you think about that in hindsight, and what your Inner Sage, Nurturer, and Warrior have to say. Example: The most extreme thing that I have ever done (and didn't want to do) to please another was: *I got breast augmentation to please my husband.* In hindsight I did this because *I was afraid I would lose him if I didn't.* The result was, *he left me anyway.* When I think about what I did, I feel *bad.* My Inner Sage says, *Learn from this that the only person you can absolutely count on is yourself, so do what is right for you, always.* My Inner Nurturer says, *It's okay, you know better now, just love yourself so much that nothing like that can ever happen again.* My Inner Warrior says, *Sometimes you have to say no.*

The most extreme thing I ever did (but didn't want to do) to please another was_____

_____

In hindsight, I did this because_____

The result was _____

When I think about what I did, I feel_____

_____

My Inner Sage says,_____

_____

My Inner Nurturer says,_____

_____

My Inner Warrior says,_____

_____

Place an X by the answers that are true for you.

_____ In order to like myself, I usually need outside approval.
_____ If I am not pleasing to those I want to love me, they will not love me.
_____ I *often* hold my true self back for fear of being disliked.
_____ I *often* go out of my way to get outside approval.
_____ I don't know who I am anymore.
_____ I spend a lot of energy trying to please others so they will continue to care for me.
_____ I wish I could be loved for who I am, instead of for what I do.
_____ I have agreed with others (another) so much I rarely have opinions of my own.
_____ When I get approval, I feel safe.
_____ I am happy *only* when I get approval.
_____ I equate approval with love.

_____ When people disagree with me, I feel horrible.
_____ I can't stand it when someone doesn't like me.
_____ I bend over backwards to get people to like me.
_____ I give into peer pressure more often than not.
_____ I usually let whomever I am with decide where we should go and what we should do.

The more X's you have, the stronger your Inner Pleaser's role in your life.

Now give your Inner Pleaser a chance to speak. Be inside the Pleaser, no matter how strong or weak it might be. Just flow as you answer the questions. Do not think or analyze too much. Feel. Let your Inner Pleaser have its say. Example: I feel a need to please _my dad_. If I don't please _my dad_, then _he might retreat from my life_, and if this happens _I will feel vulnerable and afraid_. What I'd like to do is _what is right for me without fearing my dad will with-draw his allegiance_. It's also important for me to please _my children and my friends_. In general, when I am trying to please another (others), deep down I feel _desperate for their approval_, and I think, _I am so weak and needy_. My Inner Sage says, _Embrace your intrinsic worth and your need to please will lessen_. My Inner Nurturer says, _Don't be so hard on yourself; your self-confidence will get stronger in time_. My Inner Warrior says, _It's okay to please others, but draw the line when it works against you_.

I feel a need to please_____. If I don't please_____

then_____,

and if that happens_____.

What I'd like to do is_____.

It is also important for me to please_____.

In general, when I am trying to please another (others), deep down I feel_____

_____ and I think_____

_____.

My Inner Sage says,_____

_____.

My Inner Nurturer says,_____

_____.

My Inner Warrior says,_____

_____.

Healing and Balancing Exercise for Your Inner Pleaser

Place one palm over your heart.
Place the other palm beneath your breastbone.
Concentrate deeply. Repeat silently or aloud for at least two minutes:
"I am valuable even if I don't please anyone."

Lie in a comfortable position. Play instrumental music that makes you feel good: classical, New Age, or music that is of gentle, sweeping, or dynamic beauty. When the music is playing, close your eyes. Inhale through your nose deeply, and exhale through your mouth slowly; do this eight times. Visualize that you are inhaling the power of the universe, which purifies and attunes you physically, emotionally, mentally, and metaphysically. When you exhale, all the tensions and worries leave your body and go back into the universe where they dissolve and blend into the pure life force.

Tighten and loosen your muscles slowly in this order:

Feet. Tighten. Loosen. Take a slow, deep breath, and exhale.
Calves. Tighten. Loosen. Take a slow, deep breath, and exhale.
Thighs. Tighten. Loosen. Take a slow, deep breath, and exhale.
Hips and buttocks. Tighten. Loosen. Take a slow, deep breath, and exhale.
Stomach. Tighten. Loosen. Take a slow, deep breath, and exhale.
Back. Tighten. Loosen. Take a slow, deep breath, and exhale.
Arms. Tighten. Loosen. Take a slow, deep breath, and exhale.
Hands. Tighten. Loosen. Take a slow, deep breath, and exhale.
Neck and shoulders. Tighten. Loosen. Take a slow, deep breath, and exhale.
Face. Tighten. Loosen. Take a slow, deep breath, and exhale.

Then completely relax and take eight more slow, deep breaths. Inhale the universal life energy through your nose and exhale tension through your mouth.

Set the intent: *Whoever I am, whatever I am, whatever I need, whatever is right for me—so be it. I open to insight. I open to receive.*

Now that you are completely relaxed, give your self over to the music that is playing. Focus on the center between your eyebrows and journey inward as if you are going through a tunnel into yourself. Do this for a while . . . .

As you move along, you come upon a door. Take note of the door's appearance. Open the door. Now that the door is opened you see your Inner Pleaser's world. Observe the setting. You see your Inner Pleaser. Observe its appearance and what it is doing . . . .

Approach your Inner Pleaser and stand before it. Look into its eyes. What expression is on its face? Thank it for the role it has played in an attempt to get you what you need. Looking at it now, you realize that while it may have at times appeared weak or conniving by subjugating itself to please others, it was only being true to its nature. You notice that its form seems to have a dark haze about it. You know this dark haze is a result of the times it pleased others at its own expense. Feeling empathy, you slip into the Pleaser's reality. You are your Inner Pleaser now. You feel that nagging need for approval, sometimes small, and sometimes overwhelming. You wish you didn't have it, but you do.

You feel a presence before you. It is your Inner Warrior. It hands you a sword and says, "This is the sword of individuality." As you grip the sword, you take yourself back from all those with whom you gave yourself away, because you so badly wanted their approval. The energy you gave comes back from everywhere into you, and the dark haze grows a bit lighter. You feel that you deserve to be loved for who you are, and that you don't have to become what others want you to be. The sword is absorbed into your being. Your Inner Warrior, like a spirit, moves inside you.

You now notice your Inner Nurturer standing before you, glowing with love. It reaches its hand to your heart and says, "You can get what you need by just opening your heart to the beauty all around you, the earth, the sky, the tree, the flower. The more you receive from the natural world, the less you will need from others." You feel the energy of the natural world filling your body. Your body feels charged with the natural world. You know your worth; you just do." The dark haze has almost faded.

Your Inner Nurturer, like a spirit, moves inside you, and your Inner Leader is now before you. It hands you a compass and says, "Every time you act out of self-respect, you take a step in the direction of your true path." As you hold the compass in your hand, you feel certain you will lead an exciting life because now you know that the courage you needed to act on your own behalf comes from self-respect. The dark haze is gone, and you now are glowing with a soft white light. The compass is absorbed into your being and your Inner Leader, like a spirit, moves inside you.

Now your Inner Innovator is before you. It hands you a magic wand and says, "You are an original. Allow your true self to create its masterpiece on the canvas of your life, and your charisma will attract good fortune."As you hold the magic wand, you realize that magic is what happens when we foster our talents with confidence. Your body now glows brighter because your belief in yourself has deepened. Your Inner Innovator, like a spirit, moves inside you.

One by one, your other aspects acknowledge you warmly and step inside you. You now feel yourself as your true self. A pleasant energy charges your body. It beams strongly all around you in all directions. With your Inner Warrior aligned with your Inner Pleaser, you feel secure no matter what. With your Inner Pleaser aligned with your Inner Nurturer, you feel loved no matter what. With your Inner Leader aligned with your Inner Pleaser, you can sense a life direction that is right for you. With your Inner Innovator aligned with your Inner Pleaser, you feel excited to locate and nourish your passion. Bask in this experience until the music ends . . . .

When you open your eyes, you will feel empowered, enthusiastic, and proud to be who you are.

Record your experience.

_____

_____

_____

_____

_____

_____

_____

_____

_____

Draw a picture or symbol that summarizes your experience. Example: *My arms stretched toward the sun.*

Create a key phrase that summarizes this experience. Example: *It's okay to please myself.*

_____

When needed, say the phrase silently and visualize the picture or symbol. This will reactivate the experience and generate a peaceful, empowered, clear state of mind.

Δ

Gem of Wisdom
Lasting security can only be found within.

Live the Mystery

6

Date_____

WORKSHOP SIX
THE LEADER "I am in charge."

The Leader is comfortable being in charge. It enjoys guiding, leading the way, making decisions, orchestrating, commanding, and bringing order. It shows its face in bosses, entrepreneurs, teachers, directors, organizers, explorers, officers, politicians, religious heads, and parents. Whenever we take control, whether it's over our own life situation, running a household, committee, company, or country, our Inner Leader is at the helm. When it emerges, it believes that it is best for the job.

It might emerge rarely, perhaps taking charge only in emergencies or if absolutely necessary. Or it might emerge in only in certain environments, such as performing in a supervisory capacity at work, but abdicating to the Nurturer at home. Or it might steal the spotlight, and be the boss all the time—or at least try.

We need Leaders and at times we all must lead, if only our own lives. Without Leaders there would be no change, no exploration, invention, organization, communities, or countries. Our Inner Leader is generally one, more than one, or a combination of the following types: the Noble Leader, the Trailblazer, the Creative Leader, the Corrective Leader, the Boss, the Powermonger, the Sadistic Dominant, or the Reluctant Leader. Given we all have our own nature, not all of the types will apply to you. You may however recognize them in others you know.

The Noble Leader. The Noble Leader is motivated by *honor* to make the world a better place by urging us into meaningful life directions, as well as guiding others toward harmonious ends. The Noble Leader enjoys bringing itself and the flock into greener pastures. The entrepreneur who starts a company that fosters well being in its employees and the public, is the Noble Leader. An impassioned teacher educating others to help them blossom and flourish in the world, is a Noble Leader. Noble Leaders in collaboration with the Gallant Warrior have actualized great feats such as national parks and rooftop gardens in urban areas. Whenever we take point on a groundbreaking project to better ourselves or the world, the Noble Leader is the star of our show.

The Trailblazer. The Trailblazer's motivation is *discovery*. It loves to explore and forge new paths. It is not as interested in controlling the new ground it has discovered as much as moving on and discovering more new ground. World explorers, inventers, and disease researchers are examples. When we step out of our comfort zone and take risks to have an adventure, our Trailblazing Leader has risen.

The Creative Leader. The Creative Leader's motivation is *originality*. It seeks to direct others in a creative way. Collaborating with the Innovator, it sees outside the box of the ordinary, and orchestrates others by tapping creativity, exemplified in theatrical directors, music conductors, choreographers, and marketing strategists. Or it might rise in us simply by taking charge of a situation in an imaginative way, such as a teacher putting on a show to teach, or coming up with a publicity stunt to take our business to new heights. We might even use our Creative Leader to parent our children by sparking their imagination. For example, "Mmm, those carrots will make your eyes strong to see all kinds of wonderful things a lot of people overlook." Or, "Hey, your brain is saying, 'Let's go to bed so we can have an adventure in our dreams!' "

The Corrective Leader. The Corrective Leader's motivation is to take charge of situations that need reorganizing, or *fixing*. It might help reorganize a business venture to be more profitable or its own household to run more smoothly. Our Corrective Leader is on stage when we lead the charge to fix what is flailing with tried and true solutions.

The Boss. This type of Leader is motivated by being *number one*. It is less interested in paving new paths than it is to just sit on the throne. The Boss is strong in those who are natural leaders. The Boss can be thoughtful and fair, reigning over any brood with positive results. This is evident in parents who might hold family meetings to settle disputes and generate ideas to help the household run more smoothly. It is evident in employers who sufficiently reward their employees for good work and in politicians who actually meet the needs of their constituents.

However, the Boss can also be arrogant and unjust, quashing the opinions of others and demeaning its subordinates, even if they are family members. Afraid of being vulnerable, the afflicted Boss often toots a horn that blares *I'm always right*. It will blame others for anything and everything that goes wrong. The mirror is always turned outward. It can be obstinate and insist on being the Leader even if it doesn't know what it's doing, and even if its decisions backfire.

It feels safe by being in control and will mow down anybody who vies for the driver's seat. It will hold its position, even if only to keep someone else from getting it. Somewhere in its memory is a fear that if it is not in control, it will be hurt. It doesn't need to gain more power, it just wants to keep the power it has. This is evident in the strict mother who forces her family to live by inflexible rules and has little tolerance for individuality. It is evident in the hotheaded, warm-hearted father who orders consequences for his misbehaving children, and then doesn't follow through, yet insists that the inconsistency is the way to go, despite his wife's disapproval and her PhD in child psychology.

The afflicted Boss's behavior is often generated from an early life of feeling helpless. Sometimes it is a learned behavior of witnessing one parent bully another. Though it acts superior, deep down it feels unworthy and projects its own shortcomings onto everyone around it. If it is impatient, it will claim others are impatient. If it secretly feels stupid, it will claim others are stupid.

If our Inner Boss is conflicted, and strong in our lives, we might find we are plagued with relationship problems. Nobody likes to be told what to do *all* the time, or be made to feel *always* wrong. Balance is achieved when we turn the mirror back on ourselves, behold our psychological wounds, and take responsibility to heal them. If done, our Inner Leader will have a more positive affect when it rises.

The Powermonger. The Powermonger's motivation is *to acquire power*. It not only rules the roost, but ever widens its boundaries in a tyrannical quest to become mightier than it was, with no end in sight. With the Warrior as its sidekick, it will constantly remind everyone that it is the Alpha and can demolish anyone who displeases it or gets in its way.

Powermongers who amass great power may have some good intentions, maybe even noble ones, but when their power becomes excessive, it usually fosters narcissism and corruption. Examples are dictators, gang leaders, or even ambitious CEOs who exploit their workers and play dirty to demolish the competition. These types, in general, cannot be demoted except by force or unfortunate life circumstances such as an illness. We know our Powermonger has risen when we will stoop to almost anything to force those around us into submission, and keep going for more. Today, my family, tomorrow my friends, and the next day the world.

The Sadistic Dominant. The Sadistic Dominant's motivation is to consciously or unconsciously control another or others by destroying their innocence. Colluding with the Traitor, it wants revenge for the innocence that was taken from it, usually in childhood. It might rise only on occasion, such as a scathing insult now and then, or it might regularly harm others. Whether chipping away at people's self-esteem, crushing their hopes, destructively brainwashing, or committing criminal acts, debasing others make it feel powerful. If Sadistic Dominants wind up in positions of power, such as teachers, doctors, coaches, bosses, etc. they will abuse those who trust them *because* of their social status.

The Sadistic Dominant is evident in or any who dominate others with an intent to cause harm, such as parents who are cruel to their children, one spouse abusing the other, or even in those who harm animals. It is evident in the charismatic who attract a following and lead them to self-destruct, and in serial killers too. Although it is atypical for our Inner Leader to morph into a Sadistic Dominant, if you do feel it brewing in you, somewhere, deep down, seek help—now. Your wounds can be healed, no matter how hopeless it might seem. In the center of your being, your innocence is still there. It is not dead, and you needn't hurt others to prove that it is. You can resurrect yourself; you can rise from the ashes *if* you want to. You absolutely can!

The Reluctant Leader. This type of leader is overpowered by other aspects within us. Though it is mostly dormant, it can rise with our Inner Warrior as a last resort to give us direction if we've been too long in a stale situation. For example, it might insist we stop hiding behind alcohol and make some brave life changes. Or it might insist we quit our dead end job and take steps toward a new career. It might pull us away from a bad relationship, get help for our needy child, or fuel us to exercise tough love. It enjoys feeling its power when it can, proud to come out of hiding and do something meaningful. Sometimes our Inner Leader is held back by our Inner Victim expecting to get hurt, or our Inner Scaredy Cat who is too frightened to stand out, or our Inner Pleaser who can't rock the boat.

If our Leader seldom emerges, it doesn't necessarily mean we need to make changes. As individuals we each have our own nature, which is just as it is supposed to be. Some people are more comfortable backstage, prefer to follow orders rather than give them, and submit to other leaders as long as they seem competent. The only time our Reluctant Leader needs to be nudged is if we are either in peril or plagued with inner turmoil because we won't step up to the plate.

Balancing the Inner Leader

No matter what our Leader Type, we can, if necessary, make modifications to improve our lives. If we are too controlling and people seem to fear or dislike us, we can bring our Inner Leader to balance by facing our own fears and curing our own hate. If we find ourselves doing all the work all the time, we can withhold our Inner Leader now and again, to let others, or make others, take charge. Or if we are wonderful leaders in some areas, but weak in others that result in us feeling victimized, we can develop our Inner Leader accordingly.

On the other hand, if we generally abdicate to others so much that we aren't leading our own life because all our energy is put into supporting everyone else, we can bring our Inner Leader to balance by expressing our individuality.

This workshop is designed to help you know the workings of your Inner Leader, and attune it to work for you and others in the healthiest possible way.

The Leader in a Nutshell
* Is comfortable being in charge.
* Would rather lead than follow.
* Feels more comfortable when it is in control.
* Likes to break new ground, or at least hold the ground it has.
* Strives to be on top of anything, situations, events, projects, others, and itself.

Leader Types
The Noble Leader: "Honor drives me to take charge and make things better."
The Trailblazer: "I am driven to explore new worlds and new ways."
The Creative Leader: "I lead with imagination."
The Corrective Leader: "I lead the charge with tried and true solutions to existing problems."
The Boss: "I like sitting on the throne."
The Powermonger: "More power, more!"
The Sadistic Dominant: "I use my position to hurt others."
The Reluctant Leader: "I will lead only if I must."

Exploring Your Inner Leader

Exercise One

This exercise is designed to make you more aware of the type(s) of Inner Leader that you currently tend to be. While you might be a certain kind of Leader in one situation and not another, or a few types all at once, or you might even see yourself handling things several possible ways, choose the answer that would be your *most likely* response.

Circle the letter next to the statement that best describes your most likely response.

1. I am sitting in a dark movie theater with only one seat left, and I know where it is. I see a man searching for that seat, but because the movie has begun, some patrons are agitated. I am most likely to:
    a. Stand up and call out to the man in front of everyone, "Sir, the seat is over here."
    b. Want to help but can't seem to draw attention to myself by so doing.
    c. Stand up and purposefully give the man the wrong directions just to watch him flail.
    d. Go to the manager later with a new idea for seating late patrons.
    e. Lodge a complaint against the theater's manager.
    f. Shout out to the man, "Hey, the seat is over there, third row, six seats in, hurry up."
    g. Get a game of telephone going to pass along the message to the patron who is searching for the seat.
    h. Get out of my seat quietly, go to the man, and guide him to the vacant seat.

2. When conversing with someone who challenges what I am saying, I am most likely to:
   a. Find a middle ground for us to agree upon.
   b. Be frustrated but shut down.
   c. Locate the person's Achilles heal and cripple them.
   d. Try to open the person's mind to see things a new way.
   e. Bombard the person with my superior knowledge until I get a concession.
   f. Stubbornly insist I am right.
   g. Explain my side by role playing or drawing diagrams.
   h. Listen patiently, but keep explaining my point of view.

3. My child, or a child for whom I am responsible, yells at me, "I hate you!" I am most likely to:
   a. Listen and draw out the child's feelings to understand and cure her upset.
   b. Imagine things I could do, but do nothing.
   c. Crush her with a scathing insult.
   d. Do something unexpected, like say, "Well, what can we do about that?"
   e. Ground the child for a month.
   f. Send the child to her room with a harsh tone.
   g. Suggest that the child draw a picture to express his/her feelings.
   h. Explain to the child how hurtful his/her words are, and if you hurt him/her like that, you are sorry.

4. A decision needs to be made on what outing my significant others (family, friends, etc.) and I might do on our free day together. What I want differs from what they want. I am most likely to:
   a. Strive toward a solution that suits everyone.
   b. Concede to what they want.
   c. Get my way by demeaning those who contest.
   d. Do my thing and encourage them to do theirs.
   e. Assume that what I want is what will happen and allow no discussion.
   f. Insist that I know what will be the most fun for everyone.
   g. Suggest we draw straws or flip a coin.
   h. Support whoever seems to need the outing the most.

5. If a group of unruly children (some my own) were out of control in my house, I would most likely:
   a. Blow a whistle, tell them to sit down, then explain the house rules.
   b. Go to my bedroom and close the door.
   c. Tell them the ice cream truck is outside when it isn't; then when they run out, lock the door.
   d. Take them on a challenging hike.
   e. Quiet them with a blood curdling inducement of fear.
   f. Order my children to their rooms, and the other children to go home.
   g. Tell them to all gather around because we are going to play a game.
   h. Get their attention in a courteous manner, have them gather round, and explain to them the virtue of self-control and respecting our homes.

6. If I were lost in the woods with a group of people, I would most likely:

a. Organize the group and give them each a job. (one to leave a trail, one to keep an eye out for forest food, etc.)
b. Sit back and wait for someone else to take the lead.
c. Take the lead by making others feel inept.
d. Get excited to meet the challenge.
e. Assume command in such a way that no one dare challenge me.
f. Assume command as if I've been appointed.
g. Suggest something outside the box, like for everyone to yell "Help!" all at once.
h. Call a meeting to pool our opinions on what to do.

7. If I were offered a management position that involved telling others what to do, I would:
a. Take the job gladly if I felt competent, and reject it if I didn't.
b. Wouldn't take the job if I didn't need to for financial reasons.
c. Take it, anxious to lord my position over others to make them feel small.
d. Take it, excited to implement some new ideas.
e. Take it, knowing I am one step closer to climbing an even higher rung on the ladder.
f. Take it; I love being the boss.
g. Take it as long as I will be allowed to manage those under me with my own style.
h. Take it as long as it doesn't compromise my honor or demean the people under me.

Count the number of times you circled each letter, and fill in the answer below.

a____   b____   c____   d____   e____   f____   g____   h____

If you circled mostly a's you tend to be a Corrective Leader (are compelled to fix problems).
If you circled mostly b's you tend to be a Reluctant Leader (have difficulty taking leadership).
If you circled mostly c's you tend to be a Sadistic Dominant (being mean makes you feel powerful).
If you circled mostly d's you tend to be a Trailblazer (gladly take point on any adventure).
If you circled mostly e's you tend to be a Powermonger (the more power you have, the more power you want).
If you circled mostly f's you tend to a Boss (like to be in charge).
If you circled mostly g's you tend to be a Creative Leader (imaginative in your leadership).
If you circled mostly h's you tend to be a Noble leader (take the lead to exercise what is fair).

If your answers are almost evenly mixed between two or more letters, you are a combination of those types.

Based on your answers, state your current predominant Inner Leader type(s).

_____

Exercise Two

The most common type of Leader is the Boss. There is usually one in every family, and of course, every business. When afflicted, the Boss is bossy—very very . . . bossy. Since this causes problems in most relationships, jobs, and daily life, this exercise will help you explore

GROWING WINGS SELF-DISCOVERY WORKBOOK

its workings. Whether you are a Boss-type Leader, or just know one, this exercise will generate understanding and help you better navigate your relationships.

Think of a bossy person you know or have known. What are your feelings about this person? Example #1: When I think of this bossy person, *I feel anger because he can never be wrong and blames me for everything.* Example #2: When I think of this bossy person, *I feel frustrated, because I never stood up to her.*

When I think of this bossy person, I feel_____

because_____

In general, very bossy people do not take time to empathize with those whom they are bossing. They want certain jobs to be done a certain way, and that is all they can see. In job related situations bossy bosses often make things worse because employees feel no allegiance to the Boss other than to get a paycheck. If they felt inspired by their Boss, they would actually work harder and better. In marriage, eventually, the bossed-around person will make a stand, and either leave the marriage, have an affair, or develop psychological problems. In parenting, children almost always rebel against bossy controlling parents. Contrary to popular belief, not all teens rebel. When they feel respected, honored, loved, and believed in, there is no need (usually). However, when children do rebel against what their parent(s) want of them by doing the opposite, it is actually healthier than the child who sacrifices to be compliant with the parent(s) wishes when those wishes hurt her/his well-being. There is nothing wrong with children trying spread their wings and individuate. If we help them to grow into who they are beyond our opinion of who we *think they should be,* the rebellion will subside.

Now think of an inspiring and noble Leader you know or have known (coach, teacher, mentor, employer) and express how you feel when you think of that person.

When I think of this inspiring Leader, I feel_____

because_____

When you lead (even if rarely) how do you imagine those you lead usually feel toward you? Examples: unappreciative, appreciation, hatred, they want to get away from me, respect but not warmth, warm emotional intimacy, etc.

When I lead, in general, I think what most others feel toward me is_____

_____; however, it is possible they feel_____

How does your answer make you feel? _____

If you are a bossy Boss, or if you know one, take a moment to tap your Inner Sage. What does your Sage have to say about how you or someone you know could modify the Bossy Leader toward more enriching behavior?

My Inner Sage says_____

_____

Exercise Three

Let your Inner Leader speak freely. First identify the primary kind of Leader you are (it can be a combination), your mode of operation, and why you operate that way. Then let your Inner Leader have its say about its outlook on itself, others, and life. Lastly, state the general result of your Inner Leader's actions, and what your Inner Sage has to say about this.

Example #1: I am the *Repressed Leader*. My mode of operation is *to remain hidden* because *I don't like to lead for fear I won't be liked. I am also afraid I will fail.* My outlook on myself is *I would be a good leader in certain areas, but because I prefer not to compete, I let others take over.* My outlook on most others is *to let them lead if they want to, and I will step in only if I must.* My outlook on life is *It's a jungle out there.* The general result of my Inner Leader's actions is *I am not living up to my potential.* My Inner Sage says, *Trust yourself and let the consequence be a learning experience.*

Example #2: I am the Boss. My mode of operation is *to insist people abdicate to my leadership* because *that is how I keep order, and that is how I feel safe.* My outlook on myself is *that I really do know the best way to handle everything.* My outlook on most others is *that they don't measure up to my standards.* My outlook on life is *that most people are incompetent.* The general result of my Inner Leader's actions is *many people don't like me.* My Inner Sage says, *If you give others a chance to grow and acknowledge their talents, they will appreciate you more.*

I am the_____

My mode of operation is_____

_____

because_____

_____

My outlook on myself is_____

My outlook on most others is_____

My outlook on life is_____

The general result of my Inner Leader's actions is_____

_____

My Inner Sage says, _____

_____

_____

Circle the answer that suits you best. The Leader has appeared in my life:

hardly ever   from time to time   in certain periods of my life   moderately   profusely

Healing and Balancing Exercise for Your Inner Leader

Place one palm over your heart.
Place the other palm beneath your navel.
Repeat silently or aloud for at least two minutes:
"My Inner Leader emanates from my quintessence."

Relaxation and Creative Visualization Exercise

Lie in a comfortable position. Play instrumental music that makes you feel good: classical, New Age, or music that is gentle, sweeping, or of dynamic beauty. When the music is playing, close your eyes. Inhale deeply through your nose, and exhale through slowly your mouth; do this eight times. Visualize that you are inhaling the power of the universe, which purifies and attunes you physically, emotionally, mentally, and metaphysically. When you exhale, all the tensions and worries leave your body and go back into the universe where they dissolve and blend into the pure life force.

Tighten and loosen your muscles slowly in this order:

Feet. Tighten. Loosen. Take a slow, deep breath, and exhale.
Calves. Tighten. Loosen. Take a slow, deep breath, and exhale.
Thighs. Tighten. Loosen. Take a slow, deep breath, and exhale.
Hips and buttocks. Tighten. Loosen. Take a slow, deep breath, and exhale.
Stomach. Tighten. Loosen. Take a slow, deep breath, and exhale.
Back. Tighten. Loosen. Take a slow, deep breath, and exhale.
Arms. Tighten. Loosen. Take a slow, deep breath, and exhale.
Hands. Tighten. Loosen. Take a slow, deep breath, and exhale.
Neck and shoulders. Tighten. Loosen. Take a slow, deep breath, and exhale.
Face. Tighten. Loosen. Take a slow, deep breath, and exhale.

Then completely relax and take eight more slow, deep breaths. Inhale the universal life energy through your nose and exhale tension through your mouth.

Set the intent: *Whoever I am, whatever I am, whatever I need, whatever is right for me—so be it. I open to insight. I open to receive.*

Now that you are completely relaxed, give your self over to the music that is playing. Focus on the point between your eyebrows and journey inward as if going into a tunnel within yourself. Deeper and deeper you travel into your vast inner being. Do this for a while. . . .

    You now emerge from the tunnel into the realm of your Inner Leader. Notice your surroundings. In the distance, you see your Inner Leader. Observe its appearance and what it is doing. Is it holding anything, or wearing anything that stands out? Is it in a cage, held back from emerging in your life? Or is it bold and marching about with a puffed chest? Or perhaps it radiates an ethereal light. Observe your Inner Leader for a while . . . .

    Now go to your Inner Leader. If it is in a cage, set it free. If it is a bit full of itself, get its attention. If it is Noble, let your heart swell with honor. If it is glowing an ethereal light, let your heart swell with cherish. Examine its demeanor. What expression is on its face? What attitude does it have toward you?

Look deep into its eyes. Appreciate it for the times it took charge of your life, helped you find direction, and took point in dubious situations. Even though it has helped you, you are also aware of the times it tried to take charge of others in a roughshod way and it backfired. And you are also aware of the times it did not emerge because some other aspect within you held it back. You decide it could use an alignment so that it can better lead you to fulfill your life purpose. It could do with a swim in the pool of the Quintessential Self, where all things come to balance. Feeling your intent, your Inner Leader agrees to go to the Quintessential self. It walks through a white wall of light. You follow. There before you both is a beautiful pool of glittering water, which is the Quintessential Self. Your Inner Leader moves into the pool and swims about, recharging as it ducks under the water, then comes up again, feeling rejuvenated. You can feel it realigning with your life purpose and shedding the heaviness that comes from the urge to control others. Now it only wants to control itself, and if others follow, then so be it.

Feeling an even deeper appreciation for your Inner Leader, you join it in the pool, feeling purified as you move toward it. You are feeling soothed and charged as you reach your Inner Leader. You and your Inner Leader embrace, and merge into one, experiencing attunement with the Quintessential Self, like ingredients being folded into a cake.

You feel your Inner Leader within you and how it feels its power differently: richer in honor, and clearer with an intent to help your consciousness move in directions that help you become all you can be. You feel a new resolve to put more energy into taking more charge of your own life and less charge of others.

Now just be still and listen. Bask in this experience until the music ends.

When you open your eyes, you will feel your Inner Leader charged and balanced by your Quintessence, ready to act on your behalf to help you fulfill your life purpose.

Record your experience.

_____

_____

_____

_____

_____

_____

_____

_____

Draw a picture or symbol that summarizes your experience. Example: *A compass.*

Create a key phrase that summarizes the experience. Example: *Take charge of my life.*

_____

When needed, say the phrase silently and visualize the picture or symbol. This will reactivate the experience and generate a peaceful, empowered, clear state of mind.

Δ

Gem of Wisdom
The greatest leaders do not seek followers.

Live the Mystery

7

WORKSHOP SEVEN
THE VICTIM "I have been wronged."

Stabbed in the heart, bruised to the bone, violated, unloved, unappreciated, misunderstood, or maybe just shaken, the Victim is the part of us that suffers and views that suffering as a result of being *wronged*. Although we can't get through life without incurring psychological or physical assault even if by a verbal insult or a smack on the face, feeling victimized is in the perception of the beholder. What upsets us, how deeply we are upset, and our reaction to that upset depends primarily on our view of the situation, how we see ourselves in relation to the world, and our outlook on life.

It is not always our Inner Victim that emerges when we are hurt. Sometimes it is our Inner Healer with healing guidance, our Inner Nurturer with kind self-talk, our Inner Sage making the best of the situation, or perhaps our Inner Warrior will surge forth to make a comeback. Some people never perceive themselves as victims even when the technically are, and others feel chronically victimized even when they technically aren't.

Two people in the same situation can have very different outlooks on what it means to be victimized. For example, Person A and Person B are thirty-year-old, average looking women who each live alone. Person A might feel lonely and cheated of love and turn to alcohol to ease the pain because she feels unattractive and unworthy of respect. Person B might feel independent and joyful, and though considered unattractive, radiates such dazzling self-respect that she is surrounded by adoring friends and quality suitors.

Pain thresholds vary as well, and not just physically. A verbal insult will make some writhe in anguish, mildly upset others, and some will remain unaffected. The more sensitive we are, the more easily we are hurt. Even so, it is normal, but not required, that we feel victimized when enduring a harsh event. Or at the very least, if our Inner Victim emerges, we needn't let it consume us for long. A loved one can die, and we can mourn without casting blame or inducing guilt and honor the deceased by living a full and rewarding life. When rejected, we can feel the sting for a short while, then take that energy and convert it into something productive instead of dwelling in a depressive state for months. We can be insulted and feel anger without seeking revenge, and lose a competition without feeling shortchanged. In summary, we can suffer without feeling we were "done wrong."

However, there are times when our Inner Victim has a role to play that transcends our conscious understanding. We humans are very complicated. Who's to say where our life story is meant to take us? Feeling victimized for a prolonged period might open doors for us to have a variety of experiences that on some unconscious level we need to have.

For example, our Inner Victim might serve to unearth dark secrets in the garden of our self. For instance, we get mugged and can't get over it, and after a while have flashbacks of childhood abuse. The flashbacks strengthen until the gory psychological wound is exposed, at which time we seek therapy, and afterward feel better than we ever felt in our lives. Or if we become so debilitated from a betrayal that we seek a support group that not only helps us, but generates life-long friendships. Or if we can't stop blaming ourselves for a death in the family, which lands us in mental hospital that brings our drifting family back together.

-

So, if you are going through something you feel you just can't get over, ride with it, see where it takes you. Sometimes we just need to take the journey to get to the prize.

On the other hand, we can get stuck in a life-long victim pattern, like a hamster on a wheel, unable to get off. Years go by, sometimes decades, and nothing . . . but nothing changes. How we were done wrong drives us around and around the wheel, generating ongoing resentment, and we don't really get anywhere or get on with our lives—ever. If this is you, take heart, when you get sick and tired of it, sick and tired *enough*, you will open to your Inner Hero and take steps to change your reality.

Our Inner Victim will likely fall into one, more than one, or a combination of the various types: the Helpless Victim, the Sympathy Sucker, the Woeful Victim, the Masochist, the Seething Victim, the Defensive Victim, the Lonely Victim, the Empathic Victim, or the Too-Tough-to-Tell Victim. While you may not recognize all these types in you, at least—not often, you might recognize them in others. This knowledge can serve to improve your interrelations with those in your life. By knowing your Victim nature, you might understand theirs.

The Helpless Victim. The Helpless Victim's battle cry is "I am weak." It believes it is unable to survive without constant help. *I can't make it alone; I cannot take care of myself.* Lacking confidence in its own abilities, the Helpless Victim will get others to take responsibility for its life. While the Helpless Victim might seem manipulative, it is actually terrified to be independent. Hence, it blares the "Help Me" signal, and those with a strong Inner Martyr who are into the "saving game," are usually the ones who respond. As long as others hold the Helpless Victim's head above water, it will never learn how to swim.

If the Helpless Victim is a star in our life, we will constantly feel powerless. The conundrum is, we feel we will die if others don't take care of us, but if they do, we never actually learn to help ourselves, and the helpless feeling continues. The cycle can only be broken if we elicit our Inner Warrior and Leader to help us take the plunge.

The Sympathy Sucker. The Sympathy Sucker often works in tandem with the Helpless Victim; however, it can also stand alone. The Sympathy Sucker wants everyone to feel sorry for it all the time. It thrives on sympathy and will grow angry if it doesn't get it. It might even threaten suicide to get the attention it craves. It will be happy if it gets in an accident or acquires a disease because now it can get more sympathy. It will compete with others to feel the worst and proudly proclaim the difficulties of its life. Its greatest goal is to acquire more sympathy because it equates sympathy with love. Because it corners the market on getting sympathy, it is very greedy on giving it to anyone else. It will not acknowledge that anyone's suffering can be worse than its own.

If we have a strong Sympathy Sucker in us, we will complain incessantly about how hard life is for us. *Poor me. Poor, poor me. I am struggling more than you, more than anybody. I am suffering worse than you, worse than anybody. Me. Me. Me.* In a sense, we worship our pain because it is the bait to get others to nurture us. While giving and receiving sympathy definitely has its place and can be healthy, if we are feeding off it we will eventually drain our sympathizers and their sympathy will turn to apathy.

When our Inner Sympathy Sucker begins to negatively affect our relationships, we can elicit our Inner Sage to count our blessings, and our Inner Nurturer to give back to others some of the sympathy we have sucked. Everyone goes through hardship—EVERYONE. No one can corner the market on suffering or enduring harsh situations. Pain is relative, and in every human's deepest moment of pain, it is neither less nor more than any other human on Earth. Although we are all different, we are also—all the same.

The Woeful Victim. The Woeful Victim might feel it is being treated unfairly, but it doesn't broadcast its woe. It is silently sad, not mad. It is sad for itself, and sad that people can be so cold and the world so cruel. This is natural in all of us from time to time when we are down about this or that. In general, the mood will lift as we experience or witness kinder and more beautiful occurrences.

The Masochist. The Masochist feels it deserves to be victimized. It will only accept life's pleasure if it can pay a penalty. In collusion with the Inner Traitor, it turns on itself, feeling unworthy of receiving good things unless it also is receiving bad things. If it wins a hundred bucks, it will have to give most, if not all of it away. If it is on the road to success, it might unconsciously get into an accident to set it back. In extremes, it will accept love only if the lover is also cruel, and enjoy sex only if pain is involved.

The Masochist has a strange and deep guilt that sometimes cannot be explained. We may not even feel it in us, except on rare occasions when something triggers it to rise. At those times our self-esteem is so low that we consciously or unconsciously invite people to punish us, or we might punish ourselves. Although this rings of thwarted mental health, it is more normal and natural than it seems. Most people hide this aspect from the public, but it is there in everyone from time to time, although the way it emerges, the strength behind it, and what makes it emerge can be different. It can operate on more subtle levels, such as sabotaging a good relationship or being late for meetings all the time.

When the Masochist has a lead role in our lives, we keep ourselves from flowering because we don't think we deserve it. While understanding the root cause of this self-betrayal can be helpful, we need to forgive ourselves for something we might not even remember we did, or something we did that we *perceive* as bad, but isn't bad in context with the full event. Even if not remembered, bringing our Inner Masochist to balance can be achieved by summoning our Inner Sage, Nurturer, and Healer to aid us in our endeavor to better appreciate ourselves.

The Seething Victim. This type of Victim will view everything that has ever happened to it as unfair. It is so self-consumed that even if it won a million dollars, it would feel cheated that it didn't win two million. Rewards are never enough. And the good fortune of others feels like a slap in the face. It carries a chip on its shoulder that it uses as an excuse to be abusive to others. When the Seething Victim rises, it is spiteful. It feels it has been wronged, and it is others who must make up for anything it ever lacked in its life. This can develop into narcissism: *I am the best, and you all should serve me.* And sometimes it can develop into sadism: *I will make you suffer the way I have suffered.* Or a borderline criminal personality, *It's okay to cheat others because I have been cheated. It's okay to play unfair because life has never been fair to me.* When the Seething Victim rises in us, we need our Inner Nurturer to calm this dude down.

The Defensive Victim. The Defensive Victim, powered by the Fury, views others as the enemy on the battlefield. It assumes everyone views it critically because deep down, that is how it views itself. Compliments are taken as insults. A compliment of "You were brave to make it through all that" might incite a response of "Are you making fun of me?" Suggestions are taken as criticisms. "You might feel better if you rest" might incite the response "So you think I am so stupid I can't figure that out?" A dreamy look at the beautiful outdoors might be perceived as suspicious. "You're thinking about your old lover, aren't you!"

When our Defensive Victim rises we are so beaten up inside, we can't see the forest for the trees and often wind up lonely. It is only a matter of time before people tire of us accusing them when they never meant any harm. The Defensive Victim badly needs the Inner Healer to work on its psychological wounds, and the Inner Sage to help it distinguish between those who actually hurt it and the innocent people in its current life.

The Lonely Victim. The Lonely Victim feels like no one really cares about it. This often rises in those who do not march to the beat of the common drum. If we feel we are not understood by anyone, it can feel quite lonely. Most people need to be warmly acknowledged and honored for who they truly are by at least one person. Without genuine moments of authentic emotional intimacy, we as humans start to die inside. We might even become despondent and feel unreal. We might sink into depression—and if we don't make any connections, we might think of suicide. Our Lonely Victim is thinking, *What does it matter anyway? No body cares about me . . . not really.*

Since social embrace is in our DNA, our Lonely Victim might rise on occasions where we have been singled out, rejected, betrayed, or shunned. Sometimes the Lonely Victim lashes out in a desperate attempt to get attention any way it can: emotional blackmail, tantrums, even crime. Or it might become cold and apathetic, and morph into a sociopathic personality.

Most often, however, if we develop a respectful relationship with our unique self, we can begin to move in directions that impassion us. In this, we will connect with others of like mind, and the loneliness will ease. For example, if you love waterfalls, start going to waterfalls. You will meet others who also love waterfalls. If you love Oriental culture, start taking classes, go to museums, and plan a trip to the Orient. If you love wildlife, volunteer at a wildlife preserve. In short, when we allow our individuality to flourish, it will attract special people into our lives.

The Empathic Victim. Highly sensitive people are naturally empathic, meaning they can, in varying degrees, experience other people's realties. Watching the news can send them into a tailspin. Driving past a bad accident on the road might make them feel impending doom. And if the realities of others are foreign to their own, it can create a collision of sorts within them, causing disorientation. For instance, a very drunk person might make them feel drunk, and given they didn't have a drink, confused. A psychopath's cold reality might make them feel dizzy and horrible. They can also have strong reactions to the idea of things, for instance in a fiction show or book that depicts a rape, they might tune into the concept of rape and feel it happening all over the world. Hearing the words, "broken arm," even if in a first aid class, might cause a searing pain in their arm.

When the highly empathic are unaware that their upset is not rooted in them, they often feel victimized without realizing why, other than deducing that there is something terribly wrong with them. They often unwittingly unleash the Inner Traitor and turn on themselves by thinking: *What is wrong with me? I am crazy! I am weak!* However, if they *are* aware, they can embrace their sensitivity and make the most of it. Highly sensitive people are richly sensual, brilliant in creative pursuits, and make wonderful caretakers and therapists. Furthermore, they can mitigate the down-side by learning to censor negative input and stay away from off-putting environments. Or if they stumble into someone's unsavory reality, or wind up somewhere that is having an adverse affect on them, they can summon their Inner Warrior to help them disconnect by using creative visualization, such as seeing themselves encased in armor.

We are all empathic, even if to a small degree. Sometimes, in a given situation, we might be unusually empathic, for instance, sensing a loved one in danger. Or if we just experienced a harsh event and are more vulnerable than usual, we might sense harsh events all over the world and view life as a dark experience. Even if this occurrence is rare, we know our Empathic Victim has risen when we feel overwhelmed by the dark side of life. This is easily remedied. Like a radio dial, all we need do is change the channel. Turn off the news, violent shows, and get away from negative people, negative thoughts, and irrational fears. Enjoy music and comedy, flowers and birds, a hot cup of coffee or tea, and the sweet comfort of something soft and fragrant. Amazingly, going from depressed and feeling horrible to walking with a bounce in our step and a smile on our face, is sometimes just . . . that . . . simple.

Too-Tough-to-Tell Victim. This Victim type hides its pain and acts as if nothing affects it. Though mistaken for Sage-like power, it really does, deep down, feel badly roughed up. It attributes its victimized feelings as a sign of its own weakness, and it will do anything to cover up the wound or deny it is even there. The Too-Tough-to-Tell Victim has a strong Inner Warrior whose pride in being strong will not let anyone see it cry.

When we are like this, we might secretly get drunk in the dark, cut or abuse ourselves, or gorge on comfort food. We might have lots of meaningless sex, get lost in our work, or at the very least force the tears down so hard we get a lump on our throat. No one must see we are hurting.

This Victim, when it is afflicted, might avoid its suffering by seeking revenge or by making innocent others hurt as it hurts. Or a healthier Inner Too-Tough-to-Tell Victim might just refuse to go down with the ship and give its all to a pursuit that will help it achieve a victory.

Balancing the Inner Victim

It is NOT weak to feel victimized. It does not mean you are less psychologically evolved than those who don't. No one can know the history of our hardship more than us, and what we know is often like seeing the tip of the iceberg without truly understanding the roots of our pain. Our Inner Victim isn't bad. It is HUMAN. There is no shame in feeling victimized, and it is natural to feel that way. We may want to draw the line, however, at allowing it to drive us into demeaning behaviors, such as food deprivation that makes us sick, overeating and packing on weight, incessant crying, job loss, claiming psychological disability, turning darkly cynical and making people want to flee us, having unsafe sex with strangers, developing dangerous addictions, or overdosing on drugs. And if decades pass and we still haven't done anything to overcome our woes, heal our tarnished trust, or take responsibility for making our lives better, we have chosen to stunt our psychological growth and cripple our potential to lead a rich and rewarding life.

The most powerful thing we can do to bring our Inner Victim to balance is to turn what hurts us into learning experiences to help us grow. Instead of events becoming toxic thorns in our side and letting pain eat us alive, we can transform the pain into strength to better face our future. Being mugged is a motivation to learn self-defense. Losing a job is a catalyst to pursue a career that sparks passion. Getting a serious disease is an opportunity to appreciate each moment and make the most of each day. There are countless stories of those who turned tragedy into something beautiful: the mother who lost her child to cancer generates a leap in cancer research, the once-abused woman works in a shelter and helps countless others to find their power, a man who loses everything starts from the ground up and rebuilds an even better life for himself.

Sometimes, even though we have released pain and anger of our transgressors and maybe even forgiven them, the pain still lingers. Deep wounds take time to heal, sometimes a long time, but they can never heal if we don't begin the process. It's as they say, "Time heals all wounds." And it does, eventually.

Another powerful thing we can do to bring our Inner Victim to balance is to use our Inner Sage to help us stop perceiving negative happenings as a personal affront. Events don't occur to punish us, and people who try to punish us are only projecting their Inner torment outward because they don't know what else to do. In a way, nothing wrong ever happens to us. Life happens. And there is beauty to be found in EVERYTHING that seems to have gone wrong, if only we will dare *see*.

By getting to know our Inner Victim, it will arm us with the knowledge to determine the effect it has on us and keep it from inciting more misery in our future. Bringing our Inner Victim to balance requires empowering our Inner Hero (to save us), our Healer (to repair us), our Sage (to enlighten us), our Nurturer (to love us), and our Warrior (to give us the stamina to get on with our lives.) Empowered by these aspects, our confidence need not be shaken, and our self-esteem need not ever fall. We can view all events as a *natural part of life in which no one is exempt*. This workshop is designed to help you get to know what role your Inner Victim plays in your life and determine if modifications are necessary to bring inner peace, and hence peace with your reality.

The Victim in a Nutshell
* Views its suffering as a result of something that has gone wrong.
* Perceives that it is being treated unfairly.
* Feels excessively sorry for itself.
* When given too much reign, unconsciously sets itself up for further victimization.

Victim Types.
The Helpless Victim: "I am too weak to survive on my own."
The Sympathy Sucker: "My suffering is worse than anyone else's."
The Woeful Victim: "I'm sad."
The Masochist: "I deserve to suffer."
The Seething Victim. "I've been cheated."
The Defensive Victim: "You can't possibly like me."
The Lonely Victim: "Nobody cares about me."
The Empathic Victim: "I feel everything, so I am easily hurt."
The Too-Tough-to-Tell Victim: "I will never let them see me cry."

Exploring Your Inner Victim.

Exercise One

Place an X next to the areas of your life in which you *perceive* you are being or have been victimized to a *significant degree*. For example, if your child moderately upset you once but generally treats you well, that wouldn't count. If five boyfriends jilted you and two did not, that would count. However, if you were badly scathed in an incident that happened once, but it may as well happened a thousand times for all the pain you suffered, that would count.

_____mother	_____spiritual leader(s)	_____school
_____father	_____boyfriend(s)	_____society
_____children	_____girlfriend(s)	_____animal
_____relative(s)	_____spouse(s)	_____natural disaster(s)
_____friend(s)	_____stranger(s)	_____accident(s)
_____men	_____boss(es)	_____life
_____women	_____peers	_____deity

_____the law   _____doctor(s)   _____service worker(s)
_____government   _____environment
_____teacher(s)   _____authority figure(s)
_____lawyer(s)   _____criminal(s)

___other _____   ___other_____

___other _____   ___other_____

Count your X's. How many do you have? _____

Circle the correct answer. I feel I have been victimized in _____ areas of my life.

many   a moderate amount   only a few   hardly any   none

Exercise Two

State what currently triggers your Inner Victim to emerge. Even if you feel it emerges rarely or only for a few moments before another aspect takes over, state the event anyway. Example: My Inner Victim emerges when: someone is rude, when I see other people happy, when my mom criticizes me, when I don't get the recognition I deserve. Stretch your mind to think of as many incidents as possible. However, if there are only a few, that is all right too.

1. My Victim currently emerges when_____

2. My Victim currently emerges when_____

3. My Victim currently emerges when_____

4. My Victim currently emerges when_____

5. My Victim currently emerges when_____

6. My Victim currently emerges when_____

7. My Victim currently emerges when_____

8. My Victim currently emerges when_____

9. My Victim currently emerges when_____

10. My Victim currently emerges when_____

How hard was it for you to think of what triggers your Inner Victim?

easy   moderately   difficult   really hard

How often do you view yourself as a victim?

almost always   moderately   hardly ever   never

Place a check by the *initial* thoughts that most fit what might *generally* come to mind when you are treated badly.

_____"No good deed goes unpunished." (Seething)
_____"I'll never let them see my cry." (Too-Tough-to-Tell)
_____"Bad things always happen to me." (Sympathy Sucker)
_____"It's not fair." (Seething)
_____"I deserve to feel bad." (Masochist)
_____"I am not getting the appreciation I deserve." (Woeful)
_____"The world is too rough for me." (Helpless)
_____"I need some sympathy." (Sympathy Sucker)
_____"What doesn't kill me will make me stronger." (Not a Victim)
_____"I don't measure up." (Masochist)
_____"I am not strong enough to handle this." (Helpless)
_____"I'm so tired of being hurt." (Woeful)
_____"When I watch the news on television, I get depressed." (Empathic)
_____"I'm fine, leave me alone." (Too-Tough-to-Tell)
_____"Can't anyone see I need help!" (Helpless)
_____"It's just a part of life." (Not a Victim)
_____"I know you don't really like me." (Defensive)
_____"I know you will betray me." (Defensive)
_____"No one understands me." (Lonely)
_____"I don't fit in anywhere." (Lonely)
_____"I'd rather die than show my pain." (Too-Tough-to-Tell)
_____"Their suffering hurts me." (Empathic)
_____"I'm a good person, no matter what they think." (Not a Victim)
_____"It's their loss." (Not a Victim)
_____"To hell with them." (Seething)

Based on your answers, identify the Victim type, or combination of Victim types you *most* tend to be when you *initially* feel victimized: Helpless, Masochistic, Sympathy Sucker, Seething, Empathic, Woeful, Too-Tough-to-Tell, Not a Victim.

Exercise Three

This exercise is to spotlight your sore spots and access the role your Inner Victim plays in your life. Recall times when you felt affronted on any level and still harbor some pain. The assault might have been a criticism, something that felt unfair, or a blow you felt life gave you such as the loss of a loved one. Then state how that event made you feel, what conclusion you came to as a result, and in the spirit of your Inner Sage, what you can do today to feel better about it.

Example #1: I felt affronted when *I was deemed a phony when I was being authentic.* It made me feel *sad and lonely* because *I pride myself in being authentic.* I concluded that *if I can't be accepted as a genuine person, what's the point in trying to live in this world?* I could feel better about it today if *I stop taking people's ignorance of me personally.*

Example #2: I felt affronted when *I was molested*. It made me feel *stupid* because *I should have known better*. I concluded that *I deserved it*. I could feel better about it today if *I look at the big picture and realize that back then, I really didn't know better because the molester confused me. I did not deserve what happened to me. I am still a good person. I take back the part of me that the molester took away—my dignity.*

1. I felt affronted when_____

It made me feel_____because_____

_____

I concluded that_____

_____

I could feel better about it today if I_____

_____

2. I felt affronted when_____

It made me feel_____because_____

_____

I concluded that_____

_____

I could feel better about it today if I_____

_____

3. I felt affronted when_____

It made me feel_____because_____

_____

I concluded that_____

_____

I could feel better about it today if I_____

_____

4. I felt affronted when_____

It made me feel_____because_____

_____

I concluded that_____

_____

I could feel better about it today if I_____

_____

5. I felt affronted when_____

It made me feel_____because_____

_____

I concluded that_____

_____

I could feel better about it today if I_____

Of all the experiences above, state what you most *commonly* felt after being affronted? You can have more than one answer. Examples: stupid, betrayed, enraged, deeply sad, guilty, worthless, angry at myself

_____

What is the *most* common theme(s) to what you perceive as your "victimization?" Examples: rejected by the opposite sex, sexual abuse, my friends always drop me, people laugh at me, everyone has it better than me, I always get fired, I am not treated with respect.

_____

If you pay attention to this answer, you can begin to change the behaviors that keep giving you this result. State what you can do today to stop this pattern.

_____

Circle the answer that suits you best. The Victim has appeared in my life:

hardly ever   from time to time   in certain periods of my life   moderately   profusely

Healing and Balancing Exercise for Your Inner Victim

Place one palm over your heart.
Place the other palm beneath your breastbone.

Concentrate deeply. Repeat silently or aloud for at least two minutes:
"It's not what happens to me; it's what I do with what happens to me."

Relaxation and Creative Visualization Exercise
Lie in a comfortable position. Play instrumental music that makes you feel good: classical, New Age, or music of gentle, sweeping, or dynamic beauty. When the music is playing, close your eyes. Inhale deeply through your nose, and exhale slowly through your mouth; do this eight times. Visualize that you are inhaling the power of the universe, which purifies and attunes you physically, emotionally, mentally, and metaphysically. When you exhale, all the tensions and worries leave your body and go back into the universe where they dissolve and blend into the pure life force.

Tighten and loosen your muscles slowly in this order:

Feet. Tighten. Loosen. Take a slow, deep breath, and exhale.
Calves. Tighten. Loosen. Take a slow, deep breath, and exhale.
Thighs. Tighten. Loosen. Take a slow, deep breath, and exhale.
Hips and buttocks. Tighten. Loosen. Take a slow, deep breath, and exhale.
Stomach. Tighten. Loosen. Take a slow, deep breath, and exhale.
Back. Tighten. Loosen. Take a slow, deep breath, and exhale.
Arms. Tighten. Loosen. Take a slow, deep breath, and exhale.
Hands. Tighten. Loosen. Take a slow, deep breath, and exhale.
Neck and shoulders. Tighten. Loosen. Take a slow, deep breath, and exhale.
Face. Tighten. Loosen. Take a slow, deep breath, and exhale.

Then completely relax and take eight more slow, deep breaths. Inhale the universal life energy through your nose and exhale tension through your mouth.

Set the intent: *Whoever I am, whatever I am, whatever I need, whatever is right for me—so be it. I open to insight. I open to receive.*

Now that you are completely relaxed, give your self over to the music that is playing. Focus on the center between your eyebrows and journey inward. Do this for a while . . . .
You hear sounds of someone in anguish. You move toward the sounds, and there you see, all tied up in ropes, your Inner Victim. Stand before your Inner Victim and observe its appearance, the look on its face, and the expression in its eyes. Examine it for a while . . . .
Feeling your Inner Victim's pain, your Inner Hero emerges from you like a spirit, and your Inner Warrior follows. The Hero nods to the Warrior who uses a sword to cut the ropes that bind your Inner Victim. Your Hero and Warrior stand on either side of your Inner Victim to guard and repel anything that would further upset it. Note the expression on your Inner Victim's face now that it is freed and protected.
Now your Inner Healer emerges from you like a spirit and rests its hand on your Inner Victim's head. Like a blast of buckshot, toxic thoughts and feelings fly out of your Inner Victim into the universe and are absorbed by starlight. Experience this for a moment . . . .
Your Inner Healer stands aside, and your Inner Nurturer emerges from you like a spirit and touches your Inner Victim's heart, pouring love into it. You see your Inner Victim looking lighter and brighter. Experience this for a moment . . . .
Your Inner Nurturer stands aside and your Inner Sage emerges from you like a spirit, and holds up a mirror to your Inner Victim. In the mirror, your Inner Victim sees itself

changing into a more content person because it now knows that anything that ever happened to it was a gift to catalyze it to get stronger, grow, and flower.

Now all your Inner Aspects merge into one being and you are freed from your Inner Victim's reality. You now walk a path that is yours and yours alone. You know the joy of the moment, and what it feels like to experience your intrinsic value that can never be taken away. Experience this until the music ends . . . .

When your eyes open, you will feel strong, focused on the present and free of the past.

Record your experience.

_____

_____

_____

_____

_____

_____

_____

Draw a picture or symbol that summarizes your experience. Example: *A Redwood tree.*

Create a key phrase that summarizes this experience. Example: *I am always strong.*

_____

When needed, say the phrase silently and visualize the picture or symbol. This will reactivate the experience and generate a peaceful, empowered, clear state of mind.

Δ

Gem of Wisdom
Victimization is in the eye of the beholder.

Live the Mystery

8

WORKSHOP EIGHT
THE MARTYR "I Sacrifice."

Martyrs have an innate belief that their sacrifice will benefit others and hence make them worthy. Worth is associated with being "good." Since various social groups have definitive standards for what it means to be good, the requirements may vary from culture to culture, geographic placement, genders, and even family constellation. However, the standards are basically the same for any aspiring martyr: 1. Ignore your well-being to serve others. 2. Your personal value is dependent on suffering for others. 3. The more you suffer, the more worthy you will be. 4. Believe that taking care of yourself first—is selfish. 5. Always take care of yourself *last*. 6. Believe that others *need* you to help them and will falter if you refrain. 7. Be more comfortable giving than receiving.

We all martyr ourselves in varying degrees at various times, be it rare, occasional, often, or profusely. Even those who seem self-centered do, from time to time, get overwhelmed with mercy and do something incredibly kind at their own expense. While sometimes a sacrifice can be beneficial, such as giving a sick family member a kidney, more often than not martyring ourselves depletes our energy, and/or robs others of personal growth.

Even in parenthood, the martyr role can fuel dysfunction. While good parenting requires sacrifice in a child's early years, as children grow, they need less from their parents, and more chances to find their own power and meet their own needs. No parent should ever give up so much that they are dying inside. In addition, it is good role modeling for children to watch their parents honor themselves. If not, children get one of two messages regarding the martyring parent. Message #1: I am more worthy than my parent and therefore should be served without reciprocation (the child gets spoiled). Message #2: My parent is weak and needs my protection and care (the child must be the adult).

Allowing your children to witness you taking care of yourself is to set a precedent that one day, should they have children, they too can, without guilt, take care of themselves. Or even if they don't have children, they won't equate adulthood with martyrdom. There is no reason why a family can't all take care of each other. No one should be pumping out exorbitant energy to absolve others from taking responsibility for their own lives or have a cherry on their sundae every day. And children should not have to sacrifice their childhood to take care of a parent who won't take care of her/himself. Some of us have had martyr-type parents, and some of us are martyr-type parents.

Getting to better know our Inner Martyr will shed light on how we have used it in our lives, or perhaps how others have used their Inner Martyr in ours. In this, we can determine if modifying its use might enrich our days.

In general, the Martyr falls into one, more than one, or a combination of the following types: the Reluctant Martyr, the Enabling Martyr, the Pious Martyr, the Save-the-World Martyr, or the Warrior Martyr. Given we all have our own nature, not all types will apply to you. You may, however, recognize them in others you know which can facilitate better understanding in those relationships.

The Reluctant Martyr. The Reluctant Martyr often resides in the seemingly self-centered. It views its martyr urges as a weakness that could lead to a loss of control over its own life, so it hangs back, concealed in shadow. We know we are the Reluctant Martyr when we hide behind the projected facade of "I come first," allowing our Inner Martyr to make only brief appearances, in disguise if possible, or in anonymous ways. Taking in a friend down on his/her luck is wrapped up as *I need someone to watch my dog while I am at work.* Or $20 that can barely be spared is slipped into a needy person's pocket and justified as *I don't really need the money.*

The Enabling Martyr. Contrary to the Reluctant Martyr, Enabling Martyrs unwittingly encourage those who have strong Inner Victims to depend on them. They stick out their necks and invite the chronically ailing to suck their energy as vampires suck blood. Always needing more, the chronically ailing depend upon the Enabling Martyr to get their fix, a temporary solution to release their pain. Why should they take care of themselves when they can get all the sustenance they need from someone else?

The chronic Victim says, "Help me. I need you. Give me some more energy." The Enabling Martyr who allows this coercion gets worn out because its dependents never intend to do what must be done to become strong, healthy people. Even when its reserves are overdrawn it will continue to sacrifice because the sacrifice makes it feel needed, important, worthy, and *good*. Thus, its action fosters weakness in those it is trying to save, such as the brother who continually gets into trouble waiting for the bail out, or the sister incessantly complaining about her mean husband, but will do nothing to change her situation.

While the efforts of Enabling Martyrs might appear to be the work of the Nurturer who enjoys comforting others or even the Hero who rescues with honor, it differs in that the Enabling Martyr consciously expects—but seldom sees its subjects improve, yet continues giving anyway. Eventually, these Martyrs get drained dry and must retreat from their dependents. In that withdrawal, the dependents will often cast an insult like "You don't care about me; I'm not going to talk to you anymore." At this stage, the classic response of the Enabling Martyr is "After all I have done for you, this is how you treat me?" After a recuperating hiatus, they will, in general, begin the game all over again.

Although the game enables the dependents to avoid self-examination and taking responsibility for their problems, it affords the Enabling Martyr the same thing. Blinded by all its good deeds, it feels it is already "there," and does not look at its own problems or put energy into self-development. It believes it is perfect and wonderful. After all, what would its dependents do without it? It should be appreciated, regaled even! In a way, the Enabling Martyr is full of itself and has little faith in the ability of those it tries to save—to save themselves.

We know our Enabling Martyr is on stage when we are so busy and tired from helping others that we don't have time to turn the spotlight inward to develop ourselves.

The Pious Martyr. This Martyr is not so much into saving anyone's day as it is simply doing without. If there are three steaks and four people, the Pious Martyr would say, '*You each have a steak; I will do without.* (Apparently sharing is not an option). Or, *I won't tell my children I have cancer and only six months to live; I don't want to disturb their lives.* Or, *You take the money and buy a new dress; I am happy in my rags.* The Pious Martyr only feels important when its needs *are not* met and it does without. We know our Pious Martyr is on stage when we hide in the shadows, feeling less worthy than everyone else in the world.

The Save-the-World Martyr. The Save-the-World Martyr does not take on a person here or there to "save." It's focus is on the general public and how it can improve *everyone's* lives.

It might volunteer in one or more charities or other organizations giving an exorbitant amount of energy. It will try to improve the lives of all who cross its path. For example, in overhearing a stranger talk about their troubled son, the Save-the-World-Martyr might say, "Excuse me, I heard you talking and your problem might be solved if you try . . ."

This type of Martyr sometimes has the reputation as a know-it-all and an outright buttisnksy, having helpful opinions to dole out everywhere it goes, even when unasked. We know this Martyr is on stage when we chronically march to the beat of "I can help you, and you, and you, and you . . ." Even if we get tired of offering ourselves this way, we still consider it our role in life to better *everyone's* day.

The Warrior Martyr. An often overlooked type of Martyr is the Warrior Martyr. The Warrior Martyr has a strong sense of duty to protect and/or advance the lives of others. Standing guard at the household door with little sleep and nourishment, it is fulfilled when its family inside is safe, fed, and soundly content. While there is a noble ring to all this, if taken to an extreme, the Warrior Martyr can find itself sinking in quicksand and be gone before anyone notices. The Warrior Martyr is the person who is the rock for everyone else, never revealing the toll it takes, or the parent who overworks to support the family, never complaining, but weary, falls into ill-health. The Warrior Martyr is the social activist giving everything to the cause, forfeiting a personal life, or the soldier at war who runs into harms way to constantly protect everyone else in the fray. *I must be a brave Warrior ALWAYS and be the first to sacrifice myself for others.* This can happen to soldiers who have lost comrades in war. Feeling guilty for surviving, the only way to alleviate that guilt is to keep going back to save others. We know our Warrior Martyr is on stage when we are acting out of duty and it is *hurting us,* but we hide it and do nothing to alleviate our pain.

The Selfless Martyr. This Martyr will be constantly "good-deeding" and want no recognition or reward. There is a time for this anonymous good deeding such as leaving a bag of groceries on the doorstep of a needy family who might be embarrassed to take it outright. However, if this anonymous good-deeding is done regularly to our detriment, such as going into debt to help others, or quashing our emotional needs to keep the peace, the Selfless Martyr puts us in peril.

Since in the eyes of society it is good to be selfless, the Selfless Martyr sometimes expects its family (who it views as an extension of it) to be selfless too. Instead of getting presents on holidays, donations are made to the poor. Instead of expressing needs, the children are expected to behave modestly and serve others.

When this Martyr rises, whether we work solo or expect our family to follow suit, we aspire to become selfless, as in "without a self." We do not have a life of our own. We are but a shadow of those who need and forfeit having our own adventure into the outer world. This, however, is not the sacrifice it seems. Self-development can be complicated. Adventuring into the outer world can be scary. Selfless martyrs do not have to grow into life to see what they can become. Contrary to popular belief, selfless behavior is *not* healthy. It starves our spirit, invites abuse, and keeps us from individuating into our true selves.

Balancing the Inner Martyr

When our Inner Martyr has too much control over our lives, we will feel burned out and somewhat angry that we must keep giving. This sometimes happens in demanding jobs or with busy parents who try to do it all, all the time. Deep down, when we burn out like this, sadness lurks. When will someone take care of us the way we take care of them? Secretly, our heart is breaking because we have become so depleted that we need others to give back. But since we keep our pain a secret, how can they?

Feeling bad, we might do even more for others, because that means we are "good." If we deem ourselves "good-the greatest-the best," we might feel better. Before we know it, our martyrdom has become an addiction. Although it feels good to help, everyone needs time to breathe. Every sort of martyr needs to come in out of the freezing rain and warm up by the fire. Those with strong Inner Martyr's eventually begin to feel used up because more energy goes out than comes in. This chronic act of giving energy without replenishing can lead to a break down, inciting illness, accidents, depression, and sometimes suicide. Suicide is not always conscious. One can just be too tired and get in a car accident from lack of attention. Or some might feel their sacrifices are necessary and become so malnourished and emaciated within and without that they die.

When we give in a balanced way, we feel not only energized but receptive to receiving. Being able to receive is important. Other people feel just as good to give to us as it feels for us to give to them. Healthy giving has nothing to do with martyrdom. Helpful acts sometimes are, but need not be, in tandem with self-sacrifice. We can take care of ourselves *and* others. The path to feeling better when our Inner Martyr has worn us out lies in giving less to others and more to ourselves. Sometimes we need our Inner Nurturer to nurture *us*, and our Inner Warrior to stand guard over *us*, pointing the sword with a proverbial NO to those who come knocking for our energy. *It's okay to say no.*

When our giving is balanced, we take care of ourselves first. This is NOT selfish. It is not anyone else's job to make us all right, and it is not our job to make others all right. Though a kind hand is always welcome, we feel better when we know we can depend on ourselves. And believe it or not, so do others. When it is in our hearts to offer a kind hand, now and then, to someone who needs a boost, it is a far more beautiful experience when we are full of energy and bright within ourselves.

Joy in living is found by nourishing ourselves to grow into all we can be, and while we may sacrifice to help others periodically, if done too much—everyone loses.

The Martyr in a Nutshell
* Measures its worth by how much it sacrifices.
* Equates suffering with being good.
* Feels less worthy than others.
* Has difficulty saying "no."
* Is compelled to help to the point of depletion.
* Is secretly afraid to develop itself.

Martyr Types
The Reluctant Martyr: "Sacrificing equals weakness."
The Enabling Martyr: "I need to be needed."
The Pious Martyr: "I don't need much; take all you want."
The Save-the-World Martyr: "My goal is to save everyone."
The Warrior Martyr: "I am everyone's rock; I hide my needs."
The Selfless Martyr: "I exist to serve others."

Exploring Your Inner Martyr

Exercise One

Place an X by the answers that are true for you.

____I will help anyone who asks.
____I will help others, even if it kills me.
____I have difficulty saying no.
____I am more comfortable giving than receiving.
____Sacrificing for others makes me feel good.
____I like myself the most after I am drained dry from helping someone.
____I feel important when others chronically depend on me.
____I have trouble taking a compliment.
____Even if I am tired of constantly trying to make someone feel better, I do it anyway.
____The help I give others often takes a toll on me.
____I am so busy helping others, I have little time for myself.
____I often give up what I want or need in order to make others happy.
____I am everyone's rock.
____I often hide my suffering.
____I wish I could save everyone; I really do.

By the number of checks you made, you can get a feel for the degree in which you martyr yourself and perhaps didn't even realize it. You may have felt that your Inner Martyr was the Nurturer, and that you were simply nourishing others. However, the difference is this: The Martyr gets depleted helping others, while the Nurturer feels energized. When the Nurturer can't stop trying to bring others comfort and joy and gets depleted, it crosses over into Martyr. This is not to say that an occasional Martyr act is not warranted!

Exercise Two

This next exercise is designed to help you distinguish healthy acts of giving from Martyr acts. List things you have done to help others this last year that were a sacrifice on your part, the result, how it made you feel, and what line you fed yourself. Example #1: I sacrificed to help someone this last year when *I spent time with my aging mother.* It was a sacrifice because *I had a lot of things I needed to do at home.* The result was *that my mother and I had a quality experience.* This made me feel *happy.* The line I told myself was, *Sometimes relating to the people I love is more important than getting things done.* Example #2: I sacrificed to help someone this last year when *I bailed my brother out of jail for a D.U.I. —again.* It was a sacrifice because *it drains me every time I do it.* The result was *he seemed insincere with his thanks, like it was a line.* This made me feel *exasperated and tired.* The line I told myself was, *I have to help him even though he never seems to get better, because he is my brother.*

1. I sacrificed to help someone this last year when_____

_____

It was a sacrifice because_____

_____

The result was_____

_____

This made me feel_____

The line I told myself was_____

2. I sacrificed to help someone this last year when_____

_____

It was a sacrifice because_____

_____

The result was _____

_____

This made me feel_____

The line I told myself was_____

3. I sacrificed to help someone this last year when_____

_____

It was a sacrifice because_____

_____

The result was _____

_____

This made me feel_____

The line I told myself was_____

4. I sacrificed to help someone this last year when_____

_____

It was a sacrifice because_____

_____

The result was _____

_____

This made me feel_____

The line I told myself was_____

5. I sacrificed to help someone this last year when_____

_____

It was a sacrifice because_____

_____

The result was _____

_____

This made me feel_____

The line I told myself was_____

_____

At the end of the sacrifice, how did you feel *most* of the time? (energized, depleted, angry, happy, sad)

_____

Summarize what you *most often* tell yourself after putting a lot of energy into helping another or others. Examples: I am a good person, but I'm so depleted. I did good and I feel energized.

_____

Place an X by the answer(s) that are true for you.

Most of these times listed above, my sacrifice had the following effect on me:

____I felt unappreciated and taken for granted.
____I felt fulfilled and energized.
____I felt used because the help I gave seemed only to serve as a band-aid.
____I felt overjoyed because my sacrifices really helped.
____I was drained dry but proud of myself for helping.
____Now I need someone to do something nice for me.
____I am happy I could help others, but since I did it anonymously, I feel a bit cheated.
____Other _____

Given these answers, place the number 1 by your strongest Inner Martyr type even if it makes a rare appearance. If you are more than one type, place the number 2 by the second strongest type, and so on. You might identify with only one type, or it might be all types at different times.

____Pious   ____Selfless   ____Enabling Martyr   ____Warrior Martyr

____Save-the-World Martyr   ____Reluctant Martyr

Exercise Three

Focus on your Inner Martyr. Draw a picture of it below (artwork is unimportant) and name it. Examples: Sacrificial Sam, Save-the-Day Sally, Pitifully Pious.

Name _____

Now let your Inner Martyr speak. What does it have to say? Don't think; just flow. Example: I can't stop taking care of everyone. It makes me feel important. It makes me feel in control even though I look like a martyr. I have taken in a bunch of homeless people and its bugging me to have no privacy in my own home. It is a big chore, but they deem me a hero so it is worth it . . . etc.

_____

_____

_____

_____

_____

_____

How might your life change if your Inner Martyr were more balanced?

_____

_____

What does your Inner Sage have to say about your Inner Martyr? _____

_____

Things to remember:
* If helping another depletes you, something is wrong.
* You do not need to give yourself away to know your worth.
* When you sacrifice too much for others, you rob them of personal growth.
* When you sacrifice too much for others, you rob yourself of personal growth.
* What others want from us, they eventually need to give to themselves.
* When we give too much, we become the victim of our own charity.
* When we give too much, we give others the message that it is our job to sacrifice, and if we don't, they get mad.

When your Inner Martyr has an urge to act and you do not feel it is in your own best interest, it is helpful to have a one line sentence to stop yourself. Example: "What about me?" Tune into your Inner Sage and think of a sentence that is right for you. The sentence must stir you for it to work, so take your time with this. Write the sentence below.

_____

Circle the answer that suits you best. The Martyr has appeared in my life:

hardly ever   from time to time   in certain periods of my life   moderately   profusely

Healing and Balancing Exercise for your Inner Martyr

Place one hand over your heart.
Place the other hand on the crown of your head.
Concentrate deeply. Repeat silently or aloud for at least two minutes:
"I'm important too."

Relaxation and Creative Visualization Exercise
Lie in a comfortable position. Play instrumental music that makes you feel good: classical, New Age, or music that is of gentle, sweeping, or dynamic beauty. When the music is playing, close your eyes. Inhale through your nose deeply, and exhale through your mouth slowly; do this eight times. Visualize that you are inhaling the power of the universe, which purifies and attunes you physically, emotionally, mentally, and metaphysically. When you exhale, all the tensions and worries leave your body and go back into the universe where they dissolve and blend into the pure life force.

Tighten and loosen your muscles slowly in this order:

Feet. Tighten. Loosen. Take a slow, deep breath, and exhale.
Calves. Tighten. Loosen. Take a slow, deep breath, and exhale.
Thighs. Tighten. Loosen. Take a slow, deep breath, and exhale.
Hips and buttocks. Tighten. Loosen. Take a slow, deep breath, and exhale.
Stomach. Tighten. Loosen. Take a slow, deep breath, and exhale.
Back. Tighten. Loosen. Take a slow, deep breath, and exhale.

Arms. Tighten. Loosen. Take a slow, deep breath, and exhale.
Hands. Tighten. Loosen. Take a slow, deep breath, and exhale.
Neck and shoulders. Tighten. Loosen. Take a slow, deep breath, and exhale.
Face. Tighten. Loosen. Take a slow, deep breath, and exhale.

Then completely relax and take eight more slow, deep breaths. Inhale the universal life energy through your nose and exhale tension through your mouth.

Set the intent: *Whoever I am, whatever I am, whatever I need, whatever is right for me—so be it. I open to insight. I open to receive.*

Now that you are completely relaxed, give your self over to the music that is playing. Focus on the point between your eyebrows and journey inward. Feel yourself sinking like a stone to the time you first martyred yourself. Don't try to remember, just let go. Do this for a while . . .

Now, you are your Inner Sage looking at your Inner Martyr's eyes just after it has first martyred itself. What are those eyes saying to you? Take a moment to listen. Continue gazing into the eyes of your Inner Martyr as the scene changes to the next time you martyred yourself. Keep watching as the scenes change into time after time you have martyred yourself. Notice how your Inner Martyr might change in appearance as you advance toward the present. Pay attention to the expression on your Inner Martyr's face. Do this for a while . . . .

Now you are in the present. What does your Inner Martyr look like? Look into your Inner Martyr's eyes. What are they saying to you? Take a moment to listen . . . .

Now you feel your Inner Nurturer rise within you. You take your Inner Martyr's hand and hold it kindly. You begin walking, still holding your Inner Martyr's hand. You guide it away from its sacrificial world into beautiful sunshine. The wind blows against your bodies warm and comforting as you walk down a path. You hear cries for help on the sides of the path as you walk along, but you ignore them. Your Inner Martyr is tired and needs to be replenished, so even as it turns its head to those who call, you tell your Inner Martyr, "It is all right. They will be fine without you." You lead your Inner Martyr onward toward a ball of golden light in front of you at the end of the path. Coming to this golden ball of light, you both step into it and merge into one.

Merged, you feel yourself at the top of a mountain. You look out over the land, stretch out your arms and absorb all of nature. Take time to feel how nourishing the energy of the natural world is for you. Soak it in. It feels good to receive, to finally give yourself permission to put yourself first. Say silently or aloud over and over, "I value myself." Say this until you can really feel it. Do this until the music ends . . . .

When you open your eyes you will feel refreshed. Your new rule is that you will give to others only if it does not deplete, hurt, or anger you. When giving is healthy and balanced, it will not feel bad. Old behaviors are now fading and you feel strong in your resolve to take much better care of yourself.

Record your experience.

_____

_____

_____

_____

_____

_____

_____

_____

Draw a picture or symbol that summarized your experience. Example: *Me, hugging myself.*

Create a key phrase that summarizes this experience. Example: *I matter too.*

_____

When needed, say the phrase silently and visualize the picture or symbol. This will reactivate the experience and generate a peaceful, empowered, clear state of mind.

Δ

Gem of Wisdom
Keep your own cup full and it will overflow and nourish others.

Live the Mystery

9

WORKSHOP NINE
THE SCAREDY CAT "Fear keeps me safe."

Given it is natural to fear for ourselves, our loved ones, sometimes for strangers, and sometimes the world, our Inner Scaredy Cat is a strong force that can add to or take from our lives, depending on the part we allow it to play.

Most of our life decisions are based on fear. Physically, most fear the elements, starvation, pain, and death. Without these fears we would cease to survive at a rapid rate. Emotionally, most fear failure, rejection, and being alone. Without these fears we would not strive to succeed, stand up for ourselves, or have relationships.

However, these fears can also consume our lives and thwart our psychological growth. Fearing assault, we might seldom leave our homes. Fearing poverty, we might be frugal to a fault, doing without even when the bank account is fat. We might refrain from public events for fear of catching an illness. We might stay in a debilitating, dead-end job, fearing the career ladder too steep a climb.

Fearing what *could* happen to us (even if it never has), can become so monumental, we forfeit all opportunities that might better our lives. And sometimes we so fear so badly that what *has* happened might reoccur, we forfeit promising opportunities that could enrich our lives. Extreme fear can keep us in a rut, in a gray world that consistently loses meaning. When in the rut too long, sometimes an even greater fear emerges that we will just rot on life's vine and die unfulfilled. This fear, exceeding our fear of taking chances, can push us out of the rut.

The Scaredy Cat, whether helping or hurting us, will rise and retreat at various times in a multitude of ways, with different intensities throughout our lives. Although we all behave differently when we are frightened, our Scaredy Cat will generally present itself as one, more than one, or a combination of following types: the Possum, the Posturer, Chicken Little, the Obsessive-Compulsive, the Dodger, the Phobic, the Pretender, or the Determined. Given we all have our own nature, not all of these types will apply to you. However, you may recognize them in others you know. Armed with this knowledge, it can make a difference in how you handle those relationships.

The Possum: The most passive type of Scaredy Cat is the Possum. The Possum freezes and plays dead. Still and quiet, it may not be noticed. Inert and innocuous, who would bother to hurt it? We may have used the Possum in school when the teacher asked a question in which we did not know the answer. Hoping to be overlooked, we don't move and barely breathe as the teacher's eyes scour the room. We may have used the Possum when we fear an intruder is in our house, pulling the covers over our head, too afraid to check out the questionable noise. And we may have used it in a dying relationship by acting like everything is fine, hoping the problem will vanish. Shy people have a strong Inner Possum, spending most of their lives trying *not* to be noticed. Life is just safer that way.

The Posturer. Sometimes blending into the scenery works for us, and sometimes it doesn't. A bolder brand of Scaredy Cat is the Posturer. It masks its fear with fanfare in hopes of tricking others into believing it is something that it really isn't. The fanfare might be a display of inflated happiness, conveying the message *I'm fine; don't probe me.* The fanfare might be a mighty growl, presenting a *don't tangle with me* facade. Or the fanfare might be a display of cool self-confidence, too much "together" to ever be taken apart. We may have used the Posturer to deflect our antagonists, spare our loved ones worry, or because fear doesn't suit our image. And we may have used it to fool ourselves. *I'm not afraid to get a job; I just have so much to do around the house to keep it nice for everyone!* No matter what the disguise, the Posturer hides its fear by putting on an act.

Chicken Little. Some of us are more frantic with our fear and prone to hysteria. This type of Scaredy Cat lurks in the land of Chicken Little. Chicken Little falls into a panic that surpasses all reason, imagining the worst will happen. When our Chicken Little is on stage, we might think things like, "Oh no, my son is five minute late; he must be dead!" Or, "Oh no, I have a headache; it must be a brain tumor!" Chicken Little, unable to cope with its fear, is possessed by it. We all, even if rarely, have had moments when Chicken Little ruled our roost. This is evident when we act on our terror before there is any actual evidence that we need be afraid. In this, we have pulled the rug out from under our own feet by speaking too soon, or acting too fast, and thereby causing a lot of unnecessary drama. Or to be poetic, we put the proverbial foot in our mouths, or run into a bear den to escape the dragon. If we would have just calmed down, our mouth would be free of our foot, and we might see the dragon is just a dragonfly.

This catastrophizing can lead to behaviors such as telephoning everyone we know for assurance because we fear bombing an impending interview, or running around town looking for our mate because he/she is an hour late. Racing around like a chicken with our head cut off is an attempt to prevent *imagined* impending doom. Given the caliber of its fear, Chicken Little often tries to control the people in its life and the circumstances that involve them in an attempt to keep them safe. Calling the babysitter every five minutes to check on the children is an attempt to prevent an accident that might come from the babysitter's inattentiveness. Calling 911 hysterically because our cat is in a tree, or our kid locked himself in the bedroom, or we heard a creak in the house, or we fear the wind will blow off our roof, are all attempts to make our world safer before catastrophe strikes. In short, Chicken Little, consumed with fear, overrides rational thought.

The Paranoid. A spin off of Chicken Little that has a much cooler head, or has a head and can listen to reason, will behave in a similar manner, but much more calmly. The Paranoid uses logic in a manner that keeps it rationally busy taking *excessive* preventative measure. *I have six locks on my door, three guns in my closet, and three thousand bottles of vitamins.* It can never take too much precaution. While preparing for the worst can help protect us, such as locking the doors at night, not breaking the law, informing our kids about "stranger danger," or doing a background check on someone with whom we might invest our funds, if taken to an extreme, it can monopolize our attention so much that we fail to enjoy life at all, or ever take a chance, always fearing something might happen. We know the Paranoid is on the stage of our life when we go above and beyond a reasonable amount of preventative measure, such as *never* taking our children to the park because a child molester could be lurking, or racing to the doctor for every tiny ailment that comes along (hypochondria), or experience a racing heart with all strangers, certain each one is a predator in disguise. Sometimes, though rare, if afflicted with a chemical imbalance or traumatic psychological wounds, the Paranoid can take us into psychosis. More commonly, however, if left unchecked, it can lead to obsessive-compulsive behavior.

The Obsessive-Compulsive. The type of Scaredy Cat resorts to excessive superstitious behavior and ritual as a way to cope with fear. Like Chicken Little and the Paranoid, it only feels safe if it can do something in advance to prevent a catastrophe. However, knowing it can't really prevent all catastrophe, it consoles itself by controlling what it can: the order of the house, cleanliness of the body, or a strict schedule to live by. It tells itself that if it follows certain rituals, then everything will be all right. "Everything will be all right if I wash my hands at the top of every hour." "Everything will be all right if I take three deep breaths before I walk out my door." "If I don't step on any cracks in the sidewalk, nothing bad will happen." "If I say a little rhyme every time my children leave the house, they will be safe."

When we fall into obsessive-compulsive behavior, minor or major, it is usually due to one or more of the following reasons: 1. We have an unconscious (or maybe conscious) guilt that we will be punished for something we did. 2. We are reacting to a traumatic event (remembered or not) when we were overpowered and felt helpless. 3. We have an underlying belief that the world is a cold, cruel place, and surviving is unlikely. 4. We doubt our capability to handle hardships that might come our way. 5. Feeling overwhelmed, we relieve tension by concocting mental games we can win.

Instead of resolving its fears, the Obsessive-Compulsive sticks its finger in the holes of its sinking boat with routine and superstition, instead of actually repairing the holes. While this behavior originally develops as a coping mechanism to survive trying times, if perpetuated, it can sabotage all life enjoyment.

You might recognize these behaviors in you in a more minor sense, and perhaps only occasionally when you are coping with a stressful event. Humans have used superstition since the dawn of humankind to calm down. This is very common and usually passes when our lives become less stressful. However, if this behavior is chronic and taxing you, take heart; it will begin to subside if you take a deep breath and do three things. 1. Look at the bigger picture in a *rational* way. (What are the odds, really, that what you fear would actually happen?) 2. Develop faith in yourself to cope with whatever might come. (You can handle even the worst-case scenarios better than you think.) 3. Love yourself enough to want to change behaviors that keep you on a constant edge.

The Dodger. The Dodger will throw itself into work, pastimes, or addictions to distract itself from feeling afraid. Our Dodger is on stage when we watch TV all day instead of getting a job because we can't face tomorrow, or when we spend every night out to avoid facing our angry spouse at home, or when we drink too much to avoid facing our self. From time to time, it is natural, and even helpful to dodge our fear for a while because we need time to work up the courage to face it, but if we dodge it too long, we often have a rude awakening. A never-ending procrastination of job hunting might lead to going broke. If our nights out never end because we fear facing our home life, eventually we won't have one. If we keep using alcohol to cloak our fear, we will forget who we are. Sometimes things just have to get worse before our needs override our fear. There is no shame in this! Participating in life can be scary, and it doesn't help if we let our Inner Judge crucify us for being afraid. In cases like this, our Inner Nurturer can make us feel lovable despite our fear, and our Inner Warrior can give us the courage to face our issues and do something about it.

The Pretender. The Pretender is *unaware* that it is afraid, even though it is. The woman who doesn't date due to bad relationship break-ups might proclaim, "I don't fear dating; I just prefer to be alone." The man who chronically cheats on his wife because he is overcompensating for his fear of abandonment might proclaim, "I cheat because I love women; I love the way they look, and walk, and talk, and smell." The Pretender is a master of denial and often colludes with the Inner Fabricator to create convincing stories to deceive itself. We might suspect the Pretender is playing a major role in our lives if numerous others keep confronting us about the "same" thing, over and over, and we insist they don't know what they are talking about, even though our personal growth does seem stunted. Sometimes pretending is all we can do to get by, and we just aren't ready to face the truth about ourselves. Until we are ready, no one can force us to look into the mirror.

The Phobic. Almost every human on earth has a phobia of some kind. Only when it keeps us from living a healthy life might we choose to overcome or at least minimize it. Phobias can develop due to one or more of the following reasons: 1. Sometimes we have a chemical imbalance that alters our sense of reality. 2. The phobia is indicative of a psychological issue. For example, the fear of small spaces (claustrophobia) might be a response to a fear of being psychologically trapped by controlling people. Or fear of leaving the house (agoraphobia) is really a fear of being hurt by what lurks in the outer world. Or fear of public speaking can be rooted in a fear of appearing foolish. 3. There is mounting evidence that our ancestors' life-and-death experiences are embedded in our DNA. In this, our more irrational phobias, such as fear of spiders or snakes, fire (even in a fireplace), or heights (even on a ladder), may be a residual from experiences that doomed our early ancestors. Back then, humans were victims of many things without scientific knowledge to aid them.

No matter what the cause, if phobias are disrupting your life, they can be significantly diminished through therapies such as systematic desensitization and hypnosis.

The Fatalist. The Fatalist surrenders to fear without a fight, accepting the "end," whatever that is, to come. We might only experience the Fatalist in certain situations, such as the job world. "I'm sure I will get laid off, so I might as well just quit now," or maybe just in the romance department. "Romantic love is a sham; there is no point in having a relationship that is doomed to fail." We might experience the Fatalist only briefly now and then, or chronically and fall into deep depression. The good news is, if our Inner Fatalist keeps us out in the "cold" too long, we usually succumb to our Inner Healer to help us feel the sun.

The Determined. This type of Scaredy Cat faces fear head-on, constructively dealing with the issues at hand, shoveling its way out of whatever ordeal it is in. When the Determined Scaredy Cat takes point in our lives, we feel the fear and do it anyway. Though terrified, we might go back to school to make a career change, or take a job that stretches us beyond our comfort zone. In this, our fear matriculates into the excitement of possibility.

Balancing the Inner Scaredy Cat

There is no shame in being afraid. Feeling fear is as natural as breathing. Sometimes we need fear to make us hide to survive, give us time to gather courage, or time to figure things out. The question is, is our fear being used in balance so that we live to fight another day, or is it tormenting us? Only you, in self-compassion, can sense if it is best for you to feel the fear and do it anyway, or sit this one out.

Your Inner Scaredy Cat can be brought to balance by embracing your intrinsic worth instead of basing it on outcomes. If you embrace your worth regardless of achievement, status, appearance, or approval, your fear of failure and rejection will subside. Imbued with self-respect, the subjective judgment of others has no power to wound you. You can't be emotionally hurt because you know who you are. "No matter what, I am a valuable human being." This, along with believing in your ability to handle whatever comes, will generate the confidence to survive anything. Emanating confidence, you are also less likely to be physically assaulted. Predators most often seek the vulnerable, the insecure, and the seemingly weak.

This workshop will help you discern the difference between viable fears, such a blazing inferno or a gun pointed at you, and fear that we create from our perceptions of reality, such as "I'm afraid I won't be loved." In this, you can begin to release the fears that can only hurt you if you let them, and spend more time enjoying your life.

The Scaredy Cat in a Nutshell
* Is trying to survive on some level.
* Is always doing the best it can.
* Tries to keep us and others from harm.
* Is not weak; it is afraid.

Scaredy Cat Types
The Possum: "I'm not here."
The Posturer: "I hide my fear by making others afraid."
Chicken Little: "The sky is falling, the sky is falling!"
The Paranoid: "I can never take enough precaution."
The Obsessive-Compulsive: "If I can create order through routine and superstitious behavior then my fears will not come to pass."
The Dodger: "If I distract myself from what I fear, I won't have to feel it."
The Pretender: "I am not afraid (gulp, hands trembling)."
The Phobic: "My fear doesn't make sense."
The Fatalist: "I accept my fate."
The Determined: "My fear is a signal that I must take constructive action."

Exploring Your Inner Scaredy Cat

Exercise One

This first exercise is to help you determine the nature of your Inner Scaredy Cat by examining your fears. Examples: fear of the dark, intimacy, abandonment, men, women, children, public speaking, dogs, storms, being alone, disarray, too much order, a particular person, anger, being unloved, fire, blood, death, poverty, parenthood, work, people, life, etc. Close your eyes for a moment and bring to mind what frightens you. Don't think—feel. Feel the fear in your body. Things you fear will come to mind.

State five things that scare you most, why, how you respond to that fear, and if that response helps or hurts you. Example #1: I fear *public speaking* because *I am afraid people will judge me*. When this fear rises I usually respond by *refraining from pubic speaking*. This response *hurts me* because *I could further my career if I could overcome that fear*. Example #2: I fear *childbirth* because *my mother died birthing me*. When this fear rises I usually respond by *deciding I will get pregnant anyway*. This response *helps me* because *I really want a baby one day.* Example #3: I fear *anger* because *I don't like dissension.* When this fear rises I usually respond by *stuffing my anger.* This response *hurts me* because *it is giving me an ulcer.*

1. I fear_____

because_____

When this fear rises I usually respond by_____

_____

This response _____me because_____

_____

2. I fear_____

because_____

When this fear rises I usually respond by_____

_____

This response _____me because_____

_____

3. I fear_____

because_____

When this fear rises I usually respond by_____

_____

This response _____me because_____

_____

4. I fear_____

because_____

When this fear rises I respond usually by_____

_____

This response _____me because_____

_____

5. I fear_____

because_____

When this fear rises I respond by_____

_____

This response _____me because _____

_____

Exercise Two

Place an X next to what you currently fear *beyond an average degree* that has *never* happened. Place a check next to what you currently fear *beyond an average degree* due to something that *has* happened. Place a zero next to what does *not in general* currently frighten you.

____being robbed
____sexual assault
____romantic relations
____going bankrupt
____drowning
____heights
____snakes
____crowds
____men
____women
____the police
____dogs
____the forest
____spiders
____driving a car
____school
____being laughed at
____rejection
____doctors in general
____surgery
____my mother
____my father
____my child

____disarray
____anger
____receiving love
____pain
____sex
____small places
____open places
____the dark
____public speaking
____flying in an airplane
____going hungry
____fire
____drowning
____the ocean
____the desert
____alcohol
____drugs
____being overpowered
____losing control
____bugs
____authority in general
____taking tests
____being a leader

____being left out
____poverty
____fame
____wealth
____becoming violent
____being without water
____being shamed
____substance abuse
____getting old
____looking old
____looking unattractive
____looking fat
____getting a disease
____being weak
____showing vulnerability
____trusting others
____clowns
____bars
____other_____
____other_____
____other_____
____other_____
____other_____

Number of checks_____   Number of X's _____   Number of zeroes _____

X's: If you have an abundance of X's, your Inner Scaredy Cat is likely among the more phobic types (Chicken Little, the Paranoid, the Obsessive-Compulsive, the Phobic).

Checks: If you have an abundance of checks, your Inner Scaredy Cat can be any or all of the types. Having an unbearable experience even once can lead to phobic behavior.

Zeroes: If you have an abundance of zeroes, go back to each one and ask yourself if you what you "zeroed" truly incites less than average fear, or if you are just pretending you aren't afraid or dodging that fear because you aren't ready to face it. If you are pretending or dodging, it's okay! You do not have to face these fears now. However, being aware that you really are afraid might clear up the mystery behind some of your behaviors. For example, you might be drinking excessive amounts of alcohol to calm anxiety. Or, you might be barking at anyone who confronts you on certain issues. In this, you can tell yourself it is all right to be afraid, but instead of drinking so much, you might start taking nature walks, meditate, or work out at the gym. And instead of barking at others regarding a certain topic, you can just explain, you are aware of the issue but you are not ready to deal with it. If in reviewing a topic you "zeroed" and you realize you are afraid, change it to an X or a Check.

If in reviewing the subjects you "zeroed" and most or all truly *do not* elicit above average fear, then your Inner Scaredy Cat is likely healthily tempered by other aspects within you.

X's and Checks: If you have a preponderance of X's and Checks, you can get an idea of how much time you spend being afraid. There is no right or wrong to what you fear, or to how much time you spend being afraid. Some of these fears might serve you well; others may cause you to suffer. Becoming aware of the difference can lend insight into stabilizing the fears that are making your life worse than it has to be.

Exercise Three

This exercise is designed to help you discern the difference between fears that are currently serving you and those that are deteriorating your quality of life.

List three fears that currently cause you an fair amount of suffering.

1. _____

2. _____

3. _____

What *small first steps* can you do to help alleviate each of these fears?

1. Regarding my fear of_____I can_____

_____

2. Regarding my fear of_____I can_____

_____

3. Regarding my fear of_____I can_____

_____

When we are aware that we can take small first steps to help ease our fears, we feel empowered to overcome them.

Exercise Four

No matter what we fear, by shifting our perceptions we enable ourselves to become more centered within ourselves. Share what makes you feel panicked, why, and what your Inner Sage has to say to make you feel better. Example: I feel panicked when *I think I am being judged badly,* because if that happens *I don't feel worthy.* I could make myself feel better by listening to my Inner Sage. My Inner Sage says, *Don't base your worth on the subjective perceptions of others. They don't really know you.*

1. I feel panicked when_____

_____

Because if that happens then_____

_____

I could make myself feel better by listening to my Inner Sage. My Inner Sage says,_____

_____

2. I feel panicked when_____

_____

Because if that happens then_____

_____

_____

I could make myself feel better by listening to my Inner Sage. My Inner Sage says,_____

_____

3. I feel panicked when_____

_____

Because if that happens then_____

_____

I could make myself feel better by listening to my Inner Sage. My Inner Sage says,_____

_____

What else would your Inner Sage like to say to your Inner Scaredy Cat?

_____

_____

_____

Exercise Five

When we are initially afraid, our body responds with shortness of breath, racing heart, or maybe tears. We tell ourselves that the situation is bad and we are in danger of being hurt on some level. After a while, we might move into phase two and behave differently, for example, take charge of the situation or run away.

State your *general* initial response when you are first afraid. Then state how you generally respond after some time passes. Example: When I am afraid, my most common initial behaviors are: *my heart pounds and I freeze.* I tell myself *to be quiet and still so that I won't be noticed.* After a while, I *explore what I am fearing and find a way to face it.*

When I am afraid, my most common INITIAL responses are: _____

_____

I tell myself_____

After a while, I_____

_____

Given these answers, draw two pictures of your Inner Scaredy Cat, one with your initial response, and another with your secondary response. Do not worry about the quality of your art (it can be a stick figure, a shape, or a face). If you hide your fear with rage, you might draw an angry face and a body in a hard stance with a tiny heart inside the chest. Or if you freeze, you might make yourself with big eyes and a frozen body. If you hide, you might draw yourself with a blanket over your head. Even if you are challenged in the visualization department, it will come to you if you relax and open your mind.

My Scared Self-First Response   My Scared Self-Second Response

Now, thinking of your Scaredy Cat's nature in general, come up with a name for your Inner Scaredy Cat. For instance, if you do not confront fear but go into denial, you might label yourself the "Escape Artist." If you freeze like a deer in the headlights, you might label yourself "Bambi." Or if you nervously chatter at everyone, you might label yourself "Nervous Nellie." If you act like you aren't afraid, you might label yourself "Cool Hand Luke."

My Inner Scaredy Cat's name is _____

If you could give your Inner Scaredy Cat a life of its own, imagine how it might live, and give it a voice to share how it experiences life. Example #1: "My name is Nervous Nellie. I live in a cage, pacing the floor with a nervous stomach. I am afraid of everything. I am afraid of what others think of me, if something bad is going to happen to me, if I won't be able to handle something . . . ." Example #2. "My name is Cool Hand Luke. I show no fear. But don't get too close to me or I might bite you. I don't trust you. You might hurt me. No one can penetrate my shield. I will not be vulnerable. I will not be dependent. Go away. I live in a fortress that is impenetrable. I have my guards posted and they will shoot you if you trespass. I am too afraid to let anyone in . . . ."

My name is_____. I _____

_____

_____

_____

_____

_____

_____

_____

_____

Now that you have a clearer understanding of your Inner Scaredy Cat, breathe slowly and deeply, releasing the fear. You are a strong and capable person. Whenever you feel frightened, breathe slowly and deeply while summoning your Inner Sage to help you calm down and feel centered in the core of your being. The way we breathe affects our emotions. The way we think can bring us into the calm eye of the storm where we can feel peace no matter what is going on around us. Do this for a few minutes and you will feel much better!

Circle the answer that suits you best.

The Scaredy Cat has overtaken me:

rarely   occasionally   in certain periods of my life   moderately   regularly   profusely

Healing and Balancing Exercise for Your Inner Scaredy Cat

Place one hand beneath your breastbone.
Place the other hand on the crown of your head.
Concentrate deeply. Repeat silently or aloud for at least two minutes:
"I am centered in myself, safe and calm."

Relaxation and Creative Visualization Exercise

Lie in a comfortable position. Play instrumental music that makes you feel good: classical, New Age, or music that is of gentle, sweeping, or dynamic beauty. When the music is playing, close your eyes. Inhale through your nose deeply, and exhale through your mouth slowly; do this eight times. Visualize that you are inhaling the power of the universe, which purifies and attunes you physically, emotionally, mentally, and metaphysically. When you exhale, all the tensions and worries leave your body and go back into the universe where they dissolve and blend into the pure life force.

Tighten and loosen your muscles slowly in this order:

Feet. Tighten. Loosen. Take a slow, deep breath, and exhale.
Calves. Tighten. Loosen. Take a slow, deep breath, and exhale.
Thighs. Tighten. Loosen. Take a slow, deep breath, and exhale.
Hips and buttocks. Tighten. Loosen. Take a slow, deep breath. and exhale.
Stomach. Tighten. Loosen. Take a slow, deep breath, and exhale.
Back. Tighten. Loosen. Take a slow, deep breath, and exhale.
Arms. Tighten. Loosen. Take a slow, deep breath, and exhale.
Hands. Tighten. Loosen. Take a slow, deep breath, and exhale.
Neck and shoulders. Tighten. Loosen. Take a slow, deep breath, and exhale.
Face. Tighten. Loosen. Take a slow, deep breath, and exhale.

Then completely relax and take eight more slow, deep breaths. Inhale the universal life energy through your nose and exhale tension through your mouth.

Set the intent: *Whoever I am, whatever I am, whatever I need, whatever is right for me—so be it. I open to insight. I open to receive.*

Now that you are completely relaxed, give your self over to the music that is playing. Focus on the point between your eyebrows and journey within, deeper and deeper beyond the fall-out of your life choices. Moving past the outward flowing ripples of your life choices, you journey toward where the ripples began. Do this for a while . . . .
    You now reach the point before the ripples began, before your birth. You see yourself as a seed planted in the ground. Feel yourself grow in your journey to break ground and be born. Feel your struggle, no matter if your foundation is hard and depleted or soft and nourishing. Appreciate the process. Experience this for a while . . . .
    You feel yourself break ground. What is going on around you? Is it dark, light, peaceful, lonely, or full of commotion? Experience this for a while . . . .
    Now that you are born, you continue to grow, no matter what your environment, no matter how windy, rainy, dry, hot or cold. While it feels good when nourishment comes from the

outer world, there are times when you must rely on yourself to survive. When you look at what is going on around you too much, you feel afraid. When you hang on to memories of pain you have felt, you feed the fear. But right now, you feel yourself as an extension of the seed from which you were birthed. You feel your innocence and your potential. Focus on this, and this alone. Experience this for a while . . .

This seed that you are growing from is who you were before you began analyzing the world and your relationship to it. Focus on its purity. Notice how your fear subsides. You are still who you are before you began growing. You feel your Inner Scaredy Cat stepping back into a quiet space inside you. It is calm and going into a meditative state. However, it will be there when you need it to warn you when viable danger is at hand. You appreciate it for how it has protected you, but you no longer need it to impede your growth in its effort to feel safe. You have made peace with your Inner Scaredy Cat. It no longer makes you feel sick or causes you undue stress. It is all right to be afraid. It is also all right to be unafraid.

You feel yourself now growing stronger, sprouting new growth, and flourishing into all your potential despite all odds. Experience this until the music ends . . . .

When you open your eyes, you will feel calm and confident.

Record your experience.

_____

_____

_____

_____

_____

_____

_____

_____

Draw a picture or symbol that summarizes your experience. Example: *An image of myself in the center of a circle.*

Create a key phrase that summarizes this experience. Example: *I am calm and safe in the center of my being.*

When needed, say the phrase silently and visualize the picture or symbol. This will reactivate the experience and generate a peaceful, empowered, clear state of mind.

Δ

Gem of Wisdom
An innocent heart can brave any storm.

Live the Mystery

10

WORKSHOP TEN
THE FURY "I protest."

Our rage springs from many places and rises for many reasons, however, the common denominator is a reaction to harm or threat of harm. The harm might be an attempt to undermine power, a physical blow, or an injustice. Whether the harmful element is perceived or actual—when threat comes knocking, the Fury might answer.

The Fury is a double-edged sword that cuts both ways, protecting one thing as it destroys another. It can explode like a volcano with our anger taking control of us, or bubble up in mild irritation because something isn't going our way, like the car won't start, or the cat throws up on our new rug. Sometimes the Fury inverts, and we are angry with ourselves.

Our Inner Fury will generally fall into one, more than one, or a combination of the following types: the Terminator, the Valiant Fury, the Hothead, the Deflector, the Undercover Fury, the Inverted Fury, or the Repressed Fury. Given we all have our own nature, not all types will apply to you. You may, however, recognize them in others you know, which can aid in wiser handling of those relationships.

The Terminator. The Terminator, colluding with our Inner Warrior and Inner Leader, puts empathy in a closet and wears rage like a suit of armor to repel any and all who mean harm. In a defiant stance, glaring fireball eyes, it will do what it must to survive or insure the survival of others. We know this type of Fury has risen when we become a bigger threat than those who threaten us. For instance, if our car comes out of the repair shop worse than when it went in (a ploy to get more money for further repair), the Terminator would threaten to boycott and/or sue. If a suspicious person is poking around in our backyard, the Terminator would step out of the house with a shotgun and shout, "Get off my property. I have called the police!"

Sometimes the Terminator rises less directly. For instance, a woman divorcing her husband for having an affair with an underage teenager might be infuriated when he threatens to sue for full custody of the children if she won't take a big hit in the divorce settlement. Using the Terminator, she might inform him with calm words that bite, "If you try to take the children, I'll turn you in for statutory rape."

Sometimes the Terminator can get so comfortable in its role that it torpedoes the innocent just to feel powerful. The daughter who comes home fifteen minutes late and gets grounded for a week, or the employee who makes one minor mistake and gets fired, are examples of an over-zealous Terminator at work.

The Valiant Fury. The Valiant Fury has the Terminator's fire, but unleashes its wrath only against those who would shame or degrade innocence. Sometimes we need anger to ensure we don't allow abuse. If we make excuses for those who have hurt us, we allow ourselves to be taken advantage of time and time again.

We know the Valiant Fury has risen when anger becomes our power to fight unjust treatment. We use it to defend ourselves: *I respect myself too much to EVER let you hurt me again!* We use it defend our loved ones: *I will stop the bullying of my child if it's the last thing I do!* We use it to serve as an initiator of justice for others: *I will campaign to change the law that has failed to protect innocent children!* And sometimes we use the Valiant Fury to join causes already in motion, such as a civil rights movement.

The Hothead. When the Fury controls us most of the time, the Hothead is a major star of our show. While the cause is sometimes a chemical imbalance, it is often the result of a harsh past buried in our subconscious mind. Hate and rage from old psychological wounds continually fester and bubble up onto those around us.

Hotheads are often physical with their anger, hitting others, punching walls, or kicking the dog. They frequently accuse the innocent of causing their upset. The accusation is usually a projection of what they think of themselves. For example, if they are sensitive about feeling stupid, they will easily spew to others, "You think I'm stupid, don't you? Well you don't even have a brain in your head!" This is an attempt to squash others the way they felt squashed when they incurred their psychological wounds. They will, however, almost always deny that their current anger relates to their past anger. For example, if neglect was a serious childhood issue, the Hothead, if waiting too long for a table in a restaurant, might yell to the hostess, "You are inept! I want to be seated now, do you hear me?" Believing that its anger really does belong on the hostess, the Hothead will never connect the dots that the incident is poking the old sores of childhood neglect.

Hotheads also anger easily when others won't obey their wishes. For example, if the Hothead tells his girlfriend not to pet a strange dog and she does, he might say, "I told you not to pet the dog; I hope it bites you!" Hotheads will even get angry when another's noncompliance has nothing to do with them. For instance, the Hothead might be mad at a friend who won't go out drinking with her. Instead of considering motives for noncompliance, such as the friend is trying drink less alcohol for health reasons, the Hothead will automatically take the noncompliance personally. "You're no friend of mine; you won't even go drinking with me!"

Even if something happens beyond another's control, the Hothead will still spew its toxic wrath. For example, a person showing up late for a meeting with the Hothead because a twenty-car pileup brought traffic to a prolonged standstill, will still get clobbered by the Hothead with a statement like, "You got here late just to spite me. You are irresponsible and inconsiderate!" Even if the Hothead learns of the true reason, it will likely say, "You should always leave for meetings early in case something like this should happen!"

Due to this easily triggered and constant battering, the Hothead's relationships are rocky and often short-lived because no one wants to be undeservingly battered over and over again. The relationships that last longest usually involve Significant Others who live in fear of the Hothead or have pitifully low self-esteem. Sometimes the Hothead needs to become bereft from numerous failed relationships before it is ready to deal with its past.

The untamed Hothead will eventually self-destruct. Continuing to ignore the source of its rage (a tragic past), its psychological wounds are kept raw by a sadness so horrible, it transmogrifies into a rage that filters into the Hothead's everyday life—forever. Whether the frequent anger is from a chemical imbalance or a tragic past, the Inner Healer and Sage can play a great part in cooling the Hothead's "head" through various methodologies including diet, exercise, meditation, counseling, and aid from a naturopath or physician.

The Deflector. When we use the Deflector, we deflect our anger from our private lives and hurl it onto those we don't personally know. Blowing steam on those who won't feel our heat is an easy way to release pressure without facing the true source of our rage or being met with a retaliatory response. For example, a woman fumes about a drug-addicted actress whom she doesn't know. She might spew, "That woman is an arrogant, selfish bitch." The woman's real anger likely belongs on a drug-addicted female in *her* past who hurt her. Instead of dealing with *that* rage, it is safely projected onto someone whom she will never meet. In another example, the man who angrily explodes because his favorite sports team lost the game, does so because he had projected his identity onto the team. If the team would have won, then he would have felt empowered (even though the won game wouldn't have been because of him). When the team lost, his anger from his personal life (for instance, a nagging wife, and or a critical boss) is safely hurled upon the losing team, which is in the distance and disconnected from him. Being mad at the team is easier than standing up for himself with his wife and boss. When we use the Deflector in excess, we are not dealing with our personal problems.

The Undercover Fury. When our Fury goes undercover, we express our anger on whomever has upset us, but we do it indirectly. In this, we avoid negative repercussion. A child, angry at her mother for not paying more attention to her might play sick to get it. A husband mad at his wife for nagging him might punish her by leaving the house without a word and go to a bar. While we might resort to methods like this when dealing with Hotheads, or bossy personalities, sometimes it is not only our subjects that could use modification, but us. Chronic undercover expressions of anger even with fairly understanding people is often the mark of an overpowering Inner Scaredy Cat and/or a thwarted Inner Warrior. Even though our clandestine methods of expressing anger work, they also take so much work—to work.

When ready to bring ourselves into a healthier balance (with workable people), we can have more fruitful experiences when we express our anger directly by just sharing what we feel and why without blame. For instance, saying "I am angry because I feel neglected," is so much more productive than going to all the trouble to find ways to get attention. Saying to our spouse "I am mad because I feel disrespected," will be more lucrative than spiking his/her food with hot chili peppers. Or confessing "I feel angry because you never express your love to me" will serve the marriage better than having an affair.

If we give to ourselves the love, attention, and respect we want from others, it is easier to be direct and express ourselves in a healthy manner. But sometimes we are not ready for that, and the Undercover Fury will work hard to get us what we need.

The Inverted Fury. The Inverted Fury will feel rage against other members of our Inner village, perhaps our Inner Warrior who failed to protect a loved one, or maybe our Inner Nurturer who walked into the lion's den one too many times. When our Fury is empowered by guilt, it inverts. Until the guilt is resolved, we will continue to be mad at ourselves. Guilt is a sentence passed down from our Inner Judge. Remember, the Judge is subjective, so it can never really know for sure "what is," even if it thinks it does. No matter what the Inner Judge says, there is ALWAYS a way to resolve guilt.

Resolving guilt is a matter of broadening binocular perceptions to view the greater picture. When all the elements of a situation can be seen, it is easier to understand why things happened as they did. Our life events occur like train tracks that go way back in time beginning with our first ancestor. Each track is a culmination of what proceeded it. Hence, we are all affected by our parents, and they their parents, and so on. In that, we have inherited the life stories of our genetic line (even if we were given up for adoption).

Our complicated selves, our families, our life situation, the people we meet, current social standards, the conditions of the world, and even weather are all tied up in what we do.

There is no fault—EVER, just ignorance (innocence) corrected in time by trial and error. As humans, it is impossible to know the story before we live it. Seeing it from hindsight and blaming ourselves or others for what we or they did *then* is like beating up a child for falling down when it is learning how to walk.

In the grand scheme of things, everyone deserves compassion, and though there are consequences to all our actions, everyone deserves forgiveness. In this, we can stop beating ourselves up for *anything* we have ever done.

The Repressed Fury: The Repressed Fury is captured either by the Scaredy Cat who fears the consequences of expressing anger, or by the Nurturer who can't bear to upset anyone, ever, not even in self-defense. Denying the Fury passage into our lives, even in an undercover manner, usually results in us being used and abused. Though the Fury might seem hidden, it is indeed alive and well, deep down, brewing, stewing, and waiting to erupt one day, perhaps way in the future. This pressurized explosion can be as mighty as a flood of water breaking the dam that can no longer contain it. The explosion might be a verbal explosion, or it might be lethal, as in the person who snaps and kills randomly in a crowd. Or the explosion might be an implosion, breaking our bodies down, inviting illness. Chronic anger-stuffing disintegrates our self-esteem, crucifies our dreams, our hearts, and our bodies, for not even out of respect for ourselves or others will we use our anger to make a stand. If we do not shout out *no more*, sometimes we become . . . no more.

Balancing the Inner Fury

Behind all rage lurks pain. We are angry when we've been hurt. And we get angry when those we care about have been hurt. Some people feel sad when hurt, others feel mad, and some feel mad then sad, or sad then mad. No matter what the rhythm, anger is a dragon worth facing. The Fury has a valuable part to play in our life story. It is valuable even if it's been a dirty villain that caused havoc or kept us benched from the game, for it sets us up for a greater learning experience. Eventually, our Fury catalyzes us into constructive action. It has to, for once we hit bottom with anything, there is nowhere to go but up.

Anger is often merely a symptom to make us aware that something is out of balance, be it a situation, relationship, an unresolved past, or even our hormones. It signals our other aspects for help, perhaps the Warrior to draw its sword, the Nurturer to calm a situation, or the Healer to mend an old wound.

Once we detect where our anger truly belongs and put it there, our lives go more smoothly. Nothing stirs more drama than spilling anger on those who don't deserve it. Unresolved issues always evoke some sort of bitterness. And nothing can feel more blissful than allowing anger to turn into constructive action, be it to make a needed stand, air out upsets with others in a non-blaming way, or let our Fury drive us to do something great.

This workshop is designed to help you better know your Inner Fury, the specifics that drive it, the way you use it, and to what end. What part does it play in your life? What part should it play? And how can you use it to make things better? In daring to know your Inner Fury, you are taking a huge step to make your life the best it can be.

The Fury in a Nutshell
* Rises when there are issues we must face, in ourselves, with others, or the outer world.
* Can protect us or put us in peril.
* Can destroy or foster personal growth.
* Can power through oppression or be the object of oppression.

* Can disrupt our lives if we are unaware of the underlying reasons it is evoked.
* Can deflect emotional pain—for a while.
* Can champion love and justice.

Fury Types

The Terminator: "I frighten the enemy."
The Valiant Fury: "I target injustice"
The Hothead: "I am easily angered."
The Deflector: "I project my anger onto what is outside my personal life."
The Undercover Fury: "I express my anger indirectly."
The Inverted Fury: "I am angry with myself."
The Repressed Fury: "I'm not angry." (tight jaw causing a headache)

Exploring Your Inner Fury

Exercise One

Share times when expressing your anger served you well. This does not mean your anger helped you demolish someone's self-esteem. If it served you well, it enriched your life and made you feel good about yourself. Example: My anger served me well when *I rejected my boyfriend's abusive appraisal of me and broke up with him. I was proud of myself for valuing myself enough to be with someone who treated me so badly.*

1. My anger served me well when_____

_____

I was proud of myself for_____

2. My anger served me well when_____

because_____

I was proud of myself for_____

3. My anger served me well when_____

_____

I was proud of myself for_____

Exercise Two

This exercise will help you identify the workings of your Inner Fury and allow you to examine the effect it has had in your life thus far. State what infuriates you the most, why, the past event it brings to mind, where your anger belongs, and what you can do to make things better. The reason for your rage might regard personal issues, social issues, or maybe even broader topics such as technology or pollution. There are no bounds.

Example #1: It infuriates me when *my child messes his room and won't clean it up* because *I think he won't do it just to taunt me.* The past event that comes to mind is *how as a child, I dare not leave my room messy for fear my mother would hit me because she often did.* This made me feel *like I was an unworthy slob* because *she made cleanliness more important than me.* My anger belongs *on my mother* but I take it out on *my child.* I could make things better if I *would deal with my past anger by exploring my relationship with my mother,* and my current anger by *reading some parenting books* so that *I can raise my child differently.*

Example #2: It infuriates me when *I am discounted* because *it makes me feel like my opinions aren't valued.* The past event that comes to mind is *my dad who literally discounted every opinion I ever had, insinuating I was stupid.* This made me feel *mad* because *I can't be wrong all the time.* My anger belongs on *my dad,* but I take it out on *everyone who discounts me, even once, for anything, even if my opinion actually is off base.* I could make things better if I *would deal with my past anger by resolving my father issues, learn to value my own opinion even if others don't, and realize all these other people aren't my father.*

1. It infuriates me when_____

because _____

The past event this brings to mind is_____

This made me feel_____

because_____

My anger belongs on_____

but I take it out on_____

I could feel better if I_____

_____

2. It infuriates me when_____

because _____

The past event that comes to my mind is_____

This made me feel_____

because_____

My anger belongs on_____

but I take it out on_____

I could feel better if I_____

_____

3. It infuriates me when_____

because _____

The past event that comes to my mind is_____

This made me feel_____

because_____

My anger belongs on_____

but I take it out on_____

I could feel better if I_____

_____

4. It infuriates me when_____

because_____

The past event that comes to my mind is_____

This made me feel_____

because_____

My anger belongs on_____

but I take it out on_____

I could feel better if I_____

_____

5. It infuriates me when_____

because_____

The past event that comes to my mind is_____

This made me feel_____

because_____

My anger belongs on_____

but I take it out on_____

I could feel better if I_____

_____

Exercise Three

Draw a tree with five branches. This is the ANGER TREE. On each branch, list each of the topics you wrote about in Exercise Two. On the tree trunk write the common denominator that your Inner Fury has with each.

Example #1: The branches are: people who yell at me, other people reprimanding my child, cars that cut me off in traffic, bullies, when people are aggressive with me. The trunk is BEING OVERPOWERED.

Example #2: The branches are: when my kids don't obey me, a messy house, when mechanical things fail, when people are late, when people look sloppy. The trunk is DISORDER.

Example #3: The branches: when people get sick, laziness, passive people, when people cry, when people complain. The trunk is WEAKNESS.

MY ANGER TREE

Take a moment now to look at the strongest cause of your anger. The word you wrote on the trunk of your Anger Tree is the key to understanding the sorest spot within you. Share what you understand about your sorest spot.

My sorest spot pertains to_____

_____

_____

Exercise Four

Answer the following questions.

When I express my rage, the consequence is *usually*_____

_____

When I stuff my rage, the consequence is *usually*_____

_____

Expressing our anger can work for or against us depending on how, when, and why we do it. By implementing the Eight Keys to constructively dealing with anger below, you can be assured that you will bring your Inner Fury into balance. In that, it will always work for you, not against you.

1. Meditation. When you feel angry, take time to meditate. Meditation is simply relaxing and breathing slowly to calm down and stop reacting for a moment. Learning to meditate will help you sort out where your anger is coming from, and determine if the best solution is to react or to let it blow over. By meditating first, you circumvent any angry expressions that might backfire on you.

2. Constructive self-expression. Communicating constructively will help you see if your anger belongs in the present, the past, or both. It will also have a cathartic effect and possibly better any situation. The formula is:
    1. Describe the event that angers you: "When you ignore me . . .
    2. Then state the emotion that event evokes: "I feel mad . . ."
    3. Then state why without blame: "because I matter and I need to be treated like I matter."
        So all together the sentences would be: "When you ignore me, I feel mad, because I matter and I need to be treated like I matter."
        This blameless mode of expression often catalyzes productive dialogue, but even if it doesn't, you will feel better. Expressing your feelings is less about trying to get others to change, and more about purging your feelings so they don't fester, and to promote a clear understanding about what is really going on inside you. In this, further tension generated from misunderstandings can be avoided.

3. Acknowledge your worth. Your worth is intrinsic no matter what anyone says or does to you. You can value yourself even if nobody else does.

4. Be creative. Channeling your rage into a creative outlet will not only help release it, but also transform it into an inspiring experience. Creative outlets can be anywhere from singing, writing, cooking, or making something, to reorganizing, or even tackling a problem with an original solution.

5. Exercise. Exercise boosts endorphins and burns off excess rage which can keep you from overreacting and enflaming the current problem. It also can serve as a contemplative time.

6. Nutrition. Rage is often associated with hypoglycemia which can be diminished with proper nutrition. Nutrition affects *every* aspect of our health, including mental.

7. Touch nature. The natural world always has a calming effect, even if it is in a picture or nature sounds from a recording.

8. Creative visualization. Use pleasant imagery to calm down.

Circle the answer that suits you best.

The Fury has appeared in my life:

hardly ever   from time to time   in certain periods of my life   moderately   profusely

Healing and Balancing Exercise for Your Inner Fury

Place one hand beneath your breastbone.
Place the other hand over your heart.
Concentrate deeply. Repeat silently or aloud for at least two minutes:
"I will use my rage in positive ways."

Relaxation and Creative Visualization Exercise

Lie in a comfortable position. Play instrumental music that makes you feel good: classical, New Age, or music that is of gentle, sweeping, or dynamic beauty. When the music is playing, close your eyes. Inhale through your nose deeply, and exhale through your mouth slowly; do this eight times. Visualize that you are inhaling the power of the universe, which purifies and attunes you physically, emotionally, mentally, and metaphysically. When you exhale, all the tensions and worries leave your body and go back into the universe where they dissolve and blend into the pure life force.

Tighten and loosen your muscles slowly in this order:

Feet. Tighten. Loosen. Take a slow, deep breath, and exhale.
Calves. Tighten. Loosen. Take a slow, deep breath, and exhale.
Thighs. Tighten. Loosen. Take a slow, deep breath, and exhale.
Hips and buttocks. Tighten. Loosen. Take a slow, deep breath, and exhale.
Stomach. Tighten. Loosen. Take a slow, deep breath, and exhale.
Back. Tighten. Loosen. Take a slow, deep breath, and exhale.
Arms. Tighten. Loosen. Take a slow, deep breath, and exhale.
Hands. Tighten. Loosen. Take a slow, deep breath, and exhale.
Neck and shoulders. Tighten. Loosen. Take a slow, deep breath, and exhale.
Face. Tighten. Loosen. Take a slow, deep breath, and exhale.

Then completely relax and take eight more slow, deep breaths. Inhale the universal life energy through your nose and exhale tension through your mouth.

Set the intent: *Whoever I am, whatever I am, whatever I need, whatever is right for me—so be it. I open to insight. I open to receive.*

Now that you are completely relaxed, give yourself over to the music. Focus on the point between your eyebrows and journey inward into your vast inner being. Do this for a while . . . .

Ahead of you, you see a molten fireball. This is your Inner Fury. You come closer and closer to your Inner Fury, unafraid. You want to make peace with your Inner Fury so you can use it to better your life, instead of making it harder. You now fly into the molten fireball of your Fury. As you go deeper and deeper into it, you notice how white it becomes. You have now gone so deep into your Inner Fury that you feel the pain that generates much of it. Take a moment to acknowledge this pain . . . .

Now go deeper into the molten fireball. Deeper. Deeper into the pure energy of your Fury *beyond* the pain that has generated it. Experience the pure energy of the Fury *beyond* your pain. You feel your innocence and how you have used your Fury to help you survive. From here you can see how you may have strayed from the path and caused unnecessary trouble for yourself or others, and you can see times when you remained on the path and championed respect for yourself or others. Now that you can see the difference, you will easily channel your Fury into constructive and healthy actions. You feel reattuned and balanced. You are still innocent. Embrace your innocence now. Do this until the music ends . . . .

When you open your eyes, your will feel at peace with your Inner Fury.

Record your experience.

_____

_____

_____

_____

_____

_____

_____

_____

Draw a picture or symbol that summarizes the experience. Example: *A heart inside a flame.*

Create a key phrase that summarizes this experience. Example: *I will use my Fury to stand my ground.*

When needed, say the phrase silently and visualize the picture or symbol. This will reactivate the experience and generate a peaceful, empowered, clear state of mind.

Δ

Gem of Wisdom
Uncontrolled rage destroys. Healthy rage protects.

Live the Mystery

11

WORKSHOP ELEVEN
THE FABRICATOR "I pretend."

Rationalizing, fibbing, tricking, or fudging the truth, the Fabricator uses illusion to fool itself or others. Whenever we create stories that skew or change the truth, the Fabricator is at play. We all use the Fabricator from time to time, in various ways, for a variety of reasons. We use it to cheer people up: "You look good!" (Red puffy eyes indicate the person had an all-night cry.) We use it to console: "Everything will be fine." (We feel the person is in for a rough ride.) We use it to keep the lid on potential explosions: "Put that gun away; your wife didn't cheat on you!" (We know for a fact she did.) We use it to keep others out of our business: "I'm doing great." (We're in trouble, but want to solve the problem privately.) We use it to fool people into liking us: "I am a healthy, financially well-off person, so you should date me." (The suitor is an alcoholic with a heart condition, on the verge of bankruptcy.) We use it to get what we want: "I cleaned the dishes, Mom; can I have my allowance?" (Dirty dishes are stashed in a cabinet.) And we use it to bury traumatic events: "My childhood was wonderful," (when it wasn't) or, "I wasn't raped; I had consensual sex," (there was no consent) in an attempt to paint over bad memories, because to go on with our lives, we must.

The Fabricator rises when we need to, for whatever reason, avoid the truth. Despite the standard morality clause *I will not tell a lie,* there are times when dodging the truth is not only the least of two evils, but the kinder and necessary thing to do.

Our Inner Fabricator has many faces: the Entertainer, the Magician, the Dream Weaver, the Extreme Optimist, the Poor-Me Fabricator, the Chosen One, the Rainbow Chaser, the Conflict-Repeller, and the Predatory Fabricator. You may or may not recognize all these faces in you; however you might recognize them in others you know. Understanding how and why the Fabricator operates can promote not only understanding and compassion for yourself, but for others.

The Entertainer. The Entertainer is, for the most part, a kind friend. Paired with the Innovator, it can bring comedic relief to those drowning in seriousness or inspiration to those in despair. Whether we use it to bring a smile to a struggling person or a little magic into the world, the Entertainer has bright intentions. It can tell stories with great finesse, shine in theatrical productions, and bring pleasure to children by perpetuating myths, such as Santa Claus or the Tooth Fairy.

The Magician. The Magician puts on a show to divert others from seeing the truth. The woman on stage isn't really being sawed in half, and the rabbit isn't really being pulled out of an empty hat. It's just an illusion. In this same way, when we play a flashy role to hide our insecurities, the Magician is on stage.

The Magician has various disguises. For instance, the class clown disguises his inability to concentrate on the assignment at hand by making his classmates laugh. *Look at me, I am funny (I don't have A.D.D.).* Or an arrogant actress hides her flaws by acting as if she is on screen all the time. *The real me is what you see on film; I am perfect.* Or a professor might conceal his emotional afflictions by perpetually shining his intellectual brilliance. *I make the social grade because of my mind; nothing else matters.* Whenever we define ourselves by creating an illusion to cover our flaws, we have enlisted the Magician.

It is natural and even beneficial to use the Magician now and then to help us get by, but when used too much, it can sabotage emotional intimacy. Emotional intimacy can only be had when two people are "real" with each other. When we insist we are the illusion we present, people can't really touch us, and when others insist they are the illusion they present, we can't touch them. And if two people are putting on an act with each other, well, their relationship is a show, and soon or later the curtain will close.

The Dream Weaver. This Fabricator spins convincing yarns that it has made itself believe. When this Fabricator rises, we allow it to fool us, by fooling others into believing our made-up narrative. Usually, somewhere, deep down, we know that some part of us is fabricating, but we adopt the story as a way to cope with life (which is too hard), to avoid personal development (which is too frightening), and to ignore our psychological wounds (which are too painful), so in desperation, we perpetuate the fantasy.

If we faced that truth, we would have to face ourselves, or more specifically the root of our discomfort that has led us to rationalize our current behavior and/or life choices. And we just aren't ready. We just can't do it, not now.

For example, we might insist to everyone that we are happy about a decision we have made by creating a bright illusion of all the good coming from our choice. In the case of a woman preparing to marry a very flawed man, she will set out to convince everyone around her that her impending marriage is the greatest thing since jellybeans when in reality, she just needs to be married. Fearing to stand on her own and be her own person, she *wants* to live in the shadow of another. So she finds a man who wants her to be his shadow. She allows herself to be absorbed into him to such an extent that she becomes a walking reflection of his thoughts and feelings. If she can marry him, the fabrication is a success.

To pull this off, she works hard to get everyone around her to believe her man is perfect for her. Those who try to discredit her fabrication with realities such as "But he's an alcoholic!" are denounced. If confronted, for example, with "You are just afraid to find out who you are, so you are hiding in the shadow of a man" she will (in danger of believing what she hears) run about and patch up any holes in the fabric of her rationalization: "No, he is my dream come true, and I am happy, so nothing else matters." She will cling to her rationalization even if it means losing significant others who won't collude with the charade. Her best allies are those who will collude and reinforce the pretense. *Tell me you know my story is true!* Those who collude are likely using their own Dream Weaver to sustain *their* fantasy. It is an unwritten agreement: *I will support your fantasy if you will support mine.*

As time passes, those who had or want a friendship with *her* and not the husband, will drift away. Secretly, deep down, she hurts from losing those who would not support the fabrication; however, getting them back means she'd have to develop her individuality and she isn't ready for that. Her fear is too great. Sustaining her fantasy over time, however, becomes increasingly difficult because truth ever knocks on the door of any denial. She must work harder to sustain the fabrication, all the while repressing her true self, fearing it will be discovered. After all, her husband fell in love with her *fabricated* self. What would happen if he found out the truth? And if she isn't found out, there is an underlying sadness that her true self will never be warmly acknowledged—or loved.

As the years progress, her secret pain grows because the authentic part of her is fading from her grasp from lack of use. At some point, she might decide the pain is too much and venture from her husband's shadow and discover her true self, or she might just endure and keep pretending, no matter what, until the day she dies.

The Dream Weaver will also take undeserved blame for another, just to keep that person in its life. For example, a man proclaims, "My girlfriend is the best! When she gets snippy, it is only because she is going through a hard time and I am bugging her. When she sleeps with other men, it is only because I have not measured up. She is not at fault; it's me." He is creating a story to justify staying with his girlfriend because breaking up with her and being alone is too scary. Eventually the man will be so left out in the cold and so nipped at he will be either be forced to leave his girlfriend or die of sadness.

The Dream Weaver can also go the other way and justify its own unsavory actions as wonderful. For example, a mother might proclaim, "I am a great mother. I love my kids more than life. I just stay out at the bar every night because if I get my needs met, I am better for them. When I drink, I am nicer and therefore a better mother. When I am gone a lot, it gives the kids time with their dad. My absence every night is a good thing." In time, this mother will likely lose them all.

We aren't failing when we use the Dream Weaver; it just means we aren't ready to face our inner demons. In a way, this Fabricator is saving us from giving up and going down the drain by giving us a way to cope with life. We might sustain the fantasy for a short or long while, or maybe a lifetime. We all get through life the best we can. However, when the fabrication begins to crumble, and it will, we will have the opportunity to unplug our ears, hear truth knocking, and open the door. We then can look at ourselves, solve our problems, and get on with living a more satisfying life.

The Extreme Optimist. A spin-off of the Dream Weaver is the Extreme Optimist. This is not to be confused with general optimism. Optimism can help us get out of bed in the morning with a bright attitude sustained by a positive outlook. We perceive the best in people, beauty in the world, and are grateful for what we have. Optimism can help make lemonade out of lemons, opportunities out of problems, and learning lessons from seeming failures.

However, the Extreme Optimist loves its rose-colored glasses that make everything appear unnaturally bright. It can't see an unsavory situation, even if drowning in it. The Extreme Optimist is abnormally cheery and can be swayed so far from the truth, it loses sight of it. A temporary vacation from what is true is one thing; however, allowing the Extreme Optimist to hijack our life is quite another. If we cling to the *I'm so happy; I have no problems* line of defense, like a rotting tooth we won't acknowledge, it will one day abscess.

"Everything is fine," she thinks, as her husband drinks himself into his nightly stupor. "He had a hard day at work and needs to unwind. I'm so lucky to have him, my beautiful man."

"Everything is fine," he thinks, as his wife threatens to leave him. "She will cool down, I don't need to do anything but wait. She is so beautiful and perfect."

"Everything is fine," the wife thinks, knowing her husband is likely having an affair. "As long as he comes home to me, it proves he loves me most. I am happy because I am the winner!"

This kind of denial is like having a sugar machine that makes everything sweet all the time. If we don't see the monster, it is hard to be afraid. If we refuse to see the ogre and pretend it isn't munching on us even when it is, we can avoid panic and confrontation. And in this, we never need to develop the skills that would enable us to enjoy life *without* rose-colored glasses. And usually, in the end, we wake up in a nightmare, and wonder how we got there.

The Poor-Me Fabricator. This type of Inner Fabricator colludes with the Inner Victim in an attempt to get others to take care of it. With a shot of embellishment on the truth, it creates illusions of helplessness that it actually believes. It will maintain that it is too crippled for one reason or another to develop in a healthy way: "I have all these handicaps; I cannot go out into the world and make it on my own." Or it can play weak: "I am too weak; I need you to do these things for me." Or it can play the injustice card: "Everyone does me wrong; I need you to do me right."

The Poor-Me Fabricator often emerges when we are hungry for attention that we don't know how to legitimately get, such as developing a skill or pursuing a career. This Poor-Me game is sometimes a learned behavior. If we are constantly coddled, why would we try to get strong?

Sometimes our impediment is a lack of confidence in our ability to develop our skills and/or fear of failing if we try. It is just easier to cry for help. In this, we become dependent on others to survive and never know the true beauty of our own flower. In addition, we eventually wear out those who love us. As time goes on, new people will often turn away from us, not wanting to walk into the role of a perpetual caretaker. However, for whatever reason, sometimes we just need to play this game and try to convince ourselves its true, even though deep down we *know it isn't*. If you have ever played this game, there is no need to beat yourself up for having played it. We humans have always used trial and error to make our way through the maze of life.

The Chosen One. While the Magician uses a facade to hide what it knows is the truth, the Chosen One creates illusions of grandeur that it genuinely believes. When this Inner Fabricator rises in us, we are certain we are the Chosen One. For example: "I have found my destiny as a predictor of disaster to save people" or "all five hundred females I slept with remember me as the one who brought them into true womanhood" or, "I have been chosen by the powers that be to save the world." The Chosen One Fabricator is desperate to feel supremely important, and feels it must affect large numbers of people to prove it.

Albeit rare, this Fabricator can lead us to extremes. For example, the Terrorist who convinces himself he must kill a mass of people in the name of an ideology or creator. Or the sadist who gathers a following by calling his fabricated sermons spiritual, only to lead his followers to their death. Or the woman who believes she is a vampire, attracting groupies whom she seduces by making them feel important, only to guide them to commit murder.

When we humans are desperate, sometimes we grab onto whatever we can to make ourselves seen in the world. As with all fallacy, however, eventually the bubble pops, and we must pay the toll that truth demands.

The Rainbow Chaser. This type of Fabricator loves to chase rainbows as a way to console itself about its unsatisfying current reality. It is always chasing a dream, certain that when the dream comes true, happiness will ensue. It gives us hope with promises like: "One day my true love will find me and I'll live happily ever after." "One day my child will be a doctor, and then I'll be happy." "When I lose weight and get thin, then my life will be wonderful." "The day I make a million dollars, I will be content."

When we live for a future, and a future only, we escape the present. The drawback is that our imagined futures often don't actualize, and we miss out on years of joy that could be had in the here and now. And if our imagined future does actualize, our happiness is generally short-lived, because the root of our discomfort is never beheld.

For example, a woman who keeps getting cosmetic surgery in an attempt to measure up to the ideal socially desired prototype, designed and perpetuated by commercial enterprise, will only be happy for a while before discovering another flaw that needs to be fixed. She continues to get plastic surgery for the rest of her life because she can't love her true self. Her justification is *Everyone does it. You have to look young and beautiful in this world if you want to be deemed worthy.* While she spends her whole life rainbow chasing, she misses out on genuine connections, not only with others, but with herself. It is just easier to get surgery than to develop a sense of self-worth from within. The person who made a million will then need to make two million. The mother whose child becomes the doctor will continue investing her happiness in the child's success, creating tension in that relationship and an increasing loneliness in herself.

It is natural to chase rainbows, even fun, and indeed consoling, but when the rainbow-chasing is so extensive that we cannot behold our present reality, we are missing our own story. Too much rainbow chasing cheats us of the happiness we can have today, perhaps by enjoying our garden, or something funny the cat did, or a warm conversation with another. When we shift our eyeballs from the far-away mountain to the tip of our nose, we can discover treasures right in front of us.

The Conflict-Repeller. The Conflict-Repeller lies to keep the peace. It will say whatever it needs to say to avoid an argument. It has no mal intent; it just tries to find a peaceful way to get its needs met. For instance, a woman might buy a new dress when it isn't in the budget, but tell her husband her mother gave it to her. Or the grown child will tell his mother everything is fine, even when it isn't, so she won't worry about him. Or a woman will tell her mate she didn't have an affair (that she regrets) to spare him pain and keep him from leaving her.

The Conflict-Repeller rises in us when say we are doing well (when we aren't) because we want to be left alone, or when we tell others we agree with them (even when we don't) because we aren't in the mood to defend ourselves. These are all natural behaviors, often used out of self-respect, and sometimes out of fear, and sometimes for personal gain. We know if this type of Inner Fabricator is helping or hurting us by the state of agitation or peace we feel *within* ourselves and by the consequences yet to come.

The Predatory Fabricator. This type of Inner Fabricator, in collusion with the Inner Traitor, has an *intent* to harm or take advantage of others and lies to benefit itself. Preying on the innocent, it will work to pull the wool over another's eyes, as in a dirty sales pitch or the work of a con artist. It might use the line that it needs help, or can give help, only to lure the unsuspecting into its trap.

It might draw the line at minor transactions like telling someone, "I love you more than I have ever loved anyone" to procure a one-night stand, or it might go the distance and swindle masses out of their fortunes, as in a Pondzi scheme.

The Predatory Fabricator doesn't actually believe it is bad; it either believes it *must* do what it is doing to survive, or that others are stupid, or that life owes it, or that that its targets have it coming for one reason or another.

If we find ourselves in this behavior, we are likely justifying why it is all right. This is the mode we have adopted to cope with life. It is an easy method to get what we think we deserve, even though others pay the price. Sooner or later, however, *we* pay the price. For example, manipulating a loved one out of money will lead to distrust and damage in that relationship. A trumped-up sale of a dud car might be returned and/or our reputation besmirched all over town. Conning an old lady out of her money or tricking someone into a sexual experience can land us in jail. The greater toll, however, is that our psychological wounds continue to bleed and cause continued maladaptive behavior, getting us into deeper and deeper trouble. This suffering can be alleviated only when we face our psychological infection and commit to finding a cure without hurting others.

Balancing the Inner Fabricator

We have all experienced using our Fabricator now and then to cheer others, dodge conflict, fool ourselves, or deceive whom we feel we must. The Fabricator is not bad or good. It is the part of us that can create illusion—that's all. In short, the Fabricator can be used to spark joy and imagination. It can *help us* buy time to accept a shocking event or to incubate until we are ready to face certain fears. And it can be used as a tool to survive. However, when it is in the driver's seat of our lives for long periods, it can cross us over into mental illness and mummify us so that we never have to accept certain truths that would catalyze us to move on with our lives. It is not unusual for anyone to have crossed that line temporarily at some point as an attempt to cope with trauma.

Yet, if an afflicted Fabricator *runs* our life, it will eventually run us right off the edge of a cliff while convincing us the cliff isn't there. Sometimes truths are just too hard to face and we must cling to a fabrication to justify our escapist behavior. Trying to understand this is often like trying to understand the iceberg by its tip without beholding what lies beneath. However much we understand or don't, our mind will churn thoughts like: "If I am myself, no one will love me." "If I am truthful, I will be hurt." "I must believe my fabrication in order to like myself." "I must convince others of my fabrication to get them to support me." or "I must fool people if I expect to get ahead in life."

Eventually, we humans wear ourselves out with this thinking that generates a fabricated life. Most of us, in time, will acknowledge and face our fears. And when we do . . . we can accept who we are and love ourselves for *that*. We need not pretend away our past, blind ourselves to our present, or try to force a fantasy future. We can, if we choose, allow ourselves to unfold, and with excitement, discover who we are. The natural world has a cycle, a journey that it takes without trying to change it. The oak tree will go through its cycle, the river, even the air molecule. When we allow ourselves to go through ours and be who we are, unfold as we may, and take the journey our inner truth dictates, we can enjoy the moment and celebrate our being no matter what our past or future.

This workshop will help you examine your Inner Fabricator, the part it has played, the results, and to determine if modifications might improve your life.

The Fabricator in a Nutshell
* Uses fantasy to spread joy.
* Fools itself or others for a variety of reasons.
* Uses fabrication as a way to cope or help others cope.
* Does not trust authenticity to make things better.
* Eludes the truth.
* Twists or buries truths to get what it needs.

Fabricator Types
The Entertainer: "Let me cheer you."
The Magician: "I consciously create an illusion to cover the truth."
The Dream Weaver: "I *must* pretend!"
The Extreme Optimist: "I love my rose-colored glasses!"
The Poor Me Fabricator: "I am powerless."
The Chosen One: "I am more special than anyone else."

The Rainbow Chaser: "Everything will be all right in the future."
The Conflict Repeller: "It is easier not to tell the truth."
Predatory Fabricator: "I deceive others at their expense to get what I want."

Exploring Your Inner Fabricator

As you do the following exercises ask yourself, "Am I being honest? Is my fabrication helping me flourish in a genuine way, or am I just getting by any way I can?" If you are using your Fabricator excessively, that is okay. It is okay! But if you are ready to go deeper and transform from caterpillar into butterfly, and not just *pretend* that you are, this workshop can foster that step to the next level.

Exercise One

This first exercise will strengthen your ability to recognize the Fabricator's many faces. Preceding each sentence, state the Fabricator type which the statement depicts.

1. _____ Pete acts like a notable intellect to disguise his weaknesses.

2. _____ Harry agrees with his wife just to avoid an argument.

3. _____ Mae tells her kids that the Easter Bunny is coming.

4. _____ Jay insists he is too ill to ever hold a job.

5. _____ Pat gloats about her perfect life, closing her eyes to its flaws.

6. _____ Ben believes his good looks make him every woman's dream.

7. _____ Gayle feels she can't be happy until she finds the perfect mate.

8. _____ Brad convinces himself that his ill-behaved child is doing well.

9. _____ Alice fibbed about feeling ill so her mom would have to stay home from work.

Answers: 1. Magician   2. Conflict-Repeller 3. Entertainer 4. Poor-Me 5. Extreme Optimist 6. Chosen One 7. Rainbow Chaser 8. Dream Weaver 9. Predatory

Exercise Two

Now describe what circumstances lead you to fabricate and the kind of Fabricator that emerges to play the part. Example #1: I fabricate when *I tuck my kids in at night and make up bedtime stories that teach them lessons.* At that time, my Fabricator is *the Entertainer.* Example #2: I fabricate when *I don't want to be confronted because it's just too much work to defend myself.* At that time my Fabricator is the *Conflict-Repeller.*

1. I fabricate when _____

_____

At that time, my Fabricator is the_____

2. I fabricate when_____

_____

At that time, my Fabricator is the_____

3. I fabricate when_____

_____

At that time, my Fabricator is the_____

4. I fabricate when _____

_____

At that time, my Fabricator is the_____

5. I fabricate when_____

_____

At that time, my Fabricator is the_____

What type(s) of Inner Fabricator(s) do you tend to be?

_____

Exercise Three

Our Inner Fabricator often rises because we are afraid. Exploring these fears can help us modify our Inner Fabricator's activity, if need be. List your three *greatest* fears. Examples: stepping out into the world, rejection, poverty, failure, shame, other people getting hurt, living alone, etc.

My three *greatest* fears, in this order, are:

1. _____

2. _____

3._____

Now restate each fear and what you feel you must do to keep that fear from actualizing. Determine if you are fabricating by circling "am" or "am not." If you are fabricating, explain the fabrication. If you dig deep enough you might see that you are fabricating even though at first it doesn't seem like it. Keep in mind that it is not bad to fabricate, but human, and that fabrications can be subtle and/or clever. Even in this exercise your Inner Fabricator might be tempted to fabricate that it doesn't fabricate. If so, push past it and be honest with yourself. The goal here is to help you learn more about this part of yourself so that you can use or not use it in ways that better your life. Lastly, tap your Inner Sage and see what it has to say.

Example #1: I fear *feeling shame*, so I tell myself *that I must look nice, have a clean house, and be financially solvent if I am to be honored by others and hence honor myself*. My fabrication is that *I am not worthy until I do all these things*. My Inner Sage tells me *that it is time I deemed myself worthy no matter what*.

Example #2: I fear *being alone*, so I tell myself *that I must convince prospective mates that I am everything they are searching for, so I put on an act so that they will love me*. My fabrication is *that I must play a part in order for someone to want me*. My Inner Sage tells me *that if I can learn to enjoy my own company, then I might not need to fabricate in order to win someone's love. I will then attract a mate that is truly right for me*.

1. I fear_____, so I tell myself_____

_____

I   am / am not fabricating. If I am, then my fabrication is_____
(circle the correct answer)

_____

_____

My Inner Sage tells me_____

_____

2. I fear_____, so I tell myself_____

_____

I   am / am not fabricating. If I am, then my fabrication is_____
(circle the correct answer)

_____

_____

My Inner Sage tells me_____

_____

3. I fear_____, so I tell myself _____

_____

I am / am not   fabricating. If I am, then my fabrication is_____
(circle the correct answer)

_____

_____

My Inner Sage tells me_____

_____

Exercise Four

This exercise is designed to help you come to terms with times when your Inner Fabricator emerged and you compromised your honor, the truth behind the fabrication, how you felt afterward, and why you felt you needed to fabricate.

Sometimes fabricating, given the circumstance, is the better choice, and sometimes it leaves a bitter stain on our conscience. If you determine that the fabrication was the best choice, then you can be at peace with it and stop stewing over the situation. If you determine that the fabrication is something you wish you did not do, then by realizing that, you can change your behavior in future similar circumstances. In that, there is NO shame. We humans learn by trial and error! Whatever you did that you wish you didn't is absolutely serving a purpose to help you grow more healthily in the days to come. Be kind to yourself.

Example #1: My Inner Fabricator emerged and compromised my honor once when *I convinced my child that she was better off not having piano lessons because it would interfere with her schooling,* but the truth was that *I didn't have the money to pay for the lessons or to get a piano.* Afterward I felt *guilty* because *she probably thought I was invalidating her need to be creative with music.* I fabricated because *I was ashamed of not having the money.* I could have told the truth by saying, *If I ever can afford it, yes you can have piano lessons.* In this case, it was *not best* that I fabricated. In the future, if in a similar circumstance, I will *tell the truth because it will probably make my relationship with that person better.*

Example #2: My Inner Fabricator emerged and compromised my honor once when *I told my child that I spanked him for not cleaning her bedroom because I love him enough to try and teach him a lesson,* but the truth was that *I spanked my child because I lost my temper.* Afterward I felt *mad at myself* because *I have an anger problem and took it out on him.* I fabricated *because I knew I had lost my temper but I didn't want to admit that to my son because he might view me as weak.* I could have told the truth by saying, *I lost my temper, and I was wrong. From now on there will be no television until your bedroom is picked up.* In this case, it was *not best* that I fabricated. In the future, if in a similar circumstance, *I would not fabricate again because I don't want to hurt anyone else by trying to cover my own flaws.*

Example #3: My Inner Fabricator emerged and compromised my honor once when *I had consensual sex with a mentally unstable man (letting him think I liked him) because I was afraid if I didn't, he would kill me,* but the truth was that *I hated him for how badly he was treating me.* Afterward, I felt *horrible for having to compromise my honor, but I also felt lucky to be alive.* I could have stated the truth by saying, *I don't like how you are treating me; I am leaving.* In this case, it *was best* that I fabricated because *he was a violent man.* In the future, if in a similar circumstance, I *would* fabricate again because *sometimes you have to pick the lesser of two evils.*

1. My Inner Fabricator emerged and compromised my honor once when I_____

_____

I fabricated because_____

_____

But the truth was_____

_____

I could have told the truth by_____

_____

In this case it   was / was not   best that I fabricated.
           (circle the correct answer)

In the future if a similar circumstance occurs, I   will / will not fabricate again because
                                    (circle the correct answer)

_____

_____

2. My Inner Fabricator emerged and compromised my honor once when I_____

_____

I fabricated because_____

_____

But the truth was_____

_____

I could have told the truth by_____

_____

In this case it   was / was not   best that I fabricated.
           (circle the correct answer)

In the future if a similar circumstance occurs, I   will / will not fabricate again, because
                                  (circle the correct answer)

_____

_____

3. My Inner Fabricator emerged and compromised my honor once when I_____

_____

I fabricated because_____

_____

But the truth was_____

_____

I could have told the truth by_____

_____

In this case it   was / was not   best that I fabricated.
                (circle the correct answer)

In the future if a similar circumstance occurs, I   will / will not   fabricate again, because
                                           (circle the correct answer)

_____

_____

Take a moment now to ponder if the above actions taken by your Inner Fabricator worked against you in the _long run_. For example, the woman who lied to her child about piano lessons missed an opportunity for her child to be emotionally supportive of her stress from like of finances. Further, in continuing her methodology, her child might have been told no so often that she felt unloved. Or in the example of the parent who spanked his child. Perhaps later in life the child started hitting others when mad, emulating what his father had done, whereas if the father would have told the truth, the child would have learned it is not okay to hit when mad. In the case of the woman who felt forced into sexual relations, while in the short run it helped her, in the long run it may have hurt her. While her actions at the time were appropriate, instead of resigning herself to a future fate should a similar circumstance recur, she could examine how she got in that situation in the first place. She might also consider taking self-defense classes.

What can you do today to avoid repeating an old scenario that still bothers you?

_____

Exercise Five

1. State ways you have used your Inner Fabricator on *behalf* of others. Example: On behalf of others, I have used my Inner Fabricator to: *shield my children from harmful truths; make small children's worlds magical; make others feel hopeful by creating scenarios that could be; and divert bullies from the innocent.*

On behalf of others, I have used my Inner Fabricator to:_____

_____

_____

_____

_____

_____

Take a moment to appreciate your Inner Fabricator, realizing that no matter how things came out, that part of you has done its very best to help you or others in various circumstances.

Circle the answer that suits you best. The Fabricator appears in my life:

hardly ever   from time to time   in certain periods of my life   moderately   a lot   profusely

Healing and Balancing Exercise for Your Inner Fabricator

Place one hand over your forehead.
Place the other hand over your heart.
Concentrate deeply. Repeat silently or aloud for at least two minutes:
"My truth has merit."

Relaxation and Creative Visualization Exercise

Lie in a comfortable position. Play instrumental music that makes you feel good: classical, New Age, or music that is of gentle, sweeping, or dynamic beauty. When the music is playing, close your eyes. Inhale through your nose deeply, and exhale through your mouth slowly; do this eight times. Visualize that you are inhaling the power of the universe, which purifies and attunes you physically, emotionally, mentally, and metaphysically. When you exhale, all the tensions and worries leave your body and go back into the universe where they dissolve and blend into the pure life force.

Tighten and loosen your muscles slowly in this order:

Feet. Tighten. Loosen. Take a slow, deep breath, and exhale.
Calves. Tighten. Loosen. Take a slow, deep breath, and exhale.
Thighs. Tighten. Loosen. Take a slow, deep breath, and exhale.
Hips and buttocks. Tighten. Loosen. Take a slow, deep breath, and exhale.
Stomach. Tighten. Loosen. Take a slow, deep breath, and exhale.

Back. Tighten. Loosen. Take a slow, deep breath, and exhale.
Arms. Tighten. Loosen. Take a slow, deep breath, and exhale.
Hands. Tighten. Loosen. Take a slow, deep breath, and exhale.
Neck and shoulders. Tighten. Loosen. Take a slow, deep breath, and exhale.
Face. Tighten. Loosen. Take a slow, deep breath, and exhale.

Then completely relax and take eight slower, deep breaths. Inhale the universal life energy through your nose and exhale tension through your mouth.

Set the intent: *Whoever I am, whatever I am, whatever I need, whatever is right for me—so be it. I open to insight. I open to receive.*

Now that you are completely relaxed, give your self over to the music that is playing. Focus on the point between your eyebrows and journey inward. You are moving inward . . . deeper and deeper, heading toward your Inner Fabricator. Do this for a while . . . .

You see your Inner Fabricator in the distance. What does it look like and what is it doing? Is it wearing rose-colored glasses so it won't have to see any problems? Is it wearing dark sunglasses so no one can see the truth in its eyes? Is it almost invisible in the dark or is it shrouded in rainbow colors? Observe your Inner Fabricator for a while . . . .

As you approach your Inner Fabricator, you must traverse layers of shadow. Experience this for a while . . . .

Now you have reached your Inner Fabricator. Standing before it, you see its disguises, one layered over another and another. You look it in the eyes with heroic good will, even though it grows uncomfortable. You tell it that you know its disguises have merit, but for a moment you want to behold what is beneath the disguises. It nods and allows you to do this.

Slowly unwrap your Inner Fabricator, one disguise, then another, peeling each disguise away. Pay attention to the disguises as you do this until all the disguises are removed . . . .

The closer you get to what lies beneath the disguises, the more you begin to feel how hard your Inner Fabricator has tried to protect and preserve itself and others. Appreciate your Inner Fabricator. Do this for a while . . . .

Now your Inner Fabricator is before you, open and vulnerable without any disguise. You thank your Inner Fabricator for helping you get by, and you relieve it from having to act in ways that no longer serve you. You open your arms with compassion, and your Inner Fabricator falls into them. As you embrace, you can feel your Inner Fabricator's relief that you don't condemn it. You feel the Inner Fabricator move into your heart.

At peace with your Inner Fabricator, you hold your head high and walk proudly into a brilliant white light a few feet away from you. This is the light of your Quintessential Self. As you walk into the light, you are unashamed of any truth—even if that truth is the acknowledgement you have fabricated because you were afraid. Take a moment to experience this . . .

As the purity of your Quintessential Self fills you, you feel ready to tap your inner strength to be an authentic person and bet on the truth. However, you also reserve the right to use your inner Fabricator to bring cheer or promote healthier outcomes in certain circumstances. Relax and enjoy this experience in the beautiful light of your Quintessential Self. Do this until the music ends . . . .

When you open your eyes you will feel refreshed and very kindly toward yourself.

Record your experience.

_____

_____

_____

_____

_____

_____

_____

Draw a picture or symbol that summarizes your experience. Example: *Fireworks.*

Create a key phrase that summarizes this experience. Example: *I am free to be me.*

_____

When needed, say the phrase silently and visualize the picture or symbol. This will reactivate the experience and generate a peaceful, empowered, clear state of mind.

Δ
Gem of Wisdom
When we fabricate to dodge our true self, we lose sight of who we are.
When we fabricate to honor our true self, we step toward self-actualization.

Live the Mystery

12

WORKSHOP TWELVE
THE SKEPTIC "I doubt."

The Skeptic lives in a world of doubt, arms crossed, head cocked, staring curiously at optimistic believers, so often led astray. Hence, it is not easily deceived. Never acting on blind faith, it is adept at perceiving unhealthy circumstances or ill-motivated people. This slow to trust quality is a double-edged sword. While sparing us tragedy, it also can hinder forward movement, given any possible direction might be quicksand.

The Skeptic would like to believe, but it will not emotionally invest in what might be a pipe dream. Though never quit trusting anything or anyone, neither does it condemn or conclude that what it isn't trusting *could be* trustworthy. In its own way, it is somewhat open-minded. If backed by a strong Inner Leader, it can lead a full and interesting life, experiencing even what it doubts.

Our Inner Skeptic will generally fall into one or more, or a combination of the following types: the Philosophical Skeptic, the Cynic, or the Defeatist. Given we all have our own nature, not all of the types will apply to you. You may however recognize them in others you know which can facilitate a clearer understanding of their behavior in relation to you.

The Philosophical Skeptic. The Philosophical Skeptic questions the validity of everything, everyone, even life, even itself, while remaining open to all possibilities. This Skeptic is often wise, not willing to cement its beliefs in mere ideas of truth, and would rather remain open-minded and fluid in its perceptions. It has experiences, but doesn't define them. It has ideas, but it doesn't cement them. It touches many aspects of life, because it closes the door to none.

This Skeptic, when empowered by the Sage, can be deeply wise. However, if afflicted with anger, it can develop into the Cynic.

The Cynic. The Cynic is bitter, disappointed in its life experiences, nursing pessimistic points of view: "I don't know about that." "Yeah, right." "Yeah, yeah, whatever." It is prone to berate and bitterly denounce anything in the area in which it has been hurt. With glaring eye and foaming mouth, it proclaims such things as, "I will never trust love again. I will never hope again. I will never care again." Wearing sarcasm like a costume, it colludes with the Fury to keep things boiling.

It is natural from time to time, to let our Cynic take the helm so we can retreat for a while, like a wounded cat that finds a quiet, dark place to heal. When used like this, for relatively short periods, we can, in our solitude, air out our pain, calm our fear, then come out of hiding and step back into the social scene. *I will never love again* helps us release the experience and gives us time to heal before moving on to another relationship. Many say they will never love again . . . but they do. Feelings shared that backfired might result in the proclamation, "I will never share my opinions again." This helps us be quiet for a while to work things out internally before our opinions surface once more.

However, if we harbor deep hurts that span many areas of life, our Inner Cynic can become so acrid that it repels everyone, leaving us an island unto ourselves—isolated and alone. Devoured by the chip on our shoulder, we torpedo optimistic ideas that could carry us into a bright future. There is no future; there is only the caustic moment. If we allow the Cynic to remain in charge too long, we can sink into what feels like irreversible despair. Life is colored gray, and sometimes black. It makes us sick with grief and invites mental or physical illness.

The Defeatist. Unlike the Cynic, the Defeatist does not have a chip on its shoulder; it has sunk lower than that. It tends to slack off into what might be deemed lazy or cowardly. "Why try? I'll just be shot down." The Defeatist shields itself with the memory of either its own defeats or the defeats of others. If it has seen numerous divorces, it might convince itself to never marry. If it has been in numerous failed relationships, it might convince itself to never have another. The Defeatist is prevalent in our lives when, for example, we may have given everything to start a new business and now face bankruptcy, or loved someone purely and completely and then got jilted. Retreating into ourselves, we give no reason why we can't try again, other than it won't work. Depressed by life outcomes, we have just given up.

Bolting the door on promising life change, the Defeatist can lock us into uncomfortable situations. For example, we might not even consider leaving an abusive mate because the prospect of being alone feels so damning that we'd rather stay in a bad relationship. It is normal to feel the Defeatist from time to time in certain areas of our life, but when it controls our lives too long, it can kill our spirit to live.

Balancing the Inner Skeptic

The biggest indicator of an unbalanced Inner Skeptic is a feeling of being stalemated in our own life. It is difficult to take a leap of faith to move forward when our trust is broken. We are trapped in the dark, sealed in by a two-ton door weighted with our despair. The F word is Faith, and it just feels impossible to have. No one can open the door for us, no matter how hard they try.

Often, in time, the situation becomes unbearable and our Inner Hero will find a way to open the door and let in the light. When the light touches us, like winter that turns to spring, we feel a new lease on life. Everything looks brighter, richer and more beautiful than ever before. For what is not brighter after seeing only darkness? Like after an illness, good health feels so much better. At this point, we have brought our Skeptic into balance. The caterpillar has turned into the butterfly. The Cynic and Defeatist have morphed into the Philosophical Skeptic, flying over the small world below with a message on its wings. "Judge nothing, just ride the wave and embrace the adventure."

We all have an Inner Skeptic that plays various parts in our lives. As we each are unique, the degree is less important than *what* influence the Skeptic actually has in our life. Does it keep us isolated to a point of loneliness and depression? Does it only appear after we have been deceived and burned? Does it keep us from moving on, keep people from getting too close, or only appear when something good is on the horizon? Or perhaps it already is in fine balance, keeping us open-minded, guarding us from deception or tragedy, yet also taking a backseat when a chance, as in a new job, or new friend, or new idea, might be worth the risk.

This workshop is designed to help you understand the workings of your Skeptic that you might better understand the part it has played in your life, and most importantly how you can you use it to your advantage.

The Skeptic in a Nutshell
* Seeing is not believing

* Questions everything.
* Is not easily deceived.
* Lacks trust.
* When afflicted, can be bitter and depressed.
* When open-minded, can help us experience a fuller life.

Skeptic Types

Philosophical Skeptic: "I question everything, cling to no thing, and open to all possibility."
The Cynic: "I am bitter."
The Defeatist: "Trying leads to failure."

Exploring Your Inner Skeptic

Exercise One.

Our Inner Skeptic plays several roles. It can open our mind to possibilities. It can raise red flags to warn us of impending deception. And it can guide us to proceed, but with caution. This exercise will spotlight the roles your Inner Skeptic plays in your life. State what incites your Inner Skeptic to rise regarding: Strangers, Family/Friends, Romance, Government, and Life.

Examples regarding Strangers: My Skeptic rises *when a stranger appears at my door*. My Skeptic rises when *an email informs me that I won a prize*. My Skeptic rises when *someone gives me a compliment*.

Examples regarding Family/Friends: My Skeptic rises when *my mom says she will stop drinking*. My Skeptic rises when *my friend says she really likes my boyfriend*. My Skeptic rises when *my sister says she'll try harder to get along with me*.

Examples regarding Romance: My Skeptic rises when *a man/woman professes that they love me*. My Skeptic rises when *a man/woman shows interest in me*. My Skeptic rises when *my mate says the sex is good*.

Examples regarding Government: My Skeptic rises when *a politician is elected*. My Skeptic rises when *new rules come out for public education*.

Examples regarding Life: My Skeptic rises when *things look too hopeless*. My Skeptic rises when *something good happens to me*.

Some categories might overlap. That's all right. There is no wrong way to do this exercise. Just let go and see what comes out of you!

Strangers

My Skeptic rises when_____

My Skeptic rises when_____

My Skeptic rises when_____

Family/Friends

My Skeptic rises when_____

My Skeptic rises when_____

My Skeptic rises when_____

Romance

My Skeptic rises when_____

My Skeptic rises when_____

My Skeptic rises when_____

Government

My Skeptic rises when_____

My Skeptic rises when_____

My Skeptic rises when_____

Life

My Skeptic rises when_____

My Skeptic rises when_____

My Skeptic rises when_____

Regarding the previous exercise, circle the appropriate answer(s).

1. My Inner Skeptic felt the strongest regarding:

strangers   family/relatives   romance   government   life

2. How hard was it to think of answers to the questions?

extremely   pretty hard   moderately hard   not too hard   really easy   extremely easy

Given these answers, on a scale of 1-10 (ten being the strongest) how strong is the role your Inner Skeptic plays in your life? _____

Exercise Two

Recall when another part of yourself overpowered your Inner Skeptic. Example #1: My Skeptic told me, *Don't give money to that stranger; he's conning you,* but my Inner Nurturer said, *He needs help,* and I gave him five bucks. Example #2: My Inner Skeptic told me, *Don't fall in love with that person; you will just get used like always,* but my Inner Fabricator said, *No, he's different than the others; I'm certain,* and I went ahead and got involved.

1. My_____told me _____

_____

but my_____ said_____

_____

and I_____

2. My_____told me_____

_____

but my_____said_____

_____

and I_____

3. My_____told me_____

_____

but my_____ said_____

_____

and I_____

On a scale of 1-10 (10 is very easy), how easy is it for your other Inner Aspects to overpower your Inner Skeptic? _____

Exercise Three

Sometimes our Inner Skeptic is fueled by other aspects of ourselves, most commonly, our Inner Victim, Fury, and Sage.

When our Inner Skeptic colludes with our Inner Victim, it becomes the Defeatist. A conversation between them would go something like this:

Skeptic: "I look around and see all the happy couples, but I will never have that."
Victim: "I know, nobody loves us."
Skeptic: "Everyone else gets acclaim but me, even if I do all the work."
Victim: "I know, we always get cheated."

Skeptic: "There is no meaning in life; life is stupid."
Victim: "I know; we are trapped in this depressing existence."
Skeptic: "Everyone is out for themselves, and will leave me out in the cold.
Victim: "I know; we can't count on anyone. We are all alone, and we will always be alone."
Skeptic: "It's better that way."
Victim: "But I want love, attention, and to trust others."
Skeptic: "It will never happen; you are stuck with me."

When our Inner Skeptic colludes with our Inner Fury, it becomes the Cynic. A conversation between them would go something like this:

Skeptic: "People will inevitably burn me."
Fury: "Don't worry, we'll spit some fire and insult them first."
Skeptic: "Yes, I am done trying to be kind because no good deed goes unpunished."
Fury: "Don't worry, we won't do any good deeds, and we shall do the punishing."
Skeptic: "I agree. Let em' all go to hell."
Fury: "We'll hurl our anger and burn them all."
Skeptic: "Yes, we won't let anyone get close to us.
Fury: "You and me against the world!"

When our Inner Skeptic colludes with our Inner Sage, it becomes the Philosophical Skeptic. A conversation between them would go something like this:

Skeptic: "Nothing is as it seems."
Sage: "However, it might be."
Skeptic: "I don't believe everything I hear."
Sage: "However, what you hear could have merit."
Skeptic: "People believe what suits them."
Sage: "So what?"
Skeptic: "I am inclined to not believe in anything."
Sage: "You needn't believe, but neither need you disbelieve."
Skeptic: "I suppose I can keep in an open mind."
Sage: "Yes, that way you won't miss out on enriching life adventures."

If your Inner Skeptic is generally a Cynic or Defeatist, experiment tapping your Inner Sage to work with it and see what happens.

Circle the type of Skeptic that *best* describes you.

Philosophical   Cynic   Defeatist

Exercise Four

Let your Inner Skeptic speak. What does it have to say about you, others, and life? Do not censor anything even if it feels "dark," even if anger comes spewing out with an intensity you did not know was there, even if it doesn't really feel like you. This is just a *part* of yourself speaking!

Even if the Skeptic is not strong in you (if you are mostly trusting person), give it a chance to speak anyway. Your Inner Skeptic might only rise in certain circumstances, even if rare. Yet it is there and you can learn a lot about yourself by giving it the spotlight for a few minutes.

Let me introduce myself. I am _____'s Skeptic.

(your name)

I view life like this:

_____

_____

_____

I view love like this:

_____

_____

_____

I view most, if not all people, like this:

_____

_____

_____

My motto is: (examples: Trust no one. Don't trust authority. Proceed with caution.)

_____

The part I play in_____'s life is_____

(your name)

_____

_____

Circle the answer that suits you best. The Skeptic has appeared in my life:

hardly ever   from time to time   in certain periods of my life   moderately   profusely

Healing and Balancing Exercise for Your Inner Skeptic

Place one hand over year heart.
Place the other hand on the crown of your head.
Concentrate deeply. Repeat silently or aloud for at least two minutes:
"I open to truth beyond all possible perception."

Relaxation and Creative Visualization Exercise

Lie in a comfortable position. Play instrumental music that makes you feel good: classical, New Age, or music that is of gentle, sweeping, or dynamic beauty. When the music is playing, close your eyes. Inhale through your nose deeply, and exhale through your mouth slowly; do this eight times. Visualize that you are inhaling the power of the universe, which purifies and attunes you physically, emotionally, mentally, and metaphysically. When you exhale, all the tensions and worries leave your body and go back into the universe where they dissolve and blend into the pure life force.

Tighten and loosen your muscles slowly in this order:

Feet. Tighten. Loosen. Take a slow, deep breath, and exhale.
Calves. Tighten. Loosen. Take a slow, deep breath, and exhale.
Thighs. Tighten. Loosen. Take a slow, deep breath, and exhale.
Hips and buttocks. Tighten. Loosen. Take a slow, deep breath, and exhale.
Stomach. Tighten. Loosen. Take a slow, deep breath, and exhale.
Back. Tighten. Loosen. Take a slow, deep breath, and exhale.
Arms. Tighten. Loosen. Take a slow, deep breath, and exhale.
Hands. Tighten. Loosen. Take a slow, deep breath, and exhale.
Neck and shoulders. Tighten. Loosen. Take a slow, deep breath, and exhale.
Face. Tighten. Loosen. Take a slow, deep breath, and exhale.

Then completely relax and take eight more slow, deep breaths. Inhale the universal life energy through your nose and exhale tension through your mouth.

Set the intent: *Whoever I am, whatever I am, whatever I need, whatever is right for me—so be it. I open to insight. I open to receive.*

Now that you are completely relaxed, give your self over to the music that is playing. Focus on the point between your eyebrows and journey inward, deeper and deeper. You are moving through the corridors of your vast inner being. Do this for a while . . . .

You sense a space off to the side, and you know it is where your Skeptic resides. You move into that space, and not too far away, you notice your Inner Skeptic. Observe its appearance and its surroundings. Is it freed, or caged? Is it cloaked in rags, fire, or radiant light? Take some time to observe . . . .

Now activate your Inner Healer and feel it rise within you. Walk up to the Skeptic and look it in the eye. What expression is on its face as it sees you filled with a Healer's power? Carefully slowly move your hand to its heart. From your hand there flows a pure, golden, healing energy. Experience this for a while . . . .

Now you feel yourself as your Inner Skeptic receiving the pure, golden, healing energy into your heart. This energy goes deeper and deeper into you, seeping into your suffering. Dark pockets of resentment dissolve in this pure, healing, golden light. Black pockets of fear dissolve in this pure, healing, golden light. Red pockets of pain dissolve in this pure, healing, golden light. Experience this for a while . . . .

Something is happening. The warm golden light has filled you and is turning brilliant white. You feel embraced by what is greatest and strongest in you—your Quintessential Self. You give it allegiance. Even if you can't trust anything in the world, you can trust your Quintessential Self, and in that you are open to a rainbow of new life experiences waiting to be had. Bask in this experience until the music ends . . . .

When you open your eyes, you will feel your Inner Skeptic reattuned and ready to work for you a balanced way.

Record your experience.

_____

_____

_____

_____

_____

_____

_____

_____

Draw a picture that summarizes your experience. Example: *A rainbow*.

Create a phrase that summarizes the experience. Example: *I open my mind to wisdom*.

_____

When needed, say the phrase silently and visualize the picture or symbol. This will reactivate the experience and generate a peaceful, empowered, clear state of mind.

Δ

Gem of Wisdom
Life's bounty is more richly experienced with an open mind.

Live the Mystery

13

WORKSHOP THIRTEEN
THE TRAITOR "I punish."

Slinking about in the night, the Traitor lurks in the shadows, insecure and alone, ready to strike, or watch silently as others flail, desperate to feel its power in a dog-eat-dog world. Staring through a spyglass, seeing only a small portion of anyone or anything, including itself, it plots to cripple the competition.

The Traitor, at its core, reeks of insecurity, and will do what it must to get the attention it craves. It endorses and/or incites destruction, sometimes secretly, sometimes openly, and sometimes with a sadistic smile that makes others wonder. The Traitor lives to promote failure. It is jealous. It will try to sabotage whomever seems shinier than it. It is afraid. It will demean anyone who gets in the way of its climb to the top. It is needy. It will push others off the boat to save itself. Or it might even invert and convince us that we deserve to be punished. It will demean our Inner Nurturer, insist our Inner Sage is irrelevant, and spurn our Inner Healer with a lust to destroy.

We all have a Traitor somewhere in us. It might be passive, known only as a secret burning hope that others will fail, even if only now and then. Or it might roar inside us, controlling our lives with vigilante justice. Or it might rise, feeding on our secret shame, and become our own worst enemy.

The Traitor might seem dastardly, but beneath its mischievous eyes, it trembles in its boots, terrified it will be forgotten and sink into oblivion. Hence, it claws and scratches anything and anyone that stands between it and the sun, including certain aspects within ourselves. It is just something that the Traitor feels it must do in order to make it in the world. When our Traitor acts, it means we are desperate. And when others unleash their Traitor on us, it means they are desperate.

The Traitor's unkind acts are always the product of internal suffering. This suffering can compound, when in reflection, we feel bad for our treatment of others, or can't get over how others have treated us. Traitorous acts often leave a residue of guilt, regret, and anger. Due to the intensity of the feelings that this workshop might dust up, it is advised that if you are in therapy, you consult your therapist regarding this workshop. Although this workshop is designed to help alleviate suffering, only proceed *if* you are ready to explore the roots of your Inner Traitor. You can always revisit this workshop in the future when you are more prepared. Remember, our Inner Traitor isn't bad; it's *insecure*. As an aspect of human nature, it is bent on surviving, no matter what the cost.

As we unravel the mysteries of what drives our Inner Traitor, it will be easier to embrace it with compassion and forgiveness. While its nature will always be what it is, a rather destructive aspect of ourselves, we can keep it from acting in ways that ultimately work against us.

If you are ready, continue.

The Traitor, like all our other aspects, can operate in various ways giving rise to different types. You may recognize one, more than one, or a combination of types in you or others. In this, you will be able to better navigate through the stormy waters of any relationship. These types are as follows: the Blowfish, the Bold Avenger, the Scorpion, the Ninja, the Remorseful Traitor, the Bystander, or the Self-Inflictor.

The Blowfish. This style of Traitor balloons up to show its might. It is prone to act jealously through gossip, bullying, censuring, and mocking. It sabotages openly by making a scene, publicly denouncing its rival. It will justify its claims by exposing people's secrets: *Joe is a closet homosexual;* twist the truth: *Linda is in league with the devil!* (Linda doesn't go to church); or collude with the Fabricator to trump up charges: *She's a slut; she slept with half the football* team (the accused is a virgin). The Blowfish stars in smear campaigns whether on the home front, commercial, or political stage. Despite its puffed-up appearance, the Blowfish doesn't feel good enough about itself to toot its own horn, so instead it berates its opponent in a public way. The Bully never says, "I am great; I am wonderful," but rather, "You don't measure up; there is something wrong with you."

If you have been the victim of a Blowfish, know that it is indicative of a psychologically wounded person. By blocking the Blowfish's "blow" with your Inner Sage (not reacting), you become a mirror to the Blowfish, who not only failed to pass its pain onto you, but will be given an opportunity to behold its inner wound, and maybe, just maybe, do something about it. And if you recognize the Blowfish in you, this is your opportunity to do something about it.

The Bold Avenger. The Bold Avenger, in league with the Fury, is a more advanced form of the Blowfish, and not adverse to roaming criminal territory. It will seek retribution on any who have harmed it or another in its social circle. While the Blowfish is threatening, the Bold Avenger openly makes the threats a reality. It wants its targets to know that it was the one who brought them down. Examples would be beating up someone who beat up your friend, destroying someone's valuables while they watch, an infatuated stalker who punishes the one who will not love it, or an act of gangland revenge. And when the getting back is done, it revels in the pain it has caused in its act of revenge. Taken to an extreme, the goal is to completely destroy the life of another with a smile on its face. The Bold Avenger is often so consumed with bitterness that it never enjoys its own life and has a greater chance of landing in jail than your average citizen.

In these cases, whether you are the Bold Avenger or just know one, your Inner Sage can be your best ally. Studying meditation (the tool of the Sage) will serve to neutralize anger and fear, and lend insight to dissolve any unsavory situation.

The Scorpion. This type of Traitor is less lethal than the Bold Avenger and trickier than the Blowfish. The Scorpion wants to control its target by withholding praise and affection and inserting a sting whenever it can. It often admires its target, but has no intention of letting the target know that. It might tease meanly, but in a playful tone: "Maybe I should turn you in for a younger model," and use a verbal battering ram to cripple the target: "You're ugly, but I like you anyway." These sabotaging behaviors give a dual message. 1. *Who would want a messed-up person like you?* 2. *You are lucky you have me because unlike you, I am the cream of the crop.* This method usually works on those with low self-esteem, the very forgiving, or on those who in some way depend on the Scorpion.

The Scorpion might seem cruel, but its motive springs from fear of abandonment. In this, it tries to make the targeted person too insecure to ever leave it. The very insecurity it tries to instill in its target is the insecurity it feels deep within itself. To keep that underlying fragility a secret, it sabotages any emotional intimacy that might expose it. It's hard to get close to someone who is always putting us down. This Traitor has discovered a rather clever way to keep people under its thumb, while at the same time keep them at bay.

Typical communications between a Scorpion and its Significant Other are as follows:

> Scorpion: "Don't rinse the dishes with running water; soak them in the other side of the sink."
> Significant Other: "But they rinse better with running water."
> Scorpion: "Our water bill is going to be high; you always waste money."
>
> Significant Other: "There, the floor is mopped."
> Scorpion: "It still looks grungy. Joe's wife always has clean floors."
>
> Significant Other: "I took your clothes out of the dryer and hung them up."
> Scorpion: "Don't hang my clothes up; you do it wrong."
>
> Significant Other: "I got my hair styled. What do you think?"
> Scorpion: "You look like the bride of Frankenstein; I prefer how Janie does her hair."
>
> Significant Other: "My article got published in the newspaper."
> Scorpion: "Ah, anyone can get an article published."
>
> Significant Other: "Sorry, I woke you when I had to take that emergency call."
> Scorpion: "You disturbed my sleep! Now I will be cranky all day."

Although the Significant Other never actually did anything wrong, the Scorpion's constant digs often make the Significant Other feel wounded instead of angry at the Scorpion.

The Scorpion is also capable of getting people to lower their defenses by acting kindly, listening well, and drawing them out. Once their soft spots are revealed, the Scorpion will sting them with a biting remark. For example, Karen finally reveals to James that she had been raped. Once James gets that out of her, he says, "Women who get raped are asking for it, don't you think?"

The fate of the Scorpion, however, is to be alone, because eventually the very abandonment it fears comes to pass, because no human can withstand demeaning treatment forever. If you recognized yourself as a Scorpion, take heart. You were only trying to protect yourself. Now you know that the Scorpion's protection comes at a price. If the price of loneliness is not what you want to pay, all is not lost. By inviting your Inner Nurturer to play a greater role, you can make peace with (and maybe even win back) those you stung right out of your life. At the very least, your future relationships will be much more rewarding.

The Ninja. An even more disguised form of the Scorpion is the Ninja. The Ninja creeps around in the shadows secretly punishing those who have wounded it, or those who pose a threat, while keeping its identity a secret. It will appear innocent while secretly setting up its opponents to fail. Mary says to Sally's prospective boss, "You don't want to hire Sally for the job, she sleeps all day and is irresponsible, but don't tell her I told you so." (Sally is actually quite responsible; she just made Mary mad.) Roland, who is competing with Joe for a job promotion to be decided by who can present the best project, secretly sabotages Joe's project. Roland wins. In short, the Ninja plays dirty, but looks innocent

On the most simple level, when we badmouth those who have said or done something against us (we all do this, at least occasionally), we are, in addition to letting off steam, getting back at them. While this is natural and usually harmless, further development of our Inner Sage can help us by-pass the pain that incites these traitorous acts *if* we choose.

The Bystander. The most clandestine form of all the Traitors is the Bystander. The Bystander secretly revels in the decline of others. It withholds aid when witnessing others crash and burn because any competition that can be whittled down is a good thing. It does nothing to promote the decline, yet, it will not do anything to stop or defend the victim. Example: *My friend got dumped by her boyfriend and I am not going to comfort her. Ha ha. Let her suffer. She, unlike me, has had it too good.* A brother who witnesses her mother unfairly insult another sibling may not come to his sibling's defense if he needs his mother's approval. He might even secretly grin like a Cheshire cat, feeling he might be the new favorite. It is impossible to live a life without ever feeling this way now and then. Do not beat yourself up for it; it is perfectly natural. However, incidents of it will diminish as you focus on making your own life all it can be.

The Remorseful Traitor. This type of Traitor will throw friends and relatives under the bus to get approval from whomever it needs the most. A mother reading a bedtime story to her child might abandon the task if her husband (whose praise she needs) calls for her to come and be with him. In this case, the mother loves her child, but the need to satisfy her man, ergo reinforce his approval of her, is greater. Hence, her child is betrayed.

A son, badly needing his father's approval, might not defend his mother's actions if it will give him a leg up. Already secure with the mother's love, he doesn't have much to lose. Hence, the son betrays the mother.

When this Traitor rises in us, we might in retrospect feel guilty. However, remember that we did what we did because we were afraid. Our need for approval would have to be great to turn on those we care about. But that was then. This behavior will change if we can begin to appreciate who we are as an individual and release the need for approval.

The Self-Inflictor. This form of Traitor is strong in those who blame themselves easily and frequently, or in those who feel so much inner pain, they somehow get relief if they hurt themselves more. This Traitor rises when we are feeling inadequate or guilty, or even wounded by others. It can manifest as self-criticism, self-sabotage, self-injury (as in cutting, or even stubbing a toe), substance abuse, or other destructive addictions. If our Inner Traitor is a Self-Inflictor, it can cruelly sabotage our whole life. To some degree, sometimes, we all turn on ourselves. Accepting the criticisms of our Inner Judge, the Traitor will dole out the punishment. The solution here is always to give your Inner Nurturer, Sage, and Healer permission to override the Traitor.

Balancing the Inner Traitor

When our Inner Traitor goes to extremes, it is a sign that we have been hurt and feel a need to attack the responsible party, even if it is ourselves. When we feel shame, we have turned on ourselves, allowing our Inner Judge to condemn us and our Inner Traitor to punish us. Almost all shame is due to the perception that we have fallen short of a social expectation. That expectation can be from our family, friends, a social circle, or society itself. These expectations, while seemingly admirable, do not account for our individuality. Hence, when we don't comply to, behave as, or achieve what others decide we must, we can be harshly judged and take that judgment to heart. When we are down on ourselves, we have accepted that we don't measure up. But . . . we do. Everyone measures up. Everyone has beauty. *Everyone.*

When you feel low, perceive yourself as an original who is better off *not* adhering to everyone else's perception of what you should be. In this, you will see yourself in a better light, generate self-respect, and self-sabotaging behaviors will diminish. Even behaviors such as cutting one's self is an act of deep sadness generated by self-dislike, lack of feeling loved, or rejection.

If you feel guilt for sabotaging or enjoying the sabotage of others, do not feel bad. Our Inner Traitor can only succeed in hurting another if that person deep down *chooses* to respond as a victim. Every person we may have tried to hurt or wanted to hurt has within them the same array of characters as you do, among them . . . a Warrior, Hero, Sage, Healer, and Nurturer. They, like you, will learn by trial and error how to best deal with betrayal. If they allow their Inner Victim to rise, they will harbor ire or sadness. If they allow their Inner Sage to emerge, they can use wisdom to rise above it and move on. If they allow their Inner Healer to emerge, it can help them deal with and resolve other issues the betrayal triggered. If they allow their Inner Warrior to emerge, they might fight back; and maybe they needed to practice fighting back and you gave them the opportunity.

No one is ever so powerful that we can control another person's reality. It is never what happens to us, it is what we do with what happens to us. We each have the power to deal with our blows in an abundance of ways. We are all giants. Sometimes we don't know it until our back is against the wall. In a Herculean effort to get the pressure off us, we discover hidden strength. In this, our hardest challenges are often the most rewarding. Thus, those whom you have hurt were given opportunities to find their personal power. In a strange kind of way, your somewhat ill-behavior was a gift. This is *not* to endorse ill-behavior, but rather to see that anything that occurs between two people is really an occurrence between the various characters within themselves.

On the other side of the coin, if you still carry resentment from the blows others dealt you and are frustrated because they seem to have gotten off scot-free—don't worry, they haven't. Those who allow their Inner Traitors to rule their roost and hurt others without compunction always lament in the end. In their attempt to feel safe by standing on people's heads, they wind up alone because nobody trusts a scoundrel. While they agonize in their dark worlds, you, who have made peace with your Inner Traitor, are dancing in the sun. The traitorous behavior of others will continue until they can generate love and security within themselves. And if they can, they will change and feel so bad about their unkind deeds, it is inevitable they will be kinder to others to try and make up for it.

Isn't that what we all try to do? Make up for past behaviors that in hindsight we regret? No matter what part the Traitor has played in your life, you can now take what has happened to grow wise, strong, and more secure about your value as a human being.

Admittedly, however, it is easier to spew our toxic residue from our psychological wounds than to heal the wounds. The most major battle we fight within ourselves is "do way take the high road, or play dirty?" If we take the high road, we are choosing to heal our festering psychological infections, even if we don't remember how we got the blows. Though remembering can lend valuable insight, it is not necessary, for the solution is always the same: receive compassion from the Inner Nurturer, understanding from the Inner Sage, a remedy from the Inner Healer, develop self-honor with the Inner Hero, and use the Inner Warrior to repel those who intend harm.

Even though natural law eventually brings balance to all things, the question is . . . how do you want to experience your life *now*? Jealous, angry, and afraid, or finding your personal power to shine who you are in the world no matter what happens to you? The reality you create is at your fingertips.

The Traitor in a Nutshell
* Elevates itself on the backs of others.
* Plays dirty to survive.
* Converts negative emotions into mischief.
* Secretly wants others to suffer as it has suffered.
* In desperation, it can be ruthless.
* Will use guilt to hurt us.
* Is not bad; it is insecure.

Traitor Types
The Blowfish: "Be afraid of me."
The Bold Avenger: "I hurt you, and I want you to know I did it."
The Scorpion: Sting. Sting. Sting.
The Ninja: "I didn't do it."
The Bystander: "If others are smeared, it makes me look better."
The Remorseful Traitor: "I had to throw you under the bus to save myself."
The Self-Inflictor: "I turn on myself."

Exploring Your Inner Traitor.

Exercise One

This exercise is designed to facilitate a clearer understanding of the various Traitor types so that you can identify them in yourself or others. Fill in the blanks with the Traitor type that would make each statement.

1. _____ I hope he crashes and burns.

2. _____ I'm going to secretly steal her ring just to see her upset.

3. _____ I didn't stand up for my brother when my mate berated him, because I needed my mate's approval.

4. _____ I hate myself for what I did.

5. _____ I will make my mate feel insecure so she won't leave me.

6. _____ That guy has it too good. I will humiliate him in public.

7. _____ She stole my boyfriend. I am going to plant drugs in her house and set her up to be arrested. Then I'll insinuate to her that it was I who set her up.

Answers: 1. Bystander   2. Ninja   3. Remorseful   4. Self-Inflictor   5. Scorpion   6. Blowfish   7. Bold Avenger

Exercises Two, Three, and Four will enable you to have a better understanding of your Inner Traitor's nature, what triggers its rise, and the outcome. Since the Traitor's primary motivators are jealousy, anger, and shame, they will be examined individually. Although every Traitor usually harbors all these emotions, one is usually stronger.

Exercise Two

Jealousy. We tend to get jealous when we think someone is better than us. It is the mark of personal insecurity. In romantic relationships, a popular line goes something like, "Ah, you're jealous; I am flattered." And those who enjoy the jealousy of their partner only do so because it makes *them* feel more secure. So in a way, when one is jealous, it really flatters no one.

When children are jealous of their siblings, they fear receiving less love, mostly from their parents. When co-workers are jealous of their peers, they fear being less favored by their boss, which ignites fear of losing job security, and/or failure to be promoted.

Hence, when someone is jealous of you, it is *not* a compliment; it is simply a measure of that person's insecurity. When you are jealous of others, it is the measure of yours. And when we try to make others jealous, it is an attempt to climb higher in the pecking order of importance. In short, jealousy is a flailing of self-esteem, whether we feel it or want to make others feel it. Whenever we think, "That person is better than me," it is an act of self-betrayal by devaluing our personal worth.

In this exercise, state what makes you jealous, why, the result, and what form of Traitor is in charge or wants to be, even if it doesn't quite emerge. Then state what your Inner Sage might have to say about this.

Example: I am jealous of *beautiful women* because it *makes me feel inadequate*. When I feel this way, I *ridicule myself*. The result is I *eat sweets and gain weight*. The Self-Inflictor Traitor *is in charge*. My Inner sage says, *Stop comparing yourself to others and focus on the unique beauty of your being.*

Example #2: I am jealous of *people who make a lot of money* because *it makes me feel like a failure*. When I feel this way, I *badmouth rich people*. The result is *I spend a lot of time daydreaming about how people I know with money, might fail.* The Bystander *is in charge*. My Inner Sage says, *Celebrate yourself just as you are and be open to all the inner riches within you that you have yet to discover.*

1. I am jealous of_____because_____

_____

When I feel this way I_____

The result is_____

The Traitor in charge is: (can be a combination)

_____

My Inner Sage says_____

_____

2. I am jealous of _____because_____

_____

When I feel this way I _____

The Traitor in charge is: (can be a combination)

_____

My Inner Sage says_____

_____

3. I am jealous of_____because

_____

When I feel this way I_____

The Traitor in charge is: (can be a combination).

_____

My Inner Sage says _____

_____

Self-expression is healing, so if you have more examples, continue this exercise in your supplementary journal.

In listening to your Inner Sage, you will likely discover that the cure for jealousy is always about shifting your focus back onto your unique specialness. If you are a hummingbird instead of an eagle, enjoy your special talents that the eagle cannot. Can it stand in one place in mid air? Can it suck nectar from a flower? Upon self-examination, you will see that you have gifts that those with whom you are jealous—do not. Celebrate yourself, and your jealousy will disappear.

Exercise Three

Anger. The Traitor will have thoughts like, "I hate that person who tried to hurt me and I will make her pay," or "I am mad at myself for failing; I deserve to be punished." Answer the following questions about how your anger set your Traitor into motion, how you felt afterward, what type of Traitor was in charge, then what your Inner Sage has to say about it.

Example #1: I was mad *when my daughter didn't thank me for sending her a present, so I didn't send her anything for a year.* Afterward, I felt *guilty because it seems such a small thing to jeopardize my relationship with her*. The Traitor in charge was the *Ninja*. My Inner Sage says, *Learn from this, and in the future constructively communicate your feelings before taking action.*

Example #2: I was mad *when my boyfriend cheated on me, so I went to bed with his best friend and flaunted it in his face.* Afterward, I felt *good at first, but then felt worse because it didn't lessen the hurt of him cheating on me.* The Traitor in charge was *the Bold Avenger.* My Inner Sage says, *Learn from this by realizing it feels better to walk away and shine your inner worth brighter than ever before, than to roll around in the muck of those who betray you.*

1. I was mad when_____

_____

so I_____

Afterward I felt_____

The Traitor in charge was: (can be a combination)

_____

My Inner Sage says, _____

_____

2. I was mad when_____

_____

so I_____

Afterward I felt_____

The Traitor in charge was: (can be a combination)

_____

My Inner Sage says,_____

_____

3. I was mad when _____

_____

so I_____

Afterward I felt_____

The Traitor in charge was: (can be a combination)

My Inner Sage says,_____

_____

Self-expression is healing, so if you have more examples, continue this exercise in your supplementary journal.

You may have noticed your Inner Sage's comments involved more constructive ways to deal with your anger. When we communicate our upsets in a non-blaming way (I felt upset when you . . . .) our anger often dissipates, sometimes by just airing it and sometimes because the person involved explains themselves and that understanding changes our view of the situation. Or your Inner Sage may have directed you to shift your focus back onto what you can do to make your life better despite the one who angered you.

Exercise Four

Shame. State a time you turned on yourself (Self-Inflictor), how you felt, how you responded, if that event still triggers the bad feeling, and if so, the *current* response, and then what your Inner Sage has to say about this.

Example #1: Once I turned on myself when *my dog died because I was negligent, which resulted in his death*. I felt *guilty*. Because of this, I responded by *getting drunk*. I still *feel guilty*. I still *drink when I think about it* because *I can't get over the fact that my dog died because of me*. My Inner Sage says, *There are reasons beyond what you understand for your pet dying. Every occurrence is a part of life's synchronicity which is beautiful beyond imagination. You meant no ill-will. It's time to let it go.*

Example #2: Once I turned on myself when *I forgot my lines in the play and it wrecked the play*. I felt *inept*. Because of this, I responded by *losing my confidence and dropping out of acting*. This resulted *in my acting friends keeping a distance. I no longer feel bad about it* because *it was just a human mistake and we all make them*. My Inner Sage says, *Mistakes are just stepping stones to greater wisdom.*

1. Once I turned on myself when_____

_____

I felt_____. Because of this I responded by_____

_____

This resulted in_____

When I think of this event, I_____turn on myself because_____
               still   no longer

_____

My Inner Sage says,_____

_____

2. Once I turned on myself when_____

_____

I felt_____. Because of this I responded by_____

_____

This resulted in_____

When I think of this event, I _____turn on myself because_____
                                    still   no longer

_____

My Inner Sage says,_____

_____

3. Once I turned on myself when_____

_____

I felt_____. Because of this I responded by_____

_____

This resulted in_____

When I think of this event, I_____turn on myself because_____
                                    (still   no longer)

_____

My Inner Sage says,_____

_____

Self-expression is healing, so you have more examples, continue writing in your supplementary journal.

Circle the correct answer. When I turn on someone, it is more often on:

myself   others   about equal

Exercise Five

The purpose of this next exercise is to identify your Inner Traitor's methodology and to become more aware of the frequency in which it rises. It is imperative to keep a compassionate attitude toward this part of yourself. The Traitor betrays only as a survival technique, nothing more. In better understanding it, you can temper it with your other inner aspects.

Circle the appropriate answers.

The Traitor types below have risen in my life:

The Bold Avenger:	never	seldom	moderately	a lot
The Ninja:	never	seldom	moderately	a lot
The Blowfish:	never	seldom	moderately	a lot
The Scorpion:	never	seldom	moderately	a lot
The Remorseful Traitor:	never	seldom	moderately	a lot
The Bystander:	never	seldom	moderately	a lot
The Self-Inflictor:	never	seldom	moderately	a lot

Based on these answers, my strongest Inner Traitor type(s) is/are:

_____

Now envision your Inner Traitor. See its form. It might be human, monster-like, or some form that doesn't even have a face, such as a red blob. Just stare at it. Do not be concerned with how crisp or vague your Inner Traitor appears. Visualization comes easier with some more than others. If you haven't already, close your eyes and see your Inner Traitor. When you catch the image, open your eyes and draw a sketch below. Artwork is irrelevant.

After reading this, close your eyes again and stare at your Inner Traitor. See its face, its eyes, if it has eyes. Just keep staring into the window of its being. There is a story there, the story of how your Inner Traitor came to be. It may or may not make any sense. You might even feel you are making it up. Whether fuzzy or crystal clear, just watch the story play as if looking into an eyepiece and viewing a movie. If visualization comes easy, just watch the story unfold no matter how long it takes. If visualization is a challenge, just relax, and a frame or two will appear and you will sense the underlying story. Do this now. When you feel done, open your eyes.

Now record your Inner Traitor's appearance and the story that unfolded. Don't think, just write. Let go of your constraints. These exercises are for you, and you alone, to help make yourself feel better in the long run. There is no wrong way to do this exercise. If what you saw is elaborate and there is not enough space for you to record the whole experience, finish it in your supplemental journal. Example #1: My Inner Traitor looks like *a girl with electrified hair and angry eyes*. When I look into her, deep into her, I see *a baby who cries and cries because she is neglected . . . .* Example #2: My Traitor looks like *a man with a deadpan face.* When I look into him, deep into him, *I see scene after scene of me as a kid being left out of things and feeling unimportant. I cut off my feelings and learned to fend for him . . . .* Example #3: (for those who didn't see much). My Traitor looks like *a red blob.* When I look into the blob, deep into the blob, I see *red like goo seeping into the cracks of everything I touch to repel what might hurt me . . . .*

My Inner Traitor looks like_____

_____

When I look deep into my Inner Traitor, I see_____

_____

_____

The story that unfolds is _____

_____

_____

_____

My Inner Traitor came to be because_____

_____

Now physically hold yourself. Cross your arms at your wrists and squeeze your hands above your elbows. You can do this mentally if you prefer. Feel compassion for yourself. See your Inner Traitor and flow compassion into it. This compassion strengthens into absolute unconditional love for your Inner Traitor no matter what it has ever done. You understand that it is afraid, so afraid, and it needs your comfort. You may or may not cry. You might begin to rock your body or sit perfectly still. See your Inner Traitor, so filled with compassion it is glowing white light. If the light is blue or pink or rainbow, go with that. You are giving your Inner Traitor what it was deprived and so badly needed. Every time your Inner Traitor rises and you can feel it about to act, flood it with this compassionate light. You will feel better. Do this exercise now.

Healing and Balancing Exercise for your Inner Traitor

Place one hand beneath your breastbone.

Place the other hand over your heart.
Concentrate deeply. Repeat to yourself or aloud for at least two minutes:
"I measure up in my own special way."

Relaxation and Creative Visualization Exercise

Lie in a comfortable position. Play instrumental music that makes you feel good: classical, New Age, or music that is of gentle, sweeping, or dynamic beauty. When the music is playing, close your eyes. Inhale through your nose deeply, and exhale through your mouth slowly; do this eight times. Visualize that you are inhaling the power of the universe, which purifies and attunes you physically, emotionally, mentally, and metaphysically. When you exhale, all the tensions and worries leave your body and go back into the universe where they dissolve and blend into the pure life force.

Tighten and loosen your muscles slowly in this order:

Feet. Tighten. Loosen. Take a slow, deep breath, and exhale.
Calves. Tighten. Loosen. Take a slow, deep breath, and exhale.
Thighs. Tighten. Loosen. Take a slow, deep breath, and exhale.
Hips and buttocks. Tighten. Loosen. Take a slow, deep breath, and exhale.
Stomach. Tighten. Loosen. Take a slow, deep breath, and exhale.
Back. Tighten. Loosen. Take a slow, deep breath, and exhale.
Arms. Tighten. Loosen. Take a slow, deep breath, and exhale.
Hands. Tighten. Loosen. Take a slow, deep breath, and exhale.
Neck and shoulders. Tighten. Loosen. Take a slow, deep breath, and exhale.
Face. Tighten. Loosen. Take a slow, deep breath, and exhale.

Then completely relax and take eight more slow, deep breaths. Inhale the universal life energy through your nose, and exhale tension through your mouth.

Set the intent: *Whoever I am, whatever I am, whatever I need, whatever is right for me—so be it. I open to insight. I open to receive.*

Now that you are completely relaxed, give your self over to the music that is playing. Focus on the point between your eyebrows and journey within. Deeper and deeper you go into your vast inner being. Do this for a while . . . .

In the distance you see your Inner Traitor. Notice the setting. As you approach, its appearance becomes clearer. Nearer and nearer you come. Now you are before your Inner Traitor. What does it look like? Perhaps it is in the dark, radiating fire, or hidden beneath a Ninja mask, or maybe it is standing there with tearful eyes. Look deeper into it and see its insecurity. See the pain it secretly suffers. Feel the horror in its heart. Do this for a while. . . .

You feel your Inner Nurturer stirring within you. It rises and fills you. You are the Nurturer now looking upon your Inner Traitor beholding its torment beneath its jealousy, anger, and shame. You touch your Inner Traitor's shoulder with a loving hand. Your warm hand on its shoulder conveys the comfort and knowledge that it measures up in its own special way. Watch it soften. Do this for a while . . . .

Your Inner Traitor, needing comfort so badly, is now glowing with compassionate energy. It becomes serene and moves inside you like a spirit and nestles in your heart where it will now live in the comfort of understanding and compassion. Whenever it is riled, you can calm it down and make it feel secure. From now on it will be easier to stop it from beating you up. It will also be easier to walk away from that which threatens you because your Inner Traitor will feel the joy of its specialness even if others cannot see it. Bask in this experience until the music ends . . . .

When you open your eyes, you will feel how your inner Traitor has retired, not needing to work so hard anymore because you have given it what it needs. While it might mildly emerge from time to time, you can easily calm it by shifting your focus to self-appreciation.

Record your experience.

_____

_____

_____

_____

_____

_____

_____

Draw a picture or symbol that summarizes your experience. Example: *The moon.*

Create a key phrase that summarizes this experience. Example: *I am calm in the moon.*

_____

When needed, say the phrase silently, and visualize the picture or symbol. This will reactivate the experience and generate a peaceful, empowered, clear state of mind.

Δ

Gem of Wisdom
When we turn on anyone, we turn on ourselves.
When we turn on ourselves, we turn on life.

Live the Mystery

THE REBEL "I stand out."

There is a Rebel in us all, however buried or blaring it might be. The Rebel is often judged a lunatic, or fool, someone who is a little nuts because the moon has affected them. The Rebel can be eccentric: *I feel great when I sit on my rooftop and yodel!* The Rebel is proud to be an original: *I openly share my strange ideas.* The Rebel can be brave: *I will be true to myself despite the criticism I might incur.* The Rebel often supports the underdog: *I will not stand back idly and let discrimination continue!* The Rebel does not want to follow the crowd. *Why should I join the club just because everyone else has.* The Rebel enjoys standing out in a crowd: *I love my purple hair.*

Rebels are the shape-changers of the world, the forerunners of all things new, and the champions of original thought. As with all our inner characters, our Inner Rebel will emerge and retreat at various times in various situations, and will generally fall into one, more than one, or a combination of the following types: the Dignity-Driven Rebel, the Activist Rebel, the Oppositional Rebel, the Devil's Advocate, the Headstrong Rebel, the Spit-in-Your-Eye Rebel, the I'll-Shock-You Rebel, and the Fledgling Rebel. Given we all have our own nature, not all of the types will apply to you. You may, however, recognize them in others you know and hence better understand their realities.

Dignity-Driven Rebel. Dignity-Driven Rebels march to the beat of their own drum and often stand alone, shining integrity as they sing an original song in their little corner of the world. These Rebels are potent, deep thinkers who see and respond to what is between the lines, rather than projections of what any society deems normal. Their song is about self-confidence. *Why is everyone always trying to look young? Are they really that insecure?* Their song is often about self-respect. *I'm not going to destroy my body by smoking cigarettes just because all my friends are.* The song is often about honor. *I will not act like an animal and join the rushing crowd pushing against each other to get the few seats left.*

Sometimes this honorable behavior attracts followers. For example, the birth of new music styles that catches on like wildfire, or the university professor who gains notoriety for teaching an unpopular point of view. The Dignity-Driven Rebel boldly flies in the face of mediocrity and reaches for the stars to actualize its insight. Sometimes, teamed up with the Innovator (the visionary), the Leader (taking control) and the Warrior (persistence), it will enjoy shaking up what is already comfortably in place. For example, at one time in the Western World, the idea of an airplane was laughable, landing on the moon ludicrous, and curing an incurable disease unthinkable. If the Dignity-Driven Rebel cared about social acceptance, none of those things would have happened. Hence, the Dignity-Driven Rebel can be a powerful force in we humans.

The Activist Rebel. This Rebel, while often full of honor, is passionate about certain *issues* and will stand against the majority if need be. The quest for freedom, equality, and general well-being are spearheaded by the Activist Rebel. Compelled to revolt against norms that endorse injustice, the Activist Rebel takes on causes greater than itself.

This is not to be confused with the Fabricator, *playing* at being an activist as a means to feel important and not truly impassioned about the cause. The Activist Rebel is whole heartedly involved in whatever it takes to complete the mission, which could be anything from not buying meat because it contributes to animal slaughter to instigating (with the Leader and Warrior) an oppressive revolution. Activist Rebels, as wonderful as they might seem, tend to neglect their loved ones. They can't do it all, and sometimes their personal relationships suffer.

The Oppositional Rebel. When afflicted, Rebels have a dark side as seen in oppositional personalities. The Oppositional Rebel has to be right all the time and will not listen to reason. If the sky is proclaimed beautiful, it might respond with, "I think it's ugly," despite the rainbow that's turning heads. If invited to take a walk, it might bark, "Can't you see I'm busy!" If heated skirmishes ensue, it will insist the conflict isn't a fight, just sassy banter. Collaborating with the Leader, it strives to be the top dog in any given situation by loudly barking its oppositional opinions. This unconsciously motivated posturing protects the Oppositional Rebel from being psychologically hurt by keeping others from getting too close to it. This technique works well. After all, who wants to get close to a snarling dog?

The Devil's Advocate. Ever taking everyone else's side, the Devil's Advocate is unable to comfort anyone who turns to it for emotional support. A response to "That man hurt my feelings" might be "Well, maybe he had a point." A response to "I could never kill an animal" might be "Well, then, you don't have a right to eat meat." The Devil's Advocate has a self-righteous attitude, emanating its superiority like a peacock fanning its feathers.

The Headstrong Rebel. This Rebel will stand up for what it believes is the best solution to anything, even if it makes trouble for itself. For instance, a Headstrong Rebel might withdraw her child from public school in favor of home teaching, even though everyone else thinks it's a mistake. Or a Headstrong Rebel might drop out of the social world and go into a hiatus to find himself, even though everyone judges him to be weak and running away from life. Sometimes the Headstrong Rebel can just get stubborn with tunnel vision, forfeiting reason and productivity. It will do what it will do and no one can stop it, as in a woman who insists she must date the drug dealer even though he puts her in peril, or a business-woman sticking to an unusual marketing strategy that isn't working, even if she goes bankrupt. This kind of Rebel is *goal-driven*, such as attaining love or succeeding in business, and it will stop at nothing, despite public opinion or unsavory consequences.

The Spit-in-Your Eye Rebel. This Rebel is a bit vicious, revolting against any who try to subdue it, despite the subduers' good intentions, such as a teen defying the parent by sneaking out to a midnight drinking party in the desert, or a husband staying out all night at a bar just because his wife asked him to stay home with the family. The Spit-in-Your-Eye Rebel enjoys breaking rules just because it can. It might steal a pack of gum despite the five dollars in its pocket. Its drive is to stir trouble as proof that it can't be controlled. Telling a Spit-in-Your- Eye Rebel not to take a certain job, or date a certain person, is the quickest way to get them to do just that!

The I'll-Shock-You Rebel. The I'll-Shock-You Rebel might walk into a crowd with a python draped around its neck as if to say "I am not like the crowd, and I never will be!" This Rebel is making a statement that it will never be owned or controlled by conformity. This is the person with pink hair, a Mohawk, or crazy contact lenses. Sometimes the shock factor is not apparent in appearance, but words. A statement of "I hate war" can incite the I'll-Shock-You Rebel to respond with "I enjoy war immensely." A statement of "What you did was bad" might incite the I'll-Shock-You-Rebel to respond with "Thank you." In short, unnerving others makes it feel strong and special.

The Fledgling Rebel. This Rebel mostly daydreams about being authentic, but usually dares not. Held back by the Scaredy Cat, it is paralyzed, at least most of the time, in most areas of its life. For instance, it might emerge in issues of education, but be silent with everything else. It might rise when a certain line is crossed, or make a stand only if its back is against the wall. We know our Inner Rebel is a Fledgling if it takes a lot to stir it into action.

Balancing the Inner Rebel

We humans have unconscious depths that go beyond the reaches of analysis. It is easy to judge people by their personas without seeing what is behind them and to render opinions based on looking only at what seems obvious, but there is almost always more to the picture of each individual than can ever be understood. Rebels often have the stigma of being troublemakers, but like the iceberg, there is always more to the Rebel than meets the eye. In this, Rebels aren't "bad." People with strong Inner Rebels do not set out to be rebellious; they can't help it. Something deep within compels the Rebel to emerge, at least now and then, even with the most conservative of people.

This emergence is often symptomatic of a deep need to be "ourselves," even if we don't know what that is. There comes a time in almost all our lives when our Inner Rebel bursts forth and blows off the persona we have worn like a cloak to hide our true selves. And we let it, because deep down, we long to be authentic.

Sometimes we use our Inner Rebel to *unconsciously* set ourselves up in life situations to develop weaker aspects of our self. The woman rebelling against her family by marrying an abusive man forces herself to develop her Inner Warrior if she is to survive. The man who uses rebellious opposition like a wall to protect himself will grow lonely because no one wants his unpleasant company. In time, he will be forced to collaborate with his Inner Healer to tend the ever-bleeding psychological wound that makes him so contrary and hence emotionally unavailable. In this, he might further seek outside counseling to unearth his deep-seated anger and learn how to nurture himself and others.

Whether your Inner Rebel adds spice to your life, makes you choke, or helps you embrace your individuality, this workshop will help you examine its style, the outcome it brings, and to, if needed, make modifications.

The Rebel in a Nutshell
* Has a strong sense of personal honor.
* Is comfortable being different.
* Doesn't care if it causes commotion.
* Is comfortable standing alone.
* Disdains mediocrity.
* Has a need to express individuality.

Rebel Types:
The Dignity-Driven Rebel: "I champion my originality, unaffected by peer pressure."
The Activist Rebel: "I will create change no matter what the consequence."
The Oppositional Rebel: "You are always wrong."

The Devil's Advocate: "I am never on your side."
The Headstrong Rebel: "I'm going to do it my way, even if it works against me."
The Spit-in-Your-Eye Rebel: "I will do what you don't want me to do."
The I'll-Shock-You Rebel: "I am different, and I'll prove it!"
The Fledgling Rebel: "It takes a lot to get me on stage."

Exploring Your Inner Rebel.

Exercise One

This first exercise is to determine the strength of your Inner Rebel. Circle the letter of the answer that suits you best.

1. When I am in a crowd, I'd rather:
   a. exceedingly stand out   b. moderately stand out   c. just be myself   d. fit in

2. If I disagree with others, I:
   a. always tell them   b. often tell them   c. sometimes tell them   d. seldom tell them

3. If someone tells me *not* to do something, I:
   a. do it just to spite them   b. almost always do it   c. listen, but make my own decision
   d. almost always listen and do what I'm told

4. If I see something going on that I think is wrong, I:
   a. almost always do something about it   b. sometimes do something about it
   c. seldom do something about it   d. never do something about it

5. Regarding my sense of fashion, I generally:
   a. stand out   b. wear what I feel like wearing, despite the going fashion
   c. try to fit in   d. make sure I fit in

6. If there are two lines of people waiting to be serviced, and one is very long and the other extremely short, I:
   a. usually check out the short line first and don't care if look stupid
   b. check out the short line first even if I have to overcome looking stupid
   c. usually stand in the long line, assuming it is the correct line
   d. stand in the long line because even if the short line is viable, I don't want to look stupid

7. In school, I generally:
   a. take/took pride in *not* going with fads   b. am/was part of a clique that deviated from
      the norm   c. I was/am just myself   d. try/tried to get my peers approval

8. When family, friends, or romantic partners tell me I *should* do something, I:
   a. seldom comply just to spite them   b. comply only if it suits me   c. comply some
      times, even if it doesn't suit me   d. almost always comply

How many of each letter did you circle? a's _____   b's _____   c's _____   d's _____

If you have mostly **a's**, you have an exceedingly strong Inner Rebel.
If you have mostly **b's**, you have a strong Inner Rebel.

If you have mostly **c's,** your Inner Rebel is moderate.
If you have mostly **d's,** your Inner Rebel is generally repressed.

Exercise Two

This next exercise is to help you determine the kind of Rebel you are, despite the frequency with which it emerges. Think of the most recent arguments you have had and with whom you've had them, then share the result.

Example #1: I argued with *my spouse* about *what our child's consequence should be for coming home three hours late without calling*. The result was *I handled it my own way despite what my spouse thought*. My thinking at the time was *that I know best and I will do it even if my spouse gets mad at me*. My Inner Rebel was the *Headstrong Rebel*.

Example #2: I argued with *my mother* about *someone I am dating*. The result was *I broke off the relationship even though I think she is wrong about him*. My thinking at the time was *I don't want to lose my mother's approval of me*. My Inner Rebel was the *Fledgling Rebel*.

1. I argued with_____about_____

_____

The result was_____

My thinking at the time was_____

My Inner Rebel was the_____

2. I argued with_____about_____

_____

The result was_____

My thinking at the time was_____

My Inner Rebel was the_____

3. I argued with_____about_____

_____

The result was_____

My thinking at the time was_____

My Inner Rebel was the_____

4. I argued with_____about_____

_____

The result was_____

My thinking at the time was_____

My Inner Rebel was the_____

5. I argued with _____about_____

_____

The result was _____

My thinking at the time was _____

My Inner Rebel was the _____

Exercise Three

Part One

Based on these answers, describe what type of Rebel you _most_ tend to be and why. It can be mostly one type, or a combination of types. Then state how this Rebel has helped you, and if applicable, how it may have worked against you.

Example #1: When my Inner Rebel emerges, it is mostly the _Activist Rebel_. I know this because _I only stand out in a crowd when others are being treated unfairly. I don't want anyone to notice me in general so I usually try to fit in._ It has worked for me because _people respect me_. It has worked against me because _sometimes I take on more than I can chew._

Example #2: When my Inner Rebel emerges, it is mostly the _Ill-Shock-You Rebel_. I know this because _I always say and do things to shock people_. It has worked for me _because it makes me feel strong inside_. It has worked against me because _it has limited my employment options._

Example #3: When my Inner Rebel emerges, it is mostly the _Oppositional Rebel_. I know this because _everyone says I am argumentative, but I just naturally say the opposite. I don't know why._ This Rebel has worked for me _because I can keep people from getting too close to me so they can't hurt me_. It has worked against me because _I can't sustain a healthy relationship._

When my Rebel emerges, it is mostly the_____Rebel. I

know this because_____

_____

This Rebel has worked for me_____

This Rebel has worked against me because_____

Circle has or has not.

This Rebel has / has not adversely affected my relationships.

This Rebel has / has not adversely affected my jobs.

This Rebel has / has not adversely affected my education.

This Rebel has / has not made my life more difficult.

This Rebel has / has not improved my life.

This Rebel has / has not helped others.

This Rebel has / has not hurt others.

This Rebel has / has not hurt myself.

Circle the correct answer. Based on my answers above, my primary Inner Rebel type has *mostly* been:

an asset   a detriment   an asset and detriment

If this Inner Rebel has mostly been an asset, it is in balance. If this Inner Rebel's actions have been a detriment only occasionally, that is to be expected, as things don't always turn out as we intend. However, if this Inner Rebel's actions have backfired on you or others on a regular basis, you can (if you choose) take a clearer look at the role it has played in your life. You *can* regulate which of your Inner aspects will be in control at any given time.

Part Two

State the Rebel type that emerges in you secondarily.

When my secondary Rebel emerges, it is mostly the_____Rebel. I know

this because_____

_____

This Rebel has worked for me_____

This Rebel has worked against me because_____

Circle the correct answer. My secondary Inner Rebel type has *mostly* been:

an asset   a detriment   an asset and detriment

Close your eyes a minute and observe your Inner Rebel's general appearance.

Describe what you see. _____

_____

Focus on your Inner Rebel. Get into its character. Now, let your Inner Rebel speak its mind. Don't think, just write whatever comes out of you.

I am _____'s Inner Rebel. I_____
       (your name)

_____

_____

_____

_____

_____

What does your Inner Sage have to say about this? _____

_____

Healing and Balancing Exercise for Your Inner Rebel.

    Place one hand over your heart.
    Place the other hand on the crown of your head.
    Concentrate deeply. Repeat silently or aloud for at least two minutes:
    "I champion my inner truth."

Relaxation and Creative Visualization Exercise

Lie in a comfortable position. Play instrumental music that makes you feel good: classical, New Age, or music that is of gentle, sweeping, or dynamic beauty. When the music is playing, close your eyes. Inhale through your nose deeply, and exhale through your mouth slowly; do this eight times. Visualize that you are inhaling the power of the universe, which purifies and attunes you physically, emotionally, mentally, and metaphysically. When you exhale, all the tensions and worries leave your body and go back into the universe where they dissolve and blend into the pure life force.

Tighten and loosen your muscles slowly in this order:

Feet. Tighten. Loosen. Take a slow, deep breath, and exhale.
Calves. Tighten. Loosen. Take a slow, deep breath, and exhale.
Thighs. Tighten. Loosen. Take a slow, deep breath, and exhale.
Hips and buttocks. Tighten. Loosen. Take a slow, deep breath, and exhale.
Stomach. Tighten. Loosen. Take a slow, deep breath, and exhale.
Back. Tighten. Loosen. Take a slow, deep breath, and exhale.

Arms. Tighten. Loosen. Take a slow, deep breath, and exhale.
Hands. Tighten. Loosen. Take a slow, deep breath, and exhale.
Neck and shoulders. Tighten. Loosen. Take a slow, deep breath, and exhale.
Face. Tighten. Loosen. Take a slow, deep breath, and exhale.

Then completely relax and take eight more slow, deep breaths. Inhale the universal life energy through your nose and exhale tension through your mouth.

Set the intent: *Whoever I am, whatever I am, whatever I need, whatever is right for me—so be it. I open to insight. I open to receive.*

Now that you are completely relaxed, give your self over to the music that is playing. Focus on the point between your eyebrows and journey within yourself. You are journeying through a tunnel. When you get to the end of the tunnel, you emerge into the land of your Inner Rebel. You see your Inner Rebel in its world. Stand there a moment and observe what it looks like, the expression on its face, and its demeanor. Now examine the environment in which your Inner Rebel lives. Take note if your Inner Rebel's world is mostly indoors or out, in a crowd or an open space, alone or around others, in light or dark, amongst ice or fire, beauty or chaos? Observe your Inner Rebel's reality. Watch it behave as you would in a movie. Do this for a while . . .

Now go to your Inner Rebel. Make eye contact. Take your Rebel's hands in yours and tell it how much you appreciate it for helping you fight for your individuality . . . Now tell it that it needn't ever fight so hard that it hurts itself to prove that point. You feel your Inner Nurturer stirring inside you. Unconditional love wells in your heart, flows down your arms into your hands, and into the hands of your Inner Rebel. Your Inner Rebel is filled with this nurturing energy. Your Rebel's face softens with relief. Connected to your Inner Rebel, you both close your eyes and merge your energies. This merging strengthens your good will for each other. Experience this for a while . . . .

Your Inner Rebel conveys that it won't rebel if it is going to backfire, and you convey to it that you will always support its efforts to be an authentic being in a world that encourages conformity. This is your pact, and you are at peace with your Inner Rebel. Experience this until the music ends. . . .

When you open your eyes, you will feel pleasantly charged, knowing your Inner Rebel will work for you and not against you.

Record your experience.

_____

_____

_____

_____

_____

_____

_____

_____

_____

_____

Draw a picture or symbol that summarizes your experience. Example: *A wild ocean.*

Create a key phrase that summarizes this experience. Example: *It's okay to be me.*

_____

When needed, say the phrase silently and visualize the picture or symbol. This will reactivate the experience and generate a peaceful, empowered, clear state of mind.

Δ

Gem of Wisdom
The bravest act of rebellion is to simply speak your truth.

Live the Mystery

15

WORKSHOP FIFTEEN
THE INNOVATOR "I create."

An often underappreciated but vital character within us is the Innovator. The Innovator is a visionary. It sees abstractions, what is between the lines, and what lies beyond logic. It can move outside the box of what already is and generate something new. Imaginative, inspired, creative, and resourceful, the Innovator gives us bright ideas, original thinking, inventions, and artistic works. The Innovator, like a muse, can invigorate and enrich our lives. It is our passion, our zeal, the part of us that likes to try new things, take chances, and steer away from the same old thing. And though it can take us down primrose paths that lead to pitfalls, there is never a dull moment when the Innovator is on stage.

If you prefer the ordinary and find comfort in the status quo, you likely have a more subdued Inner Innovator that rises only occasionally in a given circumstance. Even if you don't consider yourself innovative, when put on the spot, you might surprise yourself!

Our Inner Innovator generally falls into one, more than one, or a combination of the following types: the Idea Spinner, the Artist, or the Resourceful Innovator.

The Idea Spinner. This Innovator is a brilliant strategist, problem solver, and negotiator, and is an icon for the adage "Necessity is the mother of invention." It is prevalent in entrepreneurs, advertisers, and inventors. It is there when we conjure new strategies to solve old problems, or create new possibilities when our life gets stale. It is the business-person who orchestrates deals, brings them to pass, then moves on for the thrill of putting another deal together. It is the troubleshooter who generates inspired solutions to free up metaphorical logjams. And it is the entrepreneur who finds an original way to make a living. Idea Spinners are charmed with silver tongues, talented in manipulating others to see their point of view. We use the Idea Spinner when we motivate, influence, persuade, and even sometimes when we lie, for even lies can be innovative.

The Artist. This Innovator channels its creative fires into producing original works, or through sensual expression. Passionate and highly creative, it is prevalent in artists, architects, fashion and furniture designers, writers, composers, photographers, performers and the like. It can surface when we decorate our home, our bodies, or even when we make a present for someone. It is there when we create a new recipe, or creatively present a project at work or school. It is there when our passion ignites from seeing a color, a sparkle, a smile, or a tear. The Artistic Innovator likes to please the senses and stir the heart.

The Resourceful Innovator. This Innovator is talented at making things happen even if the outlook is grim. It can assess what is and turn it into a mission accomplished. For example, parents living on a limited budget find a cost-effective way to make celebrations special for their children, or those who can temporarily fix the plumbing or appliances with inventive solutions. And it can bring a dead situation to life by inventing door number three, as in creating a job in an already established business. In short, the Resourceful Innovator makes the most of what it has and finds ways to make it better.

Balancing the Inner Innovator

When our Inner Innovator overpowers us, it can leave us a bit bereft in practical matters. The bills may not get paid, the car serviced, or the dishes done, and not being fond of lists, we might forget things. We start projects we don't finish, and spend a great deal of time thinking up clever solutions to everyone else's problems instead of paying attention to our own. When this happens, all we need do is tap our Inner Warrior. Our Inner Warrior can help us create boundaries and stay inside them long enough to take care of our own business.

Conversely, our Inner Innovator, when repressed, can leave us with a longing to be passionate about something, or anything. When every day is filled with only duty and tending to practical matters, it can make life seem rather dull and cause depression. While duty, responsibility, and practicality are important, so is creativity and innovation. It's what makes us want to get out of bed in the morning, excited about this or that. The underactive Innovator can be stimulated by tapping our Inner Sage to help us shift our focus away from the outer world to our inner world. When we turn inward, grow still, and calm the chatter in our heads, we can become aware of what is going on inside off us. In this, we will begin to sense our deepest yearning, that if met, could rejuvenate our lives in a healthy way. Our yearning is our Inner Innovator trying to punch a hole of inspiration in the thick rind of our everyday life. Even the smallest yearning signifies a natural urge to grow. Growing is creative. When we feed the sprig of desire by taking tiny steps, our Innovator will sprout new leaves and continue to flourish.

These tiny steps, such as a new hairstyle, adding decoration to our home that reflects our personality, or taking up the study of what interests us, can lead to bigger things. For example, following a passion for eagles by watching them through online sites might lead to getting physically involved at an eagle sanctuary. Following a passion for art by taking art classes might lead to opening a gallery. Acting on a longing to be free of an abusive partner by increasing personal power might lead to ending that bad relationship to clear the deck for a new life chapter. Even adhering to an urge to say what we truly think and feel can lead us into new and exciting directions.

This workshop is designed to help you better know your Inner Innovator, to assess how its presence or lack thereof has affected your life, and how it might serve to enrich your current reality.

The Innovator in a Nutshell
* Is our inspiration.
* Generates original thought and/or creative expression.
* Is our passion, zeal, and urge to grow.
* Is ingeniously resourceful.
* Is a brilliant mediator and problem solver.

Innovators Types
The Idea Spinner: "My original ideas move things forward in fresh ways."
The Artist: "I stimulate the senses to facilitate inspiration."
The Resourceful Innovator: "I creatively make things happen with limited resources."

Exploring Your Inner Innovator

Exercise One

This first exercise will help you determine your own level of innovation and whether you might benefit from having more or less of this aspect in your life. Circle the letter next to the most appropriate answer.

1. In problem solving, I am most likely to:

    a. come up with new solutions   b. draw from what has been tried, as well as exploring new solutions.   c. do what others have done   d. get another to solve the problem

2. When it comes to stories, I'd rather:

    a. write stories   b. read and write stories   c. read stories   d. not read or write stories

3. When it comes to art, I would rather:

    a. be the artist   b. be artistic and enjoy the art of others   c. enjoy the art of others
    d. I don't care about art

4. In school, my project ideas:

    a. were original   b. a combination of old and new   c. were old ideas done before
    d. I plagiarized

5. My sense of fashion is:

    a. a reflection of me   b. a combination of fad and me   c. run with the fads
    d. I don't care about fashion

6. I daydream:

    a. often   b. moderately   c. at times   d. rarely

7. When I recount a story, I:

    a. embellish exceedingly   b. embellish a lot   c. embellish a little   d. stick to the facts

8. I prefer:

    a. to be spontaneous and wing things   b. a flexible schedule most of the time   c. a set schedule sometimes and a flexible schedule in others   d. a set schedule most of the time.

9. When it comes to making lists, I:

    a. don't like lists and won't use them   b. don't like lists and seldom use them   c. don't like lists, but use them   d. like lists

10. Challenges are:

   a. exciting to me b. scary, but I look forward to them   c. anxiety-evoking, but I take the ones I can.   d. I avoid challenges whenever possible.

How many of each letter did you circle?

a's_____   b's_____   c's_____   d's_____

If you circled *mostly* **a's**, you have an exceedingly strong Innovator
If you circled **a's** and **b's** about equally, your Innovator is strong.
If you circled mostly **b's,** your Innovator is moderately strong.
If you circled mostly **c's,** using your Innovator is hard for you.
If you circled *mostly* **d's**, your Innovator is repressed.

Based on your answers, how strong is your Inner Innovator? Circle the appropriate answer.

exceedingly strong   strong   moderate   weak   repressed

List in order, strongest to weakest, the kind of Innovator you tend to be.

1. _____   2._____   3. _____

Exercise Two

List five times you recall being innovative. (Examples: I creatively decorated my house, I planned an original birthday party. I made up a song, I mediated an argument between two people and came up with a creative solution, I made up a story that everyone believed, I mixed and matched my clothes and came up with a great new outfit, I created a gourmet meal for my family for under ten bucks.)

1. _____

2._____

3. _____

4._____

5. _____

When your Inner Innovator is held back at any given time (even if you are very innovative), it is usually due to fear of something going wrong and/or lack of confidence. If you feel inhibited in a certain area that you wish you could flow more freely, focus for a moment on which of your Inner aspects might be holding you back. Example #1: The Scaredy Cat holds me back from being romantically innovative because it tells me I'll look foolish. Example #2: The Judge holds me back when it comes to decorating my home because it tells me I am not creative or inventive.

_____ holds me back in the area of_____

_____because it tells me_____

_____

Exercise Three

Quiet your mind for a moment and take a deep breath. Tune into what you are craving (excluding bodily urges such as eating, exercise, or sexual release). It might be a form of nature, such as waterfalls, mountains, the ocean, or the desert. Or perhaps you crave to be heard and understood. You might have an urge to try something new, like taking a class or a trip to somewhere you have never been. Or perhaps you yearn to do something big, like start your own business, end a bad relationship, or speak your truth. Or maybe your urge is as small, as in building a birdhouse, creating a new recipe, or getting a new hairstyle. No matter how big or small, any type of innovation can lead to greater innovation. It will at least make your life more interesting, and at most, make your life more bountiful. If you feed even the smallest flame, it will burn brighter.

Write about your yearnings and how fulfilling them would improve the quality of your life. Throw practicality to the wind and let yourself daydream. Your yearnings might be abstract, such as a yearning to be free. Or your yearnings might be tangible, such as desiring to sing well.

I yearn to_____

_____

_____

_____

_____

If I could fulfill my yearnings, the quality of my life would improve because_____

_____

_____

_____

What HEALTHY first step(s) can you take to satisfy your deepest yearning? For example, if you yearn to have a new relationship, a healthy first step would be to end the old one. If your yearning is to be artistic, a healthy first step would be to get the supplies and/or take a class. If your yearning involves the natural world, a healthy first step would be to get out there.

To satisfy my deepest yearning, a *healthy* first step would be to_____

_____

I could also_____

_____

Once these first steps are taken, let the creative current take you where it will. Don't plan too much; just flow like a river and see where it takes you!

Healing and Balancing Exercise for Your Inner Innovator

Place one hand over your forehead.
Place the other hand beneath your navel.
Concentrate deeply. Repeat silently or aloud for at least two minutes:
"I am the creative fire."

Relaxation and Creative Visualization Exercise

Lie in a comfortable position. Play instrumental music that makes you feel good: classical, New Age, or music that is of gentle, sweeping, or dynamic beauty. When the music is playing, close your eyes. Inhale through your nose deeply, and exhale through your mouth slowly; do this eight times. Visualize that you are inhaling the power of the universe, which purifies and attunes you physically, emotionally, mentally, and metaphysically. When you exhale, all the tensions and worries leave your body and go back into the universe where they dissolve and blend into the pure life force.

Tighten and loosen your muscles slowly in this order:

Feet. Tighten. Loosen. Take a slow, deep breath, and exhale.
Calves. Tighten. Loosen. Take a slow, deep breath, and exhale.
Thighs. Tighten. Loosen. Take a slow, deep breath, and exhale.
Hips and buttocks. Tighten. Loosen. Take a slow, deep breath, and exhale.
Stomach. Tighten. Loosen. Take a slow, deep breath, and exhale.
Back. Tighten. Loosen. Take a slow, deep breath, and exhale.
Arms. Tighten. Loosen. Take a slow, deep breath, and exhale.
Hands. Tighten. Loosen. Take a slow, deep breath, and exhale.
Neck and shoulders. Tighten. Loosen. Take a slow, deep breath, and exhale.
Face. Tighten. Loosen. Take a slow, deep breath, and exhale.

Then completely relax and take eight more slow, deep breaths. Inhale the universal life energy through your nose and exhale tension through your mouth.

Set the intent: *Whoever I am, whatever I am, whatever I need, whatever is right for me—so be it. I open to insight. I open to receive.*

Now that you are completely relaxed, give your self over to the music that is playing. Focus on the point between your eyebrows and journey within. You are moving toward your Quintessential Self at your core. Do this for a while and enjoy the journey . . . .

Ahead, you see your Inner Innovator in its purity splashing light and form in beauteous configurations, ever changing, always new and interesting. Watch this for a while . . . .

Now move closer to your Inner Innovator, then stop and observe. Notice if there are any obstacles that keep you from getting too close. If so, who or what are the obstacles? Observe this and what your Inner Innovator is doing . . . .

Truly behold this part of you that wants to create. It offers bright promise, like a volcano erupting to create new land, or a blank canvas that takes on design and meaning. It offers hope to grey situations and solutions to impossible problems. Behold its power for a moment . . . .

If you wish this part of you to enrich your life, it is yours. It is yours and it is you. You don't have to be afraid of it. Your Inner Warrior will temper it if it begins to burn out of control. Your Inner Sage will help you use it in healthy ways. Move toward it now even if there are obstacles in the way. The deep need you have for it to brighten your life will take you right through the obstacles. Nothing can hold you back if this is what you want. You now reach your Inner Innovator and like a spirit, you glide into it. You are now merged with your Inner Innovator. You are one. The creative fires fill your body. Your brain is nourished to spark originality. Your eyes can see what ordinarily cannot be seen. Your heart flows freely. Experience this for a while . . . .

Suddenly, you feel yourself as a strong flowing river moving toward the sea of freedom. You can feel your body, mind, and heart empowered as never before with creative energy. This forward momentum in your inner world will be reflected in the outer world, enriching your life experiences. Power comes from the inside out. Experience yourself as this free flowing river until the music ends . . . .

When you open your eyes, you will feel inspired to flow who you are into the world, and you will be excited to see what might happen. You will carry this feeling into your daily life, this feeling that anything is possible. You know now that you always have a muse—your very own . . . and the muse is YOU!

Record your experience.

_____

_____

_____

_____

_____

_____

_____

_____

_____

_____

Draw a picture or symbol that summarizes your experience. Example: *A flame.*

Create a key phrase that summarizes this experience. Example: *I am the creative fire.*

_____

When needed, say the phrase silently and visualize the picture or symbol. This will reactivate the experience and generate a peaceful, empowered, clear state of mind.

Δ

Gem of Wisdom
Creative energy rejuvenates even the stalest reality.

Live the Mystery

16

WORKSHOP SIXTEEN
THE HERO "I preserve."

Our Inner Hero rises, often unexpectedly, to save the day. Shooting out of us like a bullet, it does what it must, whether it wants to or not. It rescues the innocent from bullies, brings the endangered to safety, and pulls us up from the dregs of our own despair to create a new and better day.

The Hero lurks within us all. Even if we can't see it, it is there struggling to get out from underneath the Defeatist's big bottom. It counts on no one and relies only on belief in itself. It does not act from a need to attain love or approval, or to create and maintain an image. In this, it will not respond to self-doubt or outside criticism. Its integrity shines through the darkness.

All the great heroes and heroines that ever were began their journey in a seemingly impossible jam. Instead of giving up or giving in, they wore honor like armor, faced their fears, and pushed on.

When the path behind begins to disintegrate and the path ahead is a blazing inferno, the Hero will walk the fire. It will march through limiting perceptions, past shouting dissenters on the sideline, and be in the moment, aligned with itself, step . . . by step . . . by step. Unlike the Gallant Warrior, who is passionate about charging through danger, the Hero would prefer a quiet existence, but if it comes to do or die, it will "do." Pushing ahead, it does not look back. And when the journey gets steep, it does not look down.

Defining Heroes can be illusive, as whatever constitutes a Hero lies in the eye of the beholder. Pacifistic activists might feel heroic for championing peace and view soldiers as deluded killers. And soldiers might feel heroic fighting for freedom and view pacifistic activists as traitors to their country. An employee might feel heroic, honoring herself by quitting her stressful job, even though her employer counts on her. Her employer however, might deem her a traitor and himself the Hero for surviving the situation. It could be that all of the above are Heroes. Only the Hero knows when it is being heroic. Unlike the Traitor, who can throw others to the dogs, the Hero's self-respect forbids callous disregard.

Although we all have an Inner Hero, in this day and age it often fails to be summoned. This is not our fault. In the old days we banded together in tribes. It was expected that we each rose to our full potential and possessed a wide set of skills to insure our survival. We hunted, we gathered, we huddled together in the cold night. Survival required innovation. Each person born upped the percentage of the tribes survival. Survival was up close and personal and an everyday event, hence the Hero within us was strong and present much of the time. We saved ourselves by saving each other, and we saved each other by saving ourselves.

That was then. In today's complex and vastly populated Western World, the days of our hands in the earth, arrows in our supper, walking to get around, whole tribe skilled in protecting each other—are mostly over. Our tribes have expanded and rebanded into larger social groups mostly defined by profession. In a world that offers everything we could possibly need or want for a fee, our heroes, in general, are those *outside* our social circle or family unit.

We rely on farmers, ranchers, factories, and grocers to buy food. We rely on architects, contractors, and carpenters for our shelter, and mechanics and engineers to build our various modes of transport. We rely upon manufacturers for our furniture, clothing, and sundry other items. We rely upon our artisans to decorate our abodes and bodies, and entertainers to give us a break from our daily lives. We rely upon the police and military to protect us, and medical practitioners to heal us. We have doctors for every part of our body, even our minds. We rely on postal services, computers, and phones to communicate, gather information, and bond with others in our small social circle as well as the global stage. The marvels of the modern age make our homes more comfortable with lighting, plumbing, and all kinds of machines to keep our domiciles clean and our yards manicured.

This collaboration allows us to more readily explore life beyond survival and often in style. We have time to play, be creative, travel, fulfill our dreams, and quest the answers to life's mysteries. However, this all costs money, even if paid in taxes. And these services usually lack a heart felt bond between supplier and buyer. Hence, our reliance is upon indifferent professional tribes in which we don't belong, and who won't be our Heroes unless we pay them. Pressure mounts to earn the needed bucks, and we must, for our own survival skills have shrunk. We are less able to grow or hunt our own food, weave and sew our own clothing, protect our own back yard, entertain ourselves in creative pursuits or in our natural surroundings, or to love and feel loved just by being ourselves.

The personal touch has faded and apathy is on the rise. Hence, multitudes feel lonely, bitter, and unloved. This is one reason religious institutions are so popular. In a place of worship, you have a tribe who generally will accept you even if you're poor and don't fit the specifications that society seems to require. In this case, the religious institution is our Hero. But even then. . . even then . . . what has become of the Hero within?

In a world where advertisers bombard us with messages through television, computers, radios, magazines, and do-it-all cell phones that their products and services will make us feel better, our eye is turned away from our own power. While many services and products actually are *great* gifts and incredibly wonderful, many more will advertise using current social standards as a goal to attain and thereby perpetuate a pseudo-reality that does not resonate to the well-being of individualism. This doesn't mean the marketers are bad, for they too are often unaware, and in their own way, innocent in their transgression. They, like everyone else, are desperate to survive. And all who give them money are *their* Heroes.

This is not to demean healthy competition, as in excellent advertising for a product or service that truly promotes well-being. But given we currently live in a somewhat virtual reality projected by the mass media, it is difficult to acknowledge that we even have an Inner Hero. We have been so conditioned to expect others to take care of us, make us happy, and affirm our worth that when they don't, it creates all kinds of animosity, be it toward our government seemingly failing us, friends that don't behave the way we need them to, or a mate who isn't making us happy. It has become easy to cast blame. Again, this is not our fault. It is social programming, nothing more.

In this constant searching for Heroes to save our day, and to save *the* day, rarely are we given the belief that we can save ourselves. Feeling this loss, we tend to anesthetize ourselves with substances, reach harder toward the outer world, and scream louder to be saved.

This workshop is designed to help you empower the Hero within. In this, you can find comfort in yourself knowing that you can prevail on your own, if it comes to that. And if it does come to that . . . *if* it does, then you will embark on the greatest adventure of your life, for our most profound moments are always on the heels of surviving a harrowing challenge. Your greatest Hero is you . . . if only you believe.

The Hero in a Nutshell
* Believes in itself above all others.
* Does not expect others to save it.
* Is driven by self-respect and honor, and needs no acknowledgment.
* Does not focus on obstacles, and will give its all to any pursuit.
* Without thought of reward, aids others in peril.

Exploring Your Inner Hero.

Exercise One

Part One

This exercise will help you spotlight your Inner Hero. State times when you were brave on your own behalf and it turned out well. Then state why you needed to be brave, the result, and how the result made you feel. Example: I was brave when I *made the choice to leave my abusive mate* at a time when *I feared for my life*. This resulted in *me getting a whole new life that I really like*. I felt *relieved that I took that action to save myself*.

1. I was brave when I_____

_____

at a time when_____

This resulted in_____

_____

and I felt_____

2. I was brave when I_____

_____

at a time when_____

This resulted in_____

_____

and I felt_____

3. I was brave when I_____

_____

at a time when_____

This resulted in_____

_____

and I felt_____

4. I was brave when I_____

_____

at a time when_____

This resulted in_____

_____

and I felt_____

5. I was brave when I_____

_____

at a time when_____

This resulted in_____

_____

and I felt_____

Part Two

Now list times when you were brave, but it _didn't_ work out. Example: I was brave when I _voiced my opinion to my boss_ at a time when _I was suppressing all my feelings at work._ This didn't work out because _my boss fired me._

1. I was brave once when I_____

This didn't work out because_____

Now say to yourself: "All heroes stand on a pile of failed tries. I was a hero then, and I am a hero now."

2. I was brave once when I_____

This didn't work out because_____

Now say to yourself: "All heroes stand on a pile of failed tries. I was a hero then, and I am a hero."

3. I was brave once when I_____

This didn't work out because_____

Now say to yourself: "All heroes stand on a pile of failed tries. I was a hero then, and I am a hero now."

4. I was brave once when I_____

This didn't work out because_____

Now say to yourself: "All heroes stand on a pile of failed tries. I was a hero then, and I am a hero now."

5. I was brave once when I_____

This didn't work out because_____

Now say to yourself: "All heroes stand on a pile of failed tries. I was a hero then, and I am a hero now."

Exercise Two

Part One

List times when you were heroic on *behalf of others* and it turned out well. Exclude times when you expended energy that only kept others dependent on you. The Hero is *not* an enabler of keeping others weak. Example: I was heroic once when *a man kept harassing a female, restaurant worker. I stood up and embarrassed the man for harassing the woman, so he would leave the woman alone, and he did.* Afterward, I felt *proud I could help her.*

1. I was heroic on another's behalf when_____

_____

Afterward, I felt_____

2. I was heroic on another's behalf when_____

_____

Afterward, I felt_____

3. I was heroic on another's behalf when_____

_____

Afterward, I felt_____
4. I was heroic on another's behalf when_____

_____

Afterward, I felt_____

5. I was heroic on another's behalf when_____

_____

Afterward, I felt_____

Part Two

Now list times when you were heroic on behalf of others, and it *did not* turn out well. Example: I was heroic on behalf of *my best friend*. I helped by *encouraging him to break free from his abuse father*. This did not turn out well *because his father got more abusive and my friend killed himself.*

1. I was heroic once on behalf of_____. I helped by_____

_____

This did not turn out well because_____

Afterward, I felt_____

Say to yourself: "I had pure intentions; no matter the result, I was being Heroic."

2. I was heroic once on behalf of_____. I helped by_____

_____

This did not turn out well because_____

Afterward, I felt_____

Say to yourself: "I had pure intentions; no matter the result, I was being Heroic."

3. I was heroic once on behalf of_____. I helped by_____

_____

This did not turn out well because_____

Afterward, I felt_____

Say to yourself: "I had pure intentions; no matter the result, I was being Heroic."

4. I was heroic once on behalf of_____. I helped by_____

_____

This did not turn out well because_____

Afterward, I felt_____

Say to yourself: "I had pure intentions; no matter the result, I was being Heroic."

5. I was heroic once on behalf of_____. I helped by_____

_____

This did not turn out well because_____

Afterward, I felt_____

Say to yourself: "I had pure intentions; no matter the result, I was being Heroic."

Exercise Three

List three specific things your Inner Hero can do today to improve the health of your body.

1. _____

2. _____

3. _____

List three specific things your Inner Hero can do today to decrease your stress.

1. _____

2. _____

3. _____

List three specific things your Inner Hero can do today to make you feel joyful.

1. _____

2. _____

3. _____

List three specific things your Inner Hero can do today to bring you prosperity.

1. _____

2. _____

3. _____

Healing and Balancing Exercise for your Inner Hero

Place one hand beneath your navel.
Place the other hand over your heart.
Concentrate deeply. Repeat silently or aloud for at least two minutes:
"I can save my own day."

Relaxation and Creative Visualization Exercise

Lie in a comfortable position. Play instrumental music that makes you feel good: classical, New Age, or music that is of gentle, sweeping, or dynamic beauty. When the music is playing, close your eyes. Inhale through your nose deeply, and exhale through your mouth slowly; do this eight times. Visualize that you are inhaling the power of the universe, which purifies and attunes you physically, emotionally, mentally, and metaphysically. When you exhale, all the tensions and worries leave your body and go back into the universe where they dissolve and blend into the pure life force.

Tighten and loosen your muscles slowly in this order:

Feet. Tighten. Loosen. Take a slow, deep breath, and exhale.
Calves. Tighten. Loosen. Take a slow, deep breath, and exhale.
Thighs. Tighten. Loosen. Take a slow, deep breath, and exhale.
Hips and buttocks. Tighten. Loosen. Take a slow, deep breath, and exhale.
Stomach. Tighten. Loosen. Take a slow, deep breath, and exhale.
Back. Tighten. Loosen. Take a slow, deep breath, and exhale.
Arms. Tighten. Loosen. Take a slow, deep breath, and exhale.
Hands. Tighten. Loosen. Take a slow, deep breath, and exhale.
Neck and shoulders. Tighten. Loosen. Take a slow, deep breath, and exhale.
Face. Tighten. Loosen. Take a slow, deep breath, and exhale.

Then completely relax and take eight more slow, deep breaths. Inhale the universal life energy through your nose and exhale tension through your mouth.

Set the intent: *Whoever I am, whatever I am, whatever I need, whatever is right for me—so be it. I open to insight. I open to receive.*

Now that you are completely relaxed, give your self over to the music that is playing. Focus on the point between your eyebrows and see yourself standing with your back to the outer world. You are facing your inner world. Begin moving inward, deeper and deeper into your vast inner being, heading toward the center of yourself. You are moving through layers like an onion, beginning with dark layers, growing lighter as you travel closer to your core being. Do this for a while.

Now you arrive at the center of your being which is your Quintessential Self. Behold your Quintessential Self for a moment. See the colors, the movement. Feel the power and the beauty. Do this for a while . . . .

From your Quintessence, you see your Inner Hero emerge. Walk up to your Inner Hero. Behold what it looks like. Touch it. What happens? . . . .

Move into your Inner Hero and merge. You are one with your Inner Hero. Feel its power. Experience this for a while . . . .

Now, still merged with your Inner Hero, see yourself in your daily life. Commotion goes on about you and the currents of others move about every which way, but you are unaffected because you believe in yourself and you know that if you are pure-hearted in your endeavor, you can never lose. You are always worthy and a success, no matter what happens. This empowers you. You know you can count on your Inner Hero to see you through any challenge. While you may accept the help of others, you do not *expect* it. You are a Hero, and you have more power than you could even dream. Bask in this experience until the music ends . . . .

When you open your eyes you will feel empowered and secure, knowing that you have a mighty Hero within you who will see you through the rest of your life.

Record your experience.

_____

_____

_____

_____

_____

_____

Draw a picture or symbol that summarizes your experience. Example: *An image of myself breaking through a black wall.*

Create a key phrase that summarizes this experience. Example: *I am the Hero I wish for.*

_____

When needed, say the phrase silently and visualize the picture or symbol. This will reactivate the experience and generate a peaceful, empowered, clear state of mind.

Δ
Gem of Wisdom
The greatest Hero we can ever have is our own self.

Live the Mystery

17

WORKSHOP SEVENTEEN
THE HEALER "I regenerate."

Beneath the book learning and outer-world coaching, deep in the recesses of our Being resides our Inner Healer, there to regenerate the characters within us, and sometimes those in the global community.

Our Inner Healer senses what is healthy for us as an individual and sometimes what might be healthy for others. Healthy acts can be physical, emotional, mental, or meta physical, (meta is Latin for beyond). What is healthy for one may not be healthy for another. For example, while taking a walk might seem generally healthy; if we have a bulging bunion, a swim might be better. While constructive self-expression seems generally healthy, if we are expressing everyone's ears off, silence might give ears to our Inner world.

If we listen to our Inner Healer, really listen, we can stay current with the tides of change we undergo on a daily basis. What is healing for us one moment may not be healing for us in the next. For instance, we might study herbs and use them to feel better, but at another time we might have a hunch (our Inner Healer speaking) that we need to see a medical professional.

Sometimes our Inner Healer is overthrown by other aspects within us. Our Inner Healer might say, "Stop working so hard; you need a rest," but our Inner Leader says, "No, we must stay on top of things to maintain control." And our Inner Warrior concurs, saying, "We are strong; we will keep working!"

And sometimes our Inner Healer is unheard because the social voice (often driven by commercial interests) proclaims that the ability of others to cure us trumps our own. In this, we are often convinced that "out there" is the remedy for all our ailments and woes. For instance, in the current Western World, we are often made to feel that our worth diminishes with age. To lift us from the dregs of depression, we might hungrily digest the promise of cosmetic surgery to make us look younger. In taking that path we have decided to base our worth on our appearance. In so doing, we are continually stressed in our obsession to stop aging. Our Inner Healer, if heard, may well have said that what we really needed was to ignore the social voice and embrace our personal power through better nutrition, exercise, and an appreciation for ourselves as we are.

And while many health care professionals are knowledgeable, necessary, and indeed have helped heal millions, we are prone to blindly accept their opinions and abide, ignoring our own sense of things. For instance, if told to *take a pill*, we often do so without consulting our Inner Healer. By tuning into our Inner Healer, we might have a strong sense that better than a pill would be improved nutrition, exercise, and meditation. However, in this day and age, we commonly underestimate our ability to lead the charge in our own healing.

Our bodies are always trying to communicate with us, if only we will listen. Physical and psychological ailments are our body's way of telling us that something is off balance. The culprit might be chemical, or it might be due to stress. Stress will manifest in our bodies making us nervous, angry, afraid, depressed, or physically ill, and intensify if we don't deal with what has or is upsetting us. Sometimes the upset relates to a past event that has been triggered by an occurrence in our present. Because our bodies store memories attached to feelings, we don't have to consciously remember the past event to be affected by it. In allowing our Inner Healer to calm us, we can, however, make the connection. In realizing that what we are feeling is due to a past issue and not our current reality, we can curb our anxiety.

Current challenges can also make us feel sick. Fear can shorten our breath and increase our blood pressure. Depression makes our bodies feel weighted and disturbed. If we could but take a deep breath with closed eyes, quiet the chatter in our heads, and believe in our own Inner Healer, we could better sense the crux of the problem and how to solve it instead of jumping to conclusions and making things worse.

Inviting your Inner Healer to participate in your life decisions is to pay attention to who you are as an individual and to flow with a sense of what FEELS right. There is nothing you need do but be here now, and nothing you need to become other than who you are.

Our Inner Healer can steer us through social programming into healthy life directions. For example, you might be depressed and give yourself over to your Inner Healer. From this, you might have an urge to take a walk. After taking the walk, your metabolism is boosted and you, in a good mood, ask your daughter if she wants to do art with you. In doing art together you might have an excellent interaction that further brightens your spirits. This then puts you into the mood to sign up for that class you have been wanting to take. On and on it goes. This is moving with the flow of yourself. When you trust your Inner Healer, it will speak to you by giving you a sense of what *feels* healing, not shoulds, musts, or obvious conclusions.

This workshop is designed to empower your Inner Healer to ensure that you receive the best care possible for you as an individual, you, who are one of a kind. When your Inner Healer is activated, it does not mean you cannot reach out. Your Inner Healer might guide you to other healing professionals and help you locate the one that is best for you. You might find calm and clarity within and realize that you need to go out into the world and be more social, or find someone with whom to share thoughts and feelings. You might even figure out what is ailing you and solve your own problem. While others can have a powerful healing influence on us, so can we—upon ourselves.

The Inner Healer in a Nutshell
* Knows what is best for you as an individual.
* Has instincts about what is *not good* for you.
* Can often make you feel better without consulting others.
* Will be open to work with other healers, compatible with your personal nature.

Exploring your Inner Healer

Exercise One

Given we can make ourselves ill with our turbulent emotions, this exercise is about training yourself to naturally think in ways that make you feel better. Our emotional state often begins with how we *think*. Our thoughts generate our mood, which affects our well-being, including our physical health. Thinking constructively, such as *I did my best. Things will get resolved eventually. I'll do better next time,* we feel better. Conversely, destructive thinking, such as *Life sucks. People suck. I suck. Nobody loves me,* makes us feel worse.

State an incident that upset you, the thoughts you had, how these thoughts made you feel and why. Then restate the thought in a way that makes you feel better. If you feel resistant to restating your thought, then you are clinging to a way of thinking that keeps you feeling as you do. Push on through and do the exercise anyway. If your answers are overly positive, be aware that you might be cloaking the true way you were thinking at the time of the event. Understanding what triggers our dark thinking is key to preventing it in the future. Or perhaps you already think in a healthy manner. Stretch your thinking anyway, and see if you can kick it up a notch.

Example #1: When my romantic partner dumped me, I thought to myself, *I am a good person*. I felt *okay, but it still hurt a lot*. An even more healing way to talk to myself would have been *I am glad this happened; I don't want to be with someone who can't appreciate who I am and what is best in me. Now I am free to do whatever I want without having to make compromises. I am a treasure. I appreciate me! I really admire myself.*

Example #2: When I got passed over for the promotion I was counting on, I thought to myself, *I've been cheated. What's the use? If I can't go forward, I might as well give up.* I felt *depressed, sick to my stomach, and heart broken.* A more healing way to talk to myself would have been *Okay, so I got passed over; I need to find out why and then make a decision whether or not to find a job where I can be better appreciated. I did my best. I did not fail. I am worthy and have a lot to offer the world.*

1. When_____, I thought

to myself,_____

_____

I felt_____

A more healing way to talk to myself would have been_____

_____

_____

_____

2. When_____, I thought

to myself_____

_____

I felt_____

A more healing way to talk to myself would have been_____

_____

_____

_____

3. When_____, I thought

to myself_____

_____

I felt_____

A more healing way to talk to myself would have been_____

_____

_____

_____

4. When_____, I thought

to myself_____

_____

I felt_____

A more healing way to talk to myself would have been _____

_____

_____

_____

5. When_____, I thought

to myself_____

_____

I felt_____

A more healing way to talk to myself would have been_____

_____

_____

_____

Exercise Two

Now that you have stirred your Inner Healer, take a moment to see an image in your head that represents it. It can be a person, a symbol, or an aspect of nature, such as the ocean, a glowing ball of light, or a splash of color. Close your eyes and watch what pops up. When you get the image, draw a picture of your Inner Healer. Quality of the artwork is unimportant.

Now, whenever you want to tap your Inner Healer, see this picture, and it will be easy.

Exercise Three

Stress

Stress rises when we fear certain outcomes. These outcomes are often based on our perception of what failure and success mean by social world standards. When the pressure is on, we generally try to *force* things to go our way. Not only does this often cause conflict with those around us, but what we decide needs to happen may not really be what is healthiest for us. For example, we can put all our energy into winning someone's love, but the person whose love we are trying to win has her/his own genetic codes and plan for flowering. So try as you might, if it is not in her/his plan to dance the dance of love with you, it will fail in the end. A daisy cannot be a lily no matter how hard it tries. A cat cannot be a dog, and a mountain cannot be the sea. And when it is time for the leaves to fall from the tree, fall they will. In accepting who you are with appreciation, you will nourish your true self and grow into all that you are meant to be. You do not need to *make* anything happen. If you give your allegiance to your natural self, you will automatically take the steps needed to bring yourself into fruition. To think as such not only relieves stress, but it is also the greatest expression of health.

Focus on a current event that worries you. State your fear about the outcome and what you are telling yourself will happen if that fear should actualize. Then state what your Inner Healer has to say about this. Example: I am worried *about my daughter's behavior.* I fear that *she is going down a bad road.* I am telling myself *that her behavior is a reflection of me as a parent, and that if I can't fix it, I am a bad mother.* My Inner Healer says, *Calm down; focus on how you can help yourself and feel better no matter what your daughter does. Be the example of what you wish for her.*

1. I am worried_____

I fear that_____

I am telling myself_____

_____

My Inner Healer says, _____

_____

2. I am worried_____

I fear that_____

I am telling myself_____

_____

My Inner Healer says,_____

_____

3. I am worried_____

I fear that_____

I am telling myself_____

_____

My Inner Healer says,_____

_____

4. I am worried_____

I fear that_____

I am telling myself_____

_____

My Inner Healer says,_____

_____

5. I am worried_____

I fear that_____

I am telling myself_____

_____

My Inner Healer says,_____

_____

Exercise Four

Focus on your Inner Healer. Call it to rise within you. Let the Healer speak to you about what you, as an individual, need to feel better. Example: When I look at you, *you appear sad and afraid most of the time, always trying to be what others want you to be.* You would feel better if you *lightened up and laughed a bit. You are so serious and on edge, taking everything so personally* . . . .

When I look at you_____

_____

_____

You would feel better if you_____

_____

_____

Exercise Five

Part One

View yourself in a movie, the movie of your life. In every movie, the star of the show has ups and downs, challenges and triumphs. Write about the part of the movie you are in currently. Example #1: I am currently in the part of the movie *where I have survived a lot and I am feeling better about myself, but I still need to apply all I have learned to survive the next scene in my life.* Example #2: I am currently in the part of the movie *where everything has gone wrong and I don't know if I can pull out of it.*

I am currently at the part of the movie where_____

_____

Now let your Inner Healer advise you about what you need to do to be prepared for the next scene.

My Inner Healer says that what I need to do now to prepare for the next scene is_____

_____

Part Two

Now make the movie a comedy. Think of comedies you have seen where against a backdrop of seriousness, the struggles of the characters make us laugh. Even comedians often use world news to get people laughing. And when we make jokes about our own folly, sometimes we can get *ourselves* laughing. This is not a sign of cold-heartedness, but a way to cope with what feels overwhelming. We humans are very funny creatures just as many animals can be. However, in our seriousness, we often miss the humor.

Imagine yourself as the star of a comedy in your current life circumstance and an audience is watching. Close your eyes and do this for a moment.

Now, viewing your life as a *comedy,* write a one-line ending to your movie, starring you.

Circle the answer that suits you best. My Inner Healer has appeared in my life:

hardly ever   from time to time   in certain periods of my life   moderately   profusely

Things to Keep in Mind:
* Be your own best friend. Instead of thinking, *I have failed,*
   think, *I still worthy no matter what.*
* Put faith in yourself over others. Instead of thinking, *I need others to help me,*
   think, *There is a lot I can do to help myself.*
* Do not push to make things happen. Instead of thinking, *I WILL win that contest,*
   think, *I will do my personal best.*

How to Empower your Inner Healer

* Act in ways that *feel* healthy despite outside opinion.
* Turn inward to get a sense of what is right for you *before* turning outward.
* Be aware of how past events currently effect you.
* Breathe slowly and deeply when upset; learn diaphragmatic breathing (as singers do).
* Let self-respect be your guiding light.
* Learn to lovingly laugh at yourself and life.
* Constructively express your true thoughts and feelings without blaming others.
* Air your thoughts and feelings with at least one trusted person.
* Create a healing environment that comforts your five senses.
* Stay away from toxic environments and people whenever possible.
* Gain personal knowledge by researching what ails you.
* Seek healing professionals who best resonate with who you are as an individual.
* Spend time being creative in any manner; creativity is just generating something new.
* Touch nature; the natural world calms us down.
* Take interesting classes, or join groups that make you feel better, or take any kind of healing journey that speaks to you.
* Know when to move on and try something else.
* Accept responsibility for your well-being. While others can help, it is not *their* job to solve your problem. They have problems of their own.
* Learn to meditate (relaxation and focus). In silence and stillness it is easy to sink into your
Quintessential Self to get clarity, regenerate, and feel empowered.

Healing and Balancing Exercise for Your Inner Healer

Place one hand on the crown of your head.
Place the other hand over your forehead.

Concentrate deeply. Repeat silently or aloud for at least two minutes: "I summon my Inner Healer to help me."

Relaxation and Creative Visualization Exercise

Lie in a comfortable position. Play instrumental music that makes you feel good: classical, New Age, or music that is of gentle, sweeping, or dynamic beauty. When the music is playing, close your eyes. Inhale through your nose deeply, and exhale through your mouth slowly; do this eight times. Visualize that you are inhaling the power of the universe, which purifies and attunes you physically, emotionally, mentally, and metaphysically. When you exhale, all the tensions and worries leave your body and go back into the universe where they dissolve and blend into the pure life force.

Tighten and loosen your muscles slowly in this order:

Feet. Tighten. Loosen. Take a slow, deep breath, and exhale.
Calves. Tighten. Loosen. Take a slow, deep breath, and exhale.
Thighs. Tighten. Loosen. Take a slow, deep breath, and exhale.
Hips and buttocks. Tighten. Loosen. Take a slow, deep breath, and exhale.
Stomach. Tighten. Loosen. Take a slow, deep breath, and exhale.
Back. Tighten. Loosen. Take a slow, deep breath, and exhale.
Arms. Tighten. Loosen. Take a slow, deep breath, and exhale.
Hands. Tighten. Loosen. Take a slow, deep breath, and exhale.
Neck and shoulders. Tighten. Loosen. Take a slow, deep breath, and exhale.
Face. Tighten. Loosen. Take a slow, deep breath, and exhale.

Then completely relax and take eight more slow, deep breaths. Inhale the universal life energy through your nose, exhale tension through your mouth.

Set the intent: *Whoever I am, whatever I am, whatever I need, whatever is right for me—so be it. I open to insight. I open to receive.*

Now that you are completely relaxed, give your self over to the music that is playing. Focus inward and journey into yourself. You are walking along a path in search of your Inner Healer. Notice the environment in which you walk and what the path looks like. Do this for a while . . . .

In the distance, you see your Inner Healer. Are there obstacles between you and your Inner Healer or is the path clear to reach it? Keep moving toward your Inner Healer. If there are obstacles, move through them as if you are a ghost. Nothing will keep you from getting to your Inner Healer. Feel in your heart how badly you wish to be healed on every level. Release the need to judge what you *think* is healing for you. Your Inner Healer knows just how you need to be healed beyond your conscious perception.

Your longing to be healed in whatever way is truly right for you, is like a magnet that draws you closer and closer to your Inner Healer. You cannot be stopped. Now you reach your Inner Healer. Move into your Inner Healer. Feel you and your Inner Healer as one. You are the Healer; light floods out all around you. Feel this for a while . . . .

Now listen . . . just listen to your Inner Healer. It will tell you how to better care for yourself and help you grow into all you are meant to be. Experience this until the music ends . . . .

When you open your eyes, you will feel focused on *your* path to grow into all you can be, and committed to walk it no matter what goes on around you.

Record your experience.

_____

_____

_____

_____

_____

_____

_____

_____

Draw a symbol or picture that summarizes your experience. Example: *A green star*

Create a key phrase that summarizes this experience. Example: *I open to healing.*

_____

When needed, say the phrase silently and visualize the picture or symbol. This will reactivate the experience and generate a peaceful, empowered, clear state of mind.

Δ

Gem of Wisdom
Healing begins within.

Live the Mystery

18

WORKSHOP EIGHTEEN
THE QUINTESSENTIAL SELF "I am pure."

I, the Quintessential Self, like a crystal, shine the many faces of myself into the world as an identity, but I am more than my identity. I have a body; it helps me move, and breathe, and live. It gives me an appearance, but I am more than my physical make-up. I have a mind. It helps me work out problems, and learn, and be logical, and creative. But I am more than my thoughts. I have strong feelings, I laugh and love, hate and fear. I cry. I hurt. But I am more than my emotions.

I am the sum of all my many faces in perfect balance. I am my entire life story. I am the seed that carries what will unfold and flower into all that I am. I am all my potential. I am the mystery of myself. But I am even more than that. Made up of elements common in all life forms, I am the stars and the sea, the earth and fire. I am a bit of all things blended together refracting light in the outer world into a thousand shapes and colors that rise and fall and change every moment on at least some infinitesimal level. I am that I am, always of great importance, and yet no more important than any other thing.

My many faces, like children, sometimes swim too far away from me, from their home, and get sucked into outer-world drama. Shaken by the drama, they often feel out-of-kilter and alone, but they never are, for I am always here, waiting for them to come home to me. And when they do, I enfold them in my warmth and soak them in soothing relief, reminding them that the drama is just an experience. The drama is not who they are. They are me, the Quintessential Self. I know my worth. And when touching me, they know theirs.

Although people need people, I take responsibility for myself, growing as I am meant to grow, embracing my existence, though I know not for sure what might come of it. I do not need to know. I am like the sun; all I need do is shine . . . now . . . today. The past and the future are not what was and what will be. The past and the future are reshaped in the present. The present is the point of power, and I am always remaking myself, for I am made of creative energy. And though all things are, I as an individual can have personal experiences. I move, explore, and grow. I accept the story that is me. I embrace it. I celebrate it. I do not compare, contrast, or wish that another's story were mine. If a sunflower is a sunflower, then wishing it were a rose would only keep it from knowing its true beauty. If I live who I am, and become all that I am meant to be . . . then I am fulfilling my part in an even larger story—the story of life.

Who we are inside grows brighter in self-discovery and is not diminished with the passing of time. When we make a conscious shift from laboring to become an *image* created by the social world to cherishing our Quintessential Self, we see our beauty in its unique design, complex and masterfully woven together. In beholding this design, we can admire the trials and struggles of our life that make for a remarkable story.

Everyone's story is remarkable. *Everyone* is remarkable.

Despite societal judgment, none of us is more important than another, nor less. Worth is not measured by achievement, money, appearance, or by how many people love us. It is not measured by how good we are, or how "bad." At our core, we are all the same, just humans striving to survive in this world. Some of us use our Inner Warrior to survive, others of us abdicate to the Martyr because we don't know how to survive.

Whoever you are, whatever your way, whether you wear the Fabricator's rose-colored glasses or the Skeptic's smirk, your worth is immeasurable in the span of time and the scope of space. When at last we tap our truest self, tears of joy form in our eyes, for we have uncovered the magic of our being, our deepest pain, our greatest wish, and what we *must* do to find our way "home."

You are a unique individual, bare naked and maskless at your core, void of image and free of expectation. You are a snowflake falling through the winter sky, a crystal wonder in your own configuration, matched by no other. How sacred! How precious. How beautiful you are. You are . . . you, and isn't that a lovely thing?

The Quintessential Self in a Nutshell:
* Is pure; its worth is unshakable and eternal.
* Admires and respects all its aspects unconditionally.
* Is the essence of who we are and who we are meant to be, beyond
   conscious analysis and social programming.
* Can feel everything that all its aspects experience in the outer world.

Exercise One.

Given that all the faces of yourself have contributed to your life story, the following exercise is designed to acknowledge each member of your Inner World, beginning with the strongest and ending with the weakest. The characters you most identify with are the strongest, and the ones you are least able to relate to are the weakest. Listing these aspects of yourself in order of familiarity might prove challenging as two or more can feel equally powerful within you; however, if pondered carefully, one is usually a smidgeon stronger or weaker in you than another. As the Quintessential Self is the sum of all your many faces in perfect balance, do not involve it in this exercise.

Listed below is a list of the Inner Aspects:

The Sage. The Judge. The Warrior. The Nurturer. The Pleaser. The Victim. The Martyr. The Leader. The Scaredy Cat. The Fury. The Traitor. The Skeptic. The Rebel. The Fabricator, The Innovator. The Hero. The Healer.

1._____   2._____   3._____

4._____   5._____   6._____

7._____   8. _____   9. _____

10._____   11._____   12._____

13._____   14_____   15._____

16 _____   17._____

Exercise Two

This exercise will reunite all your aspects with your Quintessential Self. Your Quintessential Self, like a pitch pipe, will tune your selves as strings on an instrument, not only to it, but to each other. In this, you may look forward with proud anticipation at what is yet to come as the purpose of your life continues to unfold.

Share (in the order you listed) in the previous exercise what each of these inner characters has contributed to making your life story what it is. Name the character, the bright and shadow side of its contribution, and the good that has come out of the role it has played in your life. Do this exercise with reverence, for even negative events that your characters may have incited have been integral to the unfolding of your story, not yet complete.

Example #1: I acknowledge the *Inner Nurturer* in my life. On the bright side it *brought me much pleasure and helped me be close to many people. It made me a good therapist and mother and friend.* On the shadow side it *got me in trouble, inviting predators into my life. I also often over-nurtured and depleted myself.* The good that has come out of it is *that was I was forced to develop my Inner Warrior by learning how to create boundaries. Learning how to create boundaries brought balance to my life.*

Example #2: I acknowledge the *Inner Warrior* in my life. On the bright side it *kept others from hurting me. It not only helped me survive many situations, but it gave me drive to create a career for myself.* On the shadow side it *kept others from getting too close to me and I had trouble sustaining intimate relationships.* The good that has come out of it is *that after failing my relationships so many times, I finally tapped my Inner Nurturer and allowed myself to receive and express love. This made my life better.*

Example #3: I acknowledge the *Pleaser* in my life. On the bright side it *provided a way for me to feel loved and accepted. It helped me survive in situations that were too harsh for me to handle.* On the shadow side it *wore me out trying to please everyone all the time just to get others to love and protect me. I have a deep sadness about not feeling strong enough to be the real me around others.* The good that has come out of it is *that everyday I value more that little seed within me that wants and needs to grow. I am close to inviting my Inner Hero to help me—be me.*

As you move down the line to the weaker Inner characters, continue to acknowledge the bright and shadow side of the character, even though it seems to have played a small role in your life. An example of this would be: I acknowledge the *Skeptic* in my life. On the bright side it *being weak allowed me to make many alliances which gave me a lot of great life experiences.* On the shadow side *I walked into many lions dens and got deceived and hurt.* The good that has come out of it is *that I am learning to discriminate.*

1. I acknowledge the role the_____ has played in my life. On

the bright side it_____

_____

On the shadow side it_____

The good that has come out of it is_____

_____

(Close your eyes and see this character basking in the light of your Quintessential Self, soaking in the nourishment it needs. Then open your eyes and continue.)

2. I acknowledge the role the_____ has played in my life. On

the bright side it_____

_____

On the shadow side it_____

_____

The good that has come out of it is_____

_____

(Close your eyes and see this character basking in the light of your Quintessential Self, soaking in the nourishment it needs. Then open your eyes and continue.)

3. I acknowledge the role the_____ has played in my life. On

the bright side it_____

_____

On the shadow side it_____

_____

The good that has come out of it is_____

_____

(Close your eyes and see this character basking in the light of your Quintessential Self, soaking in the nourishment it needs. Then open your eyes and continue.)

4. I acknowledge the role the_____ has played in my life. On

the bright side it_____

_____

On the shadow side it_____

_____

The good that has come out of it is_____

_____

(Close your eyes and see this character basking in the light of your Quintessential Self, soaking in the nourishment it needs. Then open your eyes and continue.)

5. I acknowledge the role the_____ has played in my life. On

the bright side it_____

_____

On the shadow side it_____

_____

The good that has come out of it is_____

_____

(Close your eyes and see this character basking in the light of your Quintessential Self, soaking in the nourishment it needs. Then open your eyes and continue.)

6. I acknowledge the role the_____ has played in my life. On

the bright side it_____

_____

On the shadow side it_____

_____

The good that has come out of it is_____

_____

(Close your eyes and see this character basking in the light of your Quintessential Self, soaking in the nourishment it needs. Then open your eyes and continue.)

7. I acknowledge the role the_____ has played in my life. On

the bright side it_____

_____

On the shadow side it_____

_____

The good that has come out of it is_____

_____

(Close your eyes and see this character basking in the light of your Quintessential Self, soaking in the nourishment it needs. Then open your eyes and continue.)

8. I acknowledge the role the_____ has played in my life. On

the bright side it_____

_____

On the shadow side it_____

_____

The good that has come out of it is_____

_____

(Close your eyes and see this character basking in the light of your Quintessential Self, soaking in the nourishment it needs. Then open your eyes and continue.)

9. I acknowledge the role the_____ has played in my life. On

the bright side it_____

_____

On the shadow side it_____

_____

The good that has come out of it is_____

_____

(Close your eyes and see this character basking in the light of your Quintessential Self, soaking in the nourishment it needs. Then open your eyes and continue.)

10. I acknowledge the role the_____ has played in my life. On

the bright side it_____

_____

On the shadow side it_____

_____

The good that has come out of it is_____

_____

(Close your eyes and see this character basking in the light of your Quintessential Self, soaking in the nourishment it needs. Then open your eyes and continue.)

11. I acknowledge the role the_____ has played in my life. On

the bright side it_____

_____

On the shadow side it_____

_____

The good that has come out of it is_____

_____

(Close your eyes and see this character basking in the light of your Quintessential Self, soaking in the nourishment it needs. Then open your eyes and continue.)

12. I acknowledge the role the_____ has played in my life. On

the bright side it_____

_____

On the shadow side it_____

_____

The good that has come out of it is_____

_____

(Close your eyes and see this character basking in the light of your Quintessential Self, soaking in the nourishment it needs. Then open your eyes and continue.)

13. I acknowledge the role the_____ has played in my life. On

the bright side it_____

_____

On the shadow side it_____

_____

The good that has come out of it is_____

_____

(Close your eyes and see this character basking in the light of your Quintessential Self, soaking in the nourishment it needs. Then open your eyes and continue.)

14. I acknowledge the role the_____ has played in my life. On

the bright side it_____

_____

On the shadow side it_____

_____

The good that has come out of it is_____

_____

(Close your eyes and see this character basking in the light of your Quintessential Self, soaking in the nourishment it needs. Then open your eyes and continue.)

15. I acknowledge the role the_____ has played in my life. On

the bright side it_____

_____

On the shadow side it_____

_____

The good that has come out of it is_____

_____

(Close your eyes and see this character basking in the light of your Quintessential Self, soaking in the nourishment it needs. Then open your eyes and continue.)

16. I acknowledge the role the_____ has played in my life. On

the bright side it_____

_____

On the shadow side it_____

_____

The good that has come out of it is_____

_____

(Close your eyes and see this character basking in the light of your Quintessential Self, soaking in the nourishment it needs. Then open your eyes and continue.)

17. I acknowledge the role the_____ has played in my life. On

the bright side it_____

_____

On the shadow side it_____

_____

The good that has come out of it is_____

_____

(Close your eyes and see this character basking in the light of your Quintessential Self, soaking in the nourishment it needs. Then open your eyes and continue.)

Healing and Balancing Exercise to Tap Your Quintessential Self

Place one hand over the other on the crown of your head.
Concentrate deeply. Repeat silently or aloud for at least two minutes:
"I am my Quintessence, bright and pure."

Relaxation and Creative Visualization Exercise

Lie in a comfortable position. Play instrumental music that makes you feel good: classical, New Age, or music that is of gentle, sweeping, or dynamic beauty. When the music is playing, close your eyes. Inhale through your nose deeply, and exhale through your mouth slowly; do this eight times. Visualize that you are inhaling the power of the universe, which purifies and attunes you physically, emotionally, mentally, and metaphysically. When you exhale, all the tensions and worries leave your body and go back into the universe where they dissolve and blend into the pure life force.

Tighten and loosen your muscles slowly in this order:

Feet. Tighten. Loosen. Take a slow, deep breath, and exhale.
Calves. Tighten. Loosen. Take a slow, deep breath, and exhale.
Thighs. Tighten. Loosen. Take a slow, deep breath, and exhale.
Hips and buttocks. Tighten. Loosen. Take a slow, deep breath, and exhale.
Stomach. Tighten. Loosen. Take a slow, deep breath, and exhale.
Back. Tighten. Loosen. Take a slow, deep breath, and exhale.
Arms. Tighten. Loosen. Take a slow, deep breath, and exhale.
Hands. Take a slow, deep breath, and exhale.
Neck and shoulders. Tighten. Loosen. Take a slow, deep breath, and exhale.
Face. Tighten. Loosen. Take a slow, deep breath, and exhale.

Then completely relax and take eight more slow, deep breaths. Inhale the universal life energy through your nose and exhale tension through your mouth.

Set the intent: *Whoever I am, whatever I am, whatever I need, whatever is right for me—so be it. I open to insight. I open to receive.*

Now that you are completely relaxed, give your self over to the music that is playing. Focus on the point between your brows and journey into your vast inner world. You see a starry sky. You are flying past the stars toward your Quintessential Self. You see your Quintessential Self ahead as a brilliant ball of light as big as a house. This light is made of the pure creative life force. It is the force that birthed you into the outer world. As you come closer to it, it appears larger. Closer you come to it . . . closer . . . closer. . . . You fly into it. It feels so good, filling you with all you have craved and needed. Be still now and feel it feed you and nourish you. Take a deep breath and allow this to happen for a while. . . .

The light is absorbing all your pain, transforming it into pure energy. As your pain diminishes, you feel cool relief. Experience this for a while. . . .

Now, emptied of this pain, this regenerative energy fills each of your Inner aspects completely. The light pours into your Inner Sage. Your Sage turns brilliant white. The light pours into your Inner Judge. Your Judge turns brilliant white. The light pours into your Inner Warrior. Your Warrior turns brilliant white. The light pours into your Inner Nurturer. Your Nurturer turns brilliant white. The light pours into your Inner Pleaser. Your Pleaser turns brilliant white. The Light pours into your Inner Leader. Your Leader turns brilliant white. The light pours into your Inner Victim. Your Victim turns brilliant white. The light pours into your Inner Martyr. Your Martyr turns brilliant white. The light pours into your Inner Scaredy Cat. Your Scaredy Cat turns brilliant white. The light pours into your Inner Fury. Your Fury turns brilliant white. The light pours into your Inner Fabricator. Your Fabricator turns brilliant white. The light pours into your Inner Skeptic. Your Skeptic turns brilliant white. The light pours into your Inner Traitor. Your Traitor turns brilliant white. The light pours into your Inner Rebel. Your Rebel turns brilliant white. The Light pours into your Inner Innovator. Your Innovator turns brilliant white. The light pours into your Inner Hero. Your Hero turns brilliant white. The light pours into your Inner Healer. Your Healer turns brilliant white. All your aspects in brilliant white meld together into one Quintessential Being. You measure up. You always have. You can never not measure up. Who you are transcends earthly perceptions. You are your Quintessential Self. You now experience oneness with yourself, your purpose, and your essence. You have given yourself to yourself. You are free to be you, and whoever you are, whatever you are . . . you are. Now, without mental direction, see what happens. Watch, listen, feel. Go with the experience. If your body moves or vibrates, allow it. If words or a chant emerge—allow it. Trust yourself. Just be. Do this for a while . . . .

From now on, you will walk tall in your daily life emanating your Quintessential Self, which cannot be beaten down. It is stronger than anything in the outer world. People respect it because it rings true with something inside of them. Your true essence feels pure and wonderful, and when you shine it others don't want to hurt you because that would be like hurting themselves. You are safe now, empowered by your true essence beyond conscious analysis. You have ended an old chapter within your life story, and you are now beginning a new one, united with yourself, enlightened and strong, and eager for the next adventure! Experience your Quintessential Beauty. Know that while you are a unique individual, on another level you are one with everything that exists. You will now feel this in your life. Bask in this experience until the music ends . . . .

When you open your eyes, you will feel your individuality simultaneously with your connection to the life force.

Record your experience.

_____

_____

_____

_____

_____

_____

_____

_____

_____

_____

_____

_____

Draw a picture or symbol that captures this experience. Example: *A brilliant ball of rainbow light.*

Create a key phrase that summarizes the experience. Example: *I am my Quintessence.*

_____

When needed, say the phrase silently, and visualize the picture or symbol. This will reactivate the experience and generate a peaceful, empowered, clear state of mind.

Δ

Gem of Wisdom
The essence of all you have been, are, and always will be is—perfect and pure.

Live the Mystery

Congratulations!
You have completed Blue Wing Self-Discovery Workbook-Volume Two

About the Author

Susan D. Kalior was born in Washington State, raised in Phoenix, AZ, and currently resides in Oregon. Her first profession was a psychotherapist (individual, marriage, and family counseling) treating those suffering from depression, anxiety, panic attacks, post traumatic stress disorder, substance abuse, sexual abuse, family violence, and severe mental illness. She employed therapies such as communication skill building, relaxation training, systematic desensitization, bioenergetics, and psychodrama. She has worked in a mental hospital, a placement home for juvenile delinquents, and taught Kindergarten for a year. She has also facilitated numerous stress management, parenting, and self-discovery workshops (and still does) that have aided in the psycho-spiritual healing of many. Education and training include an M.A. in Ed. in Counseling/Human Relations and Behavior (NAU), a B.S. in Sociology (ASU), and ten months training at a Tibeten based community in Mesa Arizona (Staff Training Center) learning various psychotherapeudic methodologies and indepth meditiation techniques.

With her children grown, she is currently doing what she loves most: teaching self-discovery workshops, exploring the natural world, meditating, and writing educational and entertaining books that facilitate personal growth and transformation.

In her words: "I strive to see what is often missed, and to not miss what can't be seen. There is such a life out there, and in there—beyond all perception! So I close my eyes, feel my inner rhythm, and jump off the cliff of convention. And when I land, though I might be quaking in my boots, I gather my courage and go exploring.

Through travel, study, and work, I've gained a rich awareness of cultural differences among people and their psychosocial struggles. I have discovered that oppression often results from the unexamined adoption of outside perceptions. The healing always has been in the individual's stamina to expel outside perceptions of self and and constructively exert one's unique core being into the world. I am driven to facilitate expanded awareness that people may separate who they are from who they are told to be. Embracing personal power by loving our unique selves in our weaknesses and strengths, in sickness and in health, for richer or poorer, for better or for worse . . . forever—is a key to joyous living. My motto is: Trust your story. Live the Mystery."

For more information on Growing Wings Self-Discovery Workshops in Portland Oregon, or to arrange a workshop in your location, contact:
<u>sdk@bluewingworkshops.com</u>

Lightning Source UK Ltd.
Milton Keynes UK
UKOW021510020412

190034UK00005B/22/P